# Lecture Notes in Business Information Processing  **399**

Series Editors

Wil van der Aalst ⓘ
   *RWTH Aachen University, Aachen, Germany*
John Mylopoulos ⓘ
   *University of Trento, Trento, Italy*
Michael Rosemann ⓘ
   *Queensland University of Technology, Brisbane, QLD, Australia*
Michael J. Shaw
   *University of Illinois, Urbana-Champaign, IL, USA*
Clemens Szyperski
   *Microsoft Research, Redmond, WA, USA*

More information about this series at http://www.springer.com/series/7911

Alessandro Bozzon ·
Francisco José Domínguez Mayo ·
Joaquim Filipe (Eds.)

# Web Information Systems and Technologies

15th International Conference, WEBIST 2019
Vienna, Austria, September 18–20, 2019
Revised Selected Papers

 Springer

*Editors*
Alessandro Bozzon
Delft University of Technology
Delft, The Netherlands

Francisco José Domínguez Mayo
University of Seville
Seville, Spain

Joaquim Filipe
Polytechnic Institute of Setúbal/INSTICC
Setúbal, Portugal

ISSN 1865-1348             ISSN 1865-1356 (electronic)
Lecture Notes in Business Information Processing
ISBN 978-3-030-61749-3       ISBN 978-3-030-61750-9 (eBook)
https://doi.org/10.1007/978-3-030-61750-9

This Springer imprint is published by the registered company Springer Nature Switzerland AG
The registered company address is: Gewerbestrasse 11, 6330 Cham, Switzerland

# Preface

The present book includes extended and revised versions of a set of selected papers from the 15th International Conference on Web Information Systems and Technologies (WEBIST 2019), held in Vienna, Austria, during September 18–20, 2019.

WEBIST 2019 received 87 paper submissions from 30 countries, of which 11% were included in this book. The papers were selected by the event chairs and their selection was based on a number of criteria that included the classifications and comments provided by the Program Committee members, the session chairs' assessment, and also the program chairs' global view of all papers included in the technical program. The authors of selected papers were then invited to submit a revised and extended version of their papers having at least 30% innovative material.

The purpose of WEBIST 2019 was to bring together researchers, engineers, and practitioners interested in the technological advances and business applications of web-based information systems. The conference had five main tracks, covering different aspects of web information systems, namely Internet Technology; Web Interfaces and Applications; Society; e-Communities, and e-Business; Web Intelligence; and Mobile Information Systems.

The papers selected to be included in this book contribute to the understanding of relevant trends of current research on web information systems and technologies, including:

– Big Data and Connected Services
– Web Performance
– Context-Aware and Adaptive Web Applications
– Human Robot Collaboration and Multi-Agent Systems
– Web Application Operating Systems and Platforms
– Social Media Advertising and Enhancing Purchase Intentions
– Natural Language Query Interfaces and Semantic Web
– Human-Computer Interaction and Dynamic Web Pages

We would like to thank all the authors for their contributions and also the reviewers who helped ensure the quality of this publication.

September 2019

Alessandro Bozzon
Francisco José Domínguez Mayo
Joaquim Filipe

The original version of the book was revised: first name of the second volume editor has been corrected. The correction to the book is available at https://doi.org/10.1007/978-3-030-61750-9_11

# Organization

## Conference Chair

Joaquim Filipe          Polytechnic Institute of Setúbal and INSTICC, Portugal

## Program Co-chairs

Alessandro Bozzon       Delft University of Technology, The Netherlands
Francisco Domínguez Mayo    University of Seville, Spain

## Program Committee

| | |
|---|---|
| Mohd Helmy Abd Wahab | Universiti Tun Hussein Onn Malaysia, Malaysia |
| Mohd Abdullah | Universiti Teknologi Malaysia, Malaysia |
| Jose Aguilar | Universidad Autonoma de Sinaloa, Mexico |
| Marco Aiello | University of Stuttgart, Germany |
| Ana Margarida Almeida | Universidade de Aveiro, Portugal |
| Jesús Arias Fisteus | Universidad Carlos III de Madrid, Spain |
| Giuliano Armano | University of Cagliari, Italy |
| Débora Barbosa | Universidade Feevale, Brazil |
| Faiza Belala | LIRE Laboratory, University of Constantine 2, Algeria |
| Werner Beuschel | Technische Hochschule Brandenburg, Germany |
| Adelaide Bianchini | Universidad Simón Bolívar, Venezuela |
| Boyan Bontchev | Sofia University St. Kliment Ohridski, Bulgaria |
| Gabriela Bosetti | Liris Laboratory, Université de Lyon, France |
| Alessandro Bozzon | Delft University of Technology, The Netherlands |
| Philipp Brune | Neu-Ulm University of Applied Sciences, Germany |
| Christoph Bussler | Google, Inc., USA |
| Maria Claudia Buzzi | CNR, Italy |
| Vanessa Camilleri | University of Malta, Malta |
| Inaldo Capistrano Costa | Instituto Tecnológico de Aeronáutica, Brazil |
| Dickson Chiu | The University of Hong Kong, Hong Kong |
| Christophe Cruz | Laboratoire d'Informatique de Bourgogne, France |
| Daniel Cunliffe | University of South Wales, UK |
| Clodoveu Davis Júnior | Universidade Federal de Minas Gerais, Brazil |
| Guglielmo De Angelis | CNR-IASI, Italy |
| Valeria De Antonellis | University of Brescia, Italy |
| Sergio de Cesare | University of Westminster, UK |
| Martine De Cock | University of Washington Tacoma, USA |
| Toon De Pessemier | Ghent University, iMinds, Belgium |
| Steven Demurjian | University of Connecticut, USA |

| Enrico Denti | ESECB, Instituto Politécnico de Castelo Branco, Portugal, and Universitá di Bologna, Italy |
| Luigi Di Caro | University of Turin, Italy |
| Francisco Domínguez Mayo | University of Seville, Spain |
| Georg Dr. Schneider | Trier University of Applied Sciences, Germany |
| Martin Drlik | Constantine the Philosopher University, Slovakia |
| Karim El Guemhioui | Université du Québec en Outaouais, Canada |
| Atilla Elci | Aksaray University, Turkey |
| Larbi Esmahi | Athabasca University, Canada |
| Luis Ferreira Pires | University of Twente, The Netherlands |
| Josep-Lluis Ferrer-Gomila | Balearic Islands University, Spain |
| Alvaro Figueira | CRACS, INESC TEC, University of Porto, Portugal |
| Karla Fook | Instituto Tecnológico de Aeronáutica, Brazil |
| Geoffrey Fox | Indiana University Bloomington, USA |
| Oscar Franco-Bedoya | Universidad de Caldas, Colombia |
| Pasi Fränti | University of Eastern Finland, Finland |
| Xiang Fu | Hofstra University, USA |
| Ombretta Gaggi | Università di Padova, Italy |
| Julián García García | IWT2, Spain |
| Faiez Gargouri | ISIM Sfax, Tunisia |
| John Garofalakis | University of Patras, Greece |
| Ilche Georgievski | University of Stuttgart, Germany |
| Henrique Gil | ESECB, Instituto Politécnico de Castelo Branco, Portugal |
| Vasileios Gkioulos | Norwegian University of Science and Technology, Norway |
| Nuno Gonçalves | Politechnical Institute of Setúbal, Portugal |
| Jose Gonzalez | University of Seville, Spain |
| Annamaria Goy | University of Torino, Italy |
| Carlos Granell | Universitat Jaume I, Spain |
| Ratvinder Grewal | Laurentian University, Canada |
| Angela Guercio | Kent State University, USA |
| Francesco Guerra | University of Modena and Reggio Emilia, Italy |
| Hakim Hacid | Zayed University, UAE |
| Fayçal Hamdi | Conservatoire National des Arts et Métiers, France |
| Azza Harbaoui | RIADI-ENSI, Tunisia |
| Shanmugasundaram Hariharan | Saveetha Engineering College, India |
| Ioannis Hatzilygeroudis | University of Patras, Greece |
| A. Henten | Aalborg University, Denmark |
| Jose Herrero Agustin | University of Extremadura, Spain |
| Hanno Hildmann | TNO, The Netherlands |
| Matthias Hirth | TU Ilmenau, Germany |
| Geert-Jan Houben | Delft University of Technology, The Netherlands |
| Nuria Hurtado | University of Cadiz, Spain |
| Sergio Ilarri | University of Zaragoza, Spain |

| | |
|---|---|
| Monique Janneck | Luebeck University of Applied Sciences, Germany |
| Ivan Jelinek | Czech Technical University in Prague, Czech Republic |
| Zhuoren Jiang | Sun Yat-sen University, China |
| Ejub Kajan | State University of Novi Pazar, Serbia |
| Kennedy Kambona | Vrije Universiteit Brussels, Belgium |
| Georgia Kapitsaki | University of Cyprus, Cyprus |
| Vaggelis Kapoulas | Computer Technology Institute and Press, Greece |
| Sokratis Katsikas | Norwegian University of Science and Technology, Norway |
| Takahiro Kawamura | Japan Science and Technology Agency, Japan |
| Matthias Klusch | German Research Center for Artificial Intelligence (DFKI) GmbH, Germany |
| Hiroshi Koide | Kyushu University, Japan |
| Fotios Kokkoras | University of Thessaly, Greece |
| Andreas Komninos | University of Patras, Greece |
| Dongxi Liu | CSIRO, Australia |
| Michael Mackay | Liverpool John Moores University, UK |
| Dwight Makaroff | University of Saskatchewan, Canada |
| Kazutaka Maruyama | Meisei University, Japan |
| Andrea Mauri | Delft University of Technology, The Netherlands |
| Miroslaw Mazurek | Rzeszów University of Technology, Poland |
| Luca Mazzola | Lucerne University of Applied Sciences, Switzerland |
| Inmaculada Medina-Bulo | Universidad de Cádiz, Spain |
| Hakima Mellah | Research Center in Scientific and Technical Information, Algeria |
| Ingo Melzer | Daimler AG, Germany |
| Abdelkrim Meziane | CERIST, Algeria |
| Marzal Miguel Ángel | Universidad Carlos III de Madrid, Spain |
| Matthew Montebello | University of Malta, Malta |
| Alex Norta | Tallinn University of Technology, Estonia |
| Declan O'Sullivan | Trinity College Dublin, Ireland |
| Miguel Angel Olivero | University of Seville, Spain |
| Pankaj Pandey | Norwegian University of Science and Technology, Norway |
| Kyparisia Papanikolaou | School of Educational and Technological Education (ASPETE), Greece |
| Kalpdrum Passi | Laurentian University, Canada |
| David Paul | University of New England, Australia |
| José Pereira | Instituto Politécnico de Setúbal |
| Isidoros Perikos | University of Patras, Greece |
| Laura Po | University of Modena and Reggio Emilia, Italy |
| Simona Popa | Universidad Católica San Antonio de Murcia, Spain |
| Bhanu Prasad | Florida A&M University, USA |
| Jim Prentzas | Democritus University of Thrace, Greece |
| Birgit Pröll | Johannes Kepler University Linz, Austria |
| Claudia Raibulet | University of Milano-Bicocca, Italy |

| | |
|---|---|
| Sheila Reinehr | Pontifical Catholic University of Paraná (PUCPR), Brazil |
| Thomas Risse | University Library Johann Christian Senckenberg, Germany |
| Davide Rossi | University of Bologna, Italy |
| Roberto Saia | University of Cagliari, Italy |
| Comai Sara | Politecnico di Milano, Italy |
| Claudio Schifanella | University of Turin, Italy |
| Wieland Schwinger | Johannes Kepler University Linz, Austria |
| Jochen Seitz | Technische Universität Ilmenau, Germany |
| Pavel Shapkin | National Research Nuclear University, MEPhI, Russia |
| John Shepherd | University of New South Wales, Australia |
| Marianna Sigala | UniSA Business, University of South Australia, Australia |
| Eliza Stefanova | Sofia University, Bulgaria |
| Chang-ai Sun | University of Science and Technology Beijing, China |
| Dirk Thissen | RWTH Aachen University, Germany |
| Jörg Thomaschewski | University of Applied Sciences Emden/Leer, Germany |
| Ramona Trestian | Middlesex University, UK |
| Th. Tsiatsos | Aristotle University of Thessaloniki, Greece |
| Christopher Turner | University of Surrey, UK |
| William Van Woensel | Dalhousie University, Canada |
| Elena-Madalina Vatamanescu | National University of Political Studies and Public Administration, Romania |
| Jari Veijalainen | University of Jyväskylä, Finland |
| Maurizio Vincini | DIEF, Università di Modena e Reggio Emilia, Italy |
| Petri Vuorimaa | Aalto University, Finland |
| Fan Wang | Microsoft, USA |
| Tony Wasserman | Carnegie Mellon University, USA |
| Manuel Wimmer | Johannes Kepler University Linz, Austria |
| Marco Winckler | Nice Sophia Antipolis University, France |

## Additional Reviewers

| | |
|---|---|
| Nuno Guimarães | University of Porto, Portugal |
| Alexandr Kormiltsyn | Tallinn University of Technology, Estonia |
| Brian Setz | University of Stuttgart, Germany |

## Invited Speakers

| | |
|---|---|
| Steffen Staab | University of Koblenz-Landau, Germany |
| Karl Aberer | EPFL, Switzerland |
| Claus Pahl | Free University of Bozen-Bolzano, Italy |

# Contents

# webAppOS: Creating the Illusion of a Single Computer for Web Application Developers

Sergejs Kozlovičs[✉]

Institute of Mathematics and Computer Science, University of Latvia,
Raina blvd. 29, Riga 1459, Latvia
sergejs.kozlovics@lumii.lv

**Abstract.** Unlike traditional single-PC applications, which have access to directly attached computational resources (CPUs, memory, and I/O devices), web applications have to deal with the resources scattered across the network. Besides, web applications are intended to be accessed by multiple users simultaneously. That not only requires a more sophisticated infrastructure but also brings new challenges to web application developers.

The webAppOS platform is an operating system analog for web applications. It factors out the network and provides the illusion of a single computer, the "web computer". That illusion allows web application developers to focus on business logic and create web applications faster. Besides, webAppOS standardizes many aspects of web applications and has the potential to become a universal environment for them.

**Keywords:** Web computer · Web applications · Web application operating system · webAppOS · Web application platform

## 1 Introduction

Babbage and Turing assumed that the computer is as a single device executing one program at a time and operated by a single user. Such a way of thinking is close to the psychology of the human brain since the brain is not able to focus on multiple tasks at the same time. Today, however, multitasking, networking, and multiple concurrent users are common as air. Luckily, modern operating systems implement multitasking, multiuser management, and local resource and device management. This aids in creating single-PC desktop applications, but does not help with web-based applications since the developers still have to think about application-level protocols as well as how to manage resources (CPUs, memory, and I/O devices) scattered across the network. The question arises: is it possible to simplify the process of developing web applications by allowing the developers to retain the Babbage/Turing way of thinking?

In our recent publication, we defined the concept of the *web computer*, the illusion of a single logical computer for web applications [9]. Although it still

© Springer Nature Switzerland AG 2020
A. Bozzon et al. (Eds.): WEBIST 2019, LNBIP 399, pp. 1–21, 2020.
https://doi.org/10.1007/978-3-030-61750-9_1

requires multiple physical network nodes to operate, web applications do not access them directly, but via the intermediate layer, webAppOS (web application operating system), which makes the illusion possible.

We recall the web computer architecture and the main functions of webAppOS in the next two sections. In this paper, we extend our contribution by providing additional details on webAppOS implementation. We also describe the process of creating a new web application from scratch as well as the process of migrating two real applications, OWLGrEd and DataGalaxies, to webAppOS. Furthermore, in this paper, we also address scalability issues. We conclude by discussing how webAppOS differs from existing Google Docs-like platforms.

## 2   The Web Computer

The **web computer** is an abstraction that hides network communication and creates the illusion of a single computer. The web computer consists of the following main parts: web memory (data memory), the code space (instructions memory), web processors, and web I/O devices.

Notice that data and code memory are separate; thus, the web computer follows the Harvard architecture. That differs from most classical computers, which follow the von Neumann architecture, where data and instructions are put into the same memory. The main reason for the Harvard-based approach is security: web applications are subject to code injection attacks [1]. We intentionally protect server-side code from being altered via web memory by untrusted clients. Nevertheless, approved references to code (code pointers, which actually are strings) can be stored as data in web memory. Another reason for the Harvard-based approach emerges from the differences between existing server-side and client-side environments (e.g., server-side PHP code is meaningless for the web browser). Thus, while we can synchronize the data transparently to create the illusion of a single data memory unit, it is not necessary to synchronize code.

We continue by describing the main parts of the web computer.

### 2.1   Web Memory (Data Memory)

Web memory is represented by a formal model. It consists of classes and objects (class instances). Classes have attributes, while objects have attribute values. Besides, there are associations between classes and the corresponding links between objects. Thus, web memory is an OOP-like structure, similar to that used by Java Virtual Machine.

The main reason for such design choice comes from the fact that models, in essence, are graphs; thus, they are more suitable for synchronization than classical arrays of bytes. Besides, models can be easily formalized (e.g., using standards like MOF and ECore [11, 16]).

Since synchronization involves some overhead, web memory should not be wasted. It is an analog of classical RAM; thus, only data that are currently in use should be stored there. Larger data sets can be stored elsewhere, e.g., in web I/O devices (see Sect. 2.4).

Multiple users can connect to the server and use the same web application simultaneously. Each user can also use the same application in different contexts (e.g., editing different documents). We use the term *project* to denote each such context. Each project has its own isolated web memory instance, which we call a *slot*. Projects resemble processes in traditional operating systems. Developers of traditional single-PC applications do not have to think about multiple concurrent processes, which are managed by the OS. Similarly, developers of web applications for the web computer do not have to think about multiple users working on multiple projects, since the web computer operating system (webAppOS) manages them.

## 2.2   The Code Space

From the web computer perspective, the code space is a pool of actions. An action, in essence, is some server-side or client-side function. We use the term *web call* to denote an action invocation or, in some cases, an action definition.

The code space relies on existing programming languages and technologies. Each action definition specifies the name of the action and how to invoke the corresponding code in the following format:

```
optional_modifiers name=instruction_set:code_location
```

The action name (before the "=" symbol) is a human-readable name, which can also be used as a reference to code. After the "=" symbol, there is a URI-like string describing the implementation of the action. The protocol part (before the ":" symbol) denotes the name of the *instruction set*, which represents a set of hardware and software requirements that may be imposed by the code. The remaining part specifies the code location.

Certain modifiers can be listed before the action name. One of them specifies *calling conventions*, i.e., the way how the arguments are passed and how the result is returned. Currently, two calling conventions are supported (they are mutually exclusive):

**jsoncall** the argument and the return value are encoded as JSON objects (stringified in some cases);

**webmemcall** the argument is passed as an object in web memory; the function returns no value, but it can modify web memory and store the results there (if any).

If the action does not require access to web memory[1], it has to be marked with the **static** modifier. If the action does not require an authenticated user session, it must be marked as **public**[2].

---

[1] *jsoncall* calling convention is implied for such actions.

[2] Since only authenticated users are allowed to access web memory, all non-static actions must also be non-public.

## Example

```
public static jsoncall echo=staticjava:pkg.ClassName#echoImpl
```

The action name is *echo*. The "staticjava" instruction set implies that the action is implemented as a static Java method and that a server-side Java virtual machine is required. The method name is *echoImpl*, and it is located in Java class *pkg.ClassName*. The web call can be invoked even when the user has not been authenticated (implied from the "public" modifier). Web memory will not be used (the "static" modifier). Since "jsoncall" calling conventions are specified, the *echoImpl* function must accept a JSON argument and follow other instruction set-specific conventions (e.g., in case of Java, the JSON argument will be passed as a string; the return value has to be stringified as well).

Web memory can be compared to the global variable scope. It is accessible from all non-static (and, hence, non-public) actions in the given code space. All internal variables (regardless of their actual programming language-specific scope) used when implementing actions are considered local variables—other actions are not able to access them.

The URI part can be replaced by another URI specifying some alternative implementation of the same action. Thus, the implementation can be completely rewritten or even moved from the server to the client, or vice versa. As soon as the calling conventions and arguments match, the web call remains valid regardless of the implementation location. Thus, we say that web calls are *implementation-agnostic*.

### 2.3   Web Processors

*Web processors* are software units that are able to invoke web calls. There is usually one client-side web processor (running in the web browser) and one or more server-side web processors[3]. In some cases, remote web processors (running on remote servers) can be introduced as well. Like in traditional multi-processor and multi-core systems, developers do not need to think about which particular processor will execute a particular web call. The appropriate server-side, client-side, or remote web processor will be chosen automatically depending on the programming language and the environment required by the given web call. From the developer's point of view, the web computer resembles a multi-processor system, where web processors share the same data memory but have separate arithmetic and logic units (ALUs).

Each web processor must support at least one instruction set. Usually, multiple instruction sets available for the underlying platform are supported by a single web processor. There can be variations of instruction sets, e.g., besides generic instruction set "js" for JavaScript code, we can define also the "clientjs" instruction set for code to be executed at the client side; we can even add a

---

[3] There is no one-to-one mapping with physical processors.

version, e.g., "clientjs6". Thus, instruction sets form a hierarchy based on the following "subclass of" relation definition:

an instruction set $I_2$ is a *subclass of instruction set* $I_1$, iff code requiring environment $I_1$ can be executed also within environment $I_2$.

By convention, a web processor implementing some particular instruction set should also support its superclasses.

## 2.4   Web I/O Devices

Besides web memory, there can be other data sources and receivers, which we call web input/output devices. Access to some of them is standardized via APIs provided by webAppOS. Examples of such standardized devices[4] are:

- The server-side file system. This is a "cloud drive" for storing user home directories. Other remote cloud drives (such as iCloud, OneDrive, or Google Drive) can be mounted as well.
- Registry. This is a tree-like database to store user-specific and application-specific settings.
- E-mail sender. This web I/O device is useful for registering user accounts and for password recovery.
- Desktop. This device represents the web browser window and provides the ability to display standard dialogs and launch installed web applications.

Other non-standardized devices can be accessed via web calls implemented in platform-specific code using any appropriate device API for that. For instance, a client-side printer can be accessed via the JavaScript API provided by the browser. A server-side NVIDIA graphics card can be accessible via CUDA. A remote database, which can be considered a storage device, can have both server-side and client-side APIs. In case some device becomes widely used, a standardized API can be defined for it and standardized within webAppOS.

## 3   The Web Computer Operating System (webAppOS)

Web applications targetting the web computer do not access its main parts directly but via a set of APIs provided by the web computer OS, webAppOS. The specification of webAppOS defines:

- server-side and client-side APIs for accessing web memory;
- APIs for accessing standardized web I/O devices;
- internal APIs for drivers and services.

---

[4] We use the word "standardized" from the webAppOS API perspective.

Besides that, webAppOS specification defines how to deploy web applications and web services, how web applications are delivered to the end user, and how to access third-party scopes such as Google services. The specification also defines internal communication channels (buses), e.g., between the browser and the server or between web memory and web processors.

The webAppOS distribution contains out-of-the-box modules for user authentication, file system access, the desktop environment, and other services. The distribution also has the default server-side web processor implementing several instruction sets and the client-side web processor implementing the "clientjs" (client-side JavaScript) instruction set.

The main goal of webAppOS is to provide an infrastructure for web applications and web services. It also provides a uniform way to authenticate users to access webAppOS server-side resources or remote resources provided by third parties. Besides that, webAppOS factors out the execution environment. The following subsections provide the details.

## 3.1 Applications, Libraries, and Services

A *webAppOS application* consists of:

- a set of web calls (from the code space) implementing the business logic;
- artifacts for ensuring the communication with the end user (including delivering client-side code to the web browser).

Web calls are implemented using existing server-side and client-side technology stacks. When necessary, some exotic instruction sets can be introduced by implementing additional server-side or remote web processors having specific prerequisites installed. Some web calls can have multiple implementations for different platforms (e.g., for full-screen browsers, for mobile browsers, or for different host operating systems and processor architectures). Since web calls are implementation-agnostic, webAppOS can choose the most suitable web call implementation depending on the underlying platform.

Web calls can invoke other web calls, access web memory, access standardized web I/O devices using webAppOS APIs, access other devices using native APIs, perform computational and other tasks. Thus, the sequence of web calls resembles the execution of a classical single-PC program with traditional CALL/JUMP instructions. However, web calls can switch the execution flow between the server and the browser, which both share the same web memory state, which is being constantly and automatically synchronized.

Like classical applications, web applications can be graphical and console. We rely on HTTP to deliver graphical web applications to the end user. Similarly, we use the Web Socket protocol for delivering the output of console applications to the browser.

Classical GUI applications can be written using different technologies such as native API (Windows API or Cocoa) or using some GUI library, e.g., QT or JavaFX. Similarly, console applications can be written using native code or as scripts (shell or Python scripts). The same applies to web applications. Graphical webAppOS applications can be deployed, for example, as HTML/JS/CSS files, PHP scripts, or Java servlets. Console web applications can be implemented using, for instance, CGI-like forwarding of input/output streams or as Java web socket servlets. To support all different ways of delivering web applications to the end user, webAppOS relies on *application adapters*.

*Libraries* in webAppOS resemble dynamic (shared) libraries in traditional desktop operating systems. A web library is a set of web calls that can be re-used in multiple web applications. Each web call can access the same web memory slot as used by the main web application for the current project. Web libraries are also useful for factoring out platform-specific services, where different implementations can be provided for different platforms. Thus, web applications can be developed in a platform-independent way by delegating platform-specific web calls to such libraries.

A *webAppOS service* is a module that provides useful functionality to webAppOS or third-party applications. However, end users do not access them directly. Services can be implemented as Java servlets, as client-side JavaScript code, as non-HTTP services, as Docker containers, or using some other technology. To support different service types, webAppOS uses *service adapters*.

Services can invoke web calls and access web memory, web I/O devices, and other resources. However, when being accessed, a service may require some form of user authentication as well as the context (e.g., the current project for invoking web calls).

Let us mention webAppOS WebDAV service as an example. The service provides access to the user's home directory. It uses webAppOS FileSystem API and requires users credentials (login+password) for that. The WebDAV service is implemented as a Java servlet. End users do not access WebDAV service directly, some client-side software supporting the webDAV protocol is required for that.

## 3.2   Scopes: A Uniform Way to Access Resources

We use the term *scope* to refer to a resource or a set of resources that require some form of authentication. Each scope has some name defined by the resource provider, e.g., Google "profile" and "spreadsheets" scopes. After successful authentication, some token is stored at the client or server side, and the resources from the desired scope become accessible by passing the token to the corresponding API.

Although the underlying resources and their APIs differ, webAppOS defines a uniform Scopes API. This API relies on scopes drivers, which perform provider-specific authentication (e.g., Google authentication via the OAuth2.0 protocol) and receive access tokens. Since authorizing scopes requires user's intervention at the client-side, Scopes API is available only at the client-side. However, scopes drivers can store tokens not only at the client side (e.g., as cookies or in *localStorage*) but also at the server side (e.g., in webAppOS Registry). Thus, webAppOS applications and services that support the APIs of the underlying resources can access them via the stored token.

For some resources, webAppOS has a standardized API, e.g., File System API for accessing resources represented as file systems. Scopes drivers should implement such standardized APIs for their underlying resources whenever possible. We call such implementations *web I/O device drivers*. By relying on these drivers, webAppOS can provide deeper integration with remote scopes and resources, e.g., by providing the ability to mount remote file systems.

Scopes drivers are implemented as webAppOS web services accessible from the client side. If a scopes driver implements some web I/O device driver, it should specify where the implementation is located (e.g., the name of the Java class that implements the File System API for the underlying scope).

### Example: "google_scopes" driver

A "google_scopes" driver provides the google_scopes_driver.js script, which will be called by webAppOS whenever authentication from Google is required to access some of the Google services (e.g., "gdrive"). The google_scopes_driver.js displays the Google login window. After successful authentication, the driver stores the token in the webAppOS registry (for the given user). Besides, the "google_scopes" driver implements webAppOS File System API in some Java class (a file system driver), which takes the stored token and forwards it to Google, when the user wants to access the Google drive.

### Example: "webappos_scopes" driver

webAppOS scopes driver defines the "login" scope, which displays the login page. After successful authentication, the user can access certain web I/O devices (e.g., the user's home file system) and make private web calls. The "project_id" scope extends "login". In addition, it initializes access to web memory for some webAppOS project (if the project has not been specified in the URL, the user can choose it).

## 3.3   Execution Environments

Typically, webAppOS runs in the *web environment*, having on or more servers that are accessed by multiple concurrent users from their browsers. By bundling the web server and the web browser component into a single desktop application, webAppOS can be launched as a standalone desktop application (we say that webAppOS runs in the *desktop environment*). If client-side code that creates graphical presentations is re-written to support small screen sizes and touch events, we can try to launch webAppOS applications in the *mobile environment*.

As a special use case, certain web applications can be created using only client-side parts of webAppOS. Such applications can rely on webAppOS client-side APIs and access third-party services, without the need to launch a webAppOS server. From the webAppOS point of view, such applications are *serverless*. Such applications can be deployed as a folder with static files that can be opened locally or served by a tiny web server.

# 4   Examples

In this section, we describe the steps required to create the "Hello, World!" webAppOS application and share the experience of migrating two existing applications to webAppOS, namely, OWLGrEd and DataGalaxies.

## 4.1   The "Hello, World!" Application

We describe how to create a simple application, where the server-side code (written in Java) stores a message in web memory and invokes a client-side web call (implemented in JavaScript) that displays that message to the end user.

A webAppOS application is deployed as a directory. It contains the webapp.properties file, where application-specific settings are specified, such as the extension for projects, application delivery type (e.g., "html" for the HTML/JS/CSS client side) and paths for finding the code (e.g., Java classpaths). The most important setting is "main", which specifies the initial web call, which will be invoked each time the project is created or opened:

```
main=HelloWorldMain
```

Since we are going to implement the main web call in Java, we declare it in the HelloWorld.webcalls file as follows:

```
webmemcall HelloWorldMain=staticjava:\
    org.webappos.apps.helloworld.HelloWorld#initial
```

According to this declaration, we have to create the HelloWorld Java class containing the static initial method:

```
package org.webappos.apps.helloworld;
...
public class HelloWorld {
    public static void initial(IWebMemory webmem, String project_id, long r) {
    ...
```

Since the HelloWorldMain web call uses the *webmemcall* calling conventions, the "staticjava" web calls adapter will pass to it the pointer to web memory, the current project id, and the reference $r$ to some object in web memory (for initial web calls, $r = 0$).

To be able to store data in web memory, we have to define our data metamodel (e.g., in XML-based ECore syntax). Suppose we defined the HelloWorld-Metamodel.ecore file containing the *HelloWorld* class having the *message* property of type *EString*. Since metamodel files are found and loaded into web memory automatically by webAppOS, the initial web call will be able to access the *HelloWorld* class right away via the *webmem* pointer[5].

However, using the web memory pointer directly is considered a low-level approach since the corresponding API resembles the assembly language. A more convenient approach is to generate Java classes that correspond to the desired web memory structure. The generator[6] can be invoked from the command line as follows:

---

[5] For non-Java code, a shared library for accessing web memory from Windows, Linux, and macOS native code is available.

[6] It is bundled into the webAppOS distribution.

```
../../bin/ecore2java HelloWorldMetamodel.ecore src
```

(here *src* is the target directory for Java classes).

After elevating the *webmem* pointer, we can access web memory classes as Java classes. In the following listing, we find or create a *HelloWorld* instance and set the value for the *message* property.

```
HelloWorldMetamodelFactory factory =
  webmem.elevate(HelloWorldMetamodelFactory.class);

HelloWorld objectWithMessage = HelloWorld.firstObject(factory);
if (objectWithMessage==null) {
  objectWithMessage = factory.createHelloWorld();
  objectWithMessage.setMessage("Hello for the first time!");
}
else
  objectWithMessage.setMessage("Hello again!");
```

To invoke another web call from Java, we use the server-side function *API.webCaller.enqueue*. It takes one argument, a web call seed, which specifies information about the web call.

```
WebCallSeed seed2 = new WebCallSeed();
seed2.actionName = "ShowMessageFromWebMemory";
seed2.project_id = project_id;
seed2.webmemArgument = objectWithMessage.getRAAPIReference();
seed2.callingConventions = IWebCaller.CallingConventions.WEBMEMCALL;
API.webCaller.enqueue(seed2);
```

We define the client-side *ShowMessageFromWebMemory* web call in HelloWorld.webcalls as follows:

```
webmemcall ShowMessageFromWebMemory=clientjs:helloFromWebMemory
```

Then we define the *helloFromWebMemory* function (e.g., in the script tag of index.html), which takes a web memory object as an argument and displays the message:

```
<script>
...
function helloFromWebMemory(obj) {
        alert(obj.getMessage());
}
...
</script>
```

We do not need to generate JavaScript classes (or object prototypes) to be able to access web memory from the client side—these classes (and the corresponding properties such as *getMessage*) will be created automatically on web memory synchronization.

However, to be able to use web memory at the client side, it has to be initialized via Scopes API as follows:

```
<script>
...
webappos.request_scopes("webappos_scopes", "project_id").then(
  // web-memory initialized
);
...
</script>
```

The corresponding webAppOS scopes driver will request user credentials (via the login page) and ask for the project to create or open. Then it will initialize and synchronize web memory that will become accessible as JavaScript property *webmem*.

## 4.2  OWLGrEd

OWLGrEd[7] is a powerful graphical editor for OWL 2.0 ontologies [2,12]. It has a high evaluation among the semantic web community [4]. Since the desktop version of OWLGrEd has been available for Windows only, we conduct an experiment of migrating OWLGrEd to the web, thus, making it accessible from multiple platforms.

First, we decided to retain the code implementing the business logic of OWLGrEd. That could not only save time but also minimize maintenance costs of existing OWLGrEd features, which must be supported in both desktop and web versions of OWLGrEd. Since the business logic code was written in Lua, we developed the "lua" web calls adapter to be used by the default server-side web processor to invoke Lua web calls. The adapter has been implemented using the LuaJ[8] library. In addition, we have created a LuaJ module for accessing web memory from Lua. This module provides the same data access API used by desktop OWLGrEd. As a result, the Lua code itself remained mostly unchanged.

However, to be able to visualize diagrams and dialog windows in the web browser, we had to re-write the corresponding graphical OWLGrEd components in JavaScript as client-side web libraries. We used the *ajoo* library for editing graph-like diagrams [14] and the DoJo Toolkit[9] for visualizing dialog windows. In addition, we used Google Web Toolkit[10] to move our layout library (for calculating coordinates of diagram elements and dialog widgets) to the web [6].

To ensure the communication between the server-side Lua code and client-side web libraries, we had to declare web calls to be triggered on certain user events (such as clicks). All technical aspects (such as data synchronization and invocations of web calls) are managed by webAppOS. Besides, webAppOS provides default dialogs for uploading, downloading, and opening projects in a way similar to opening files in classical desktop applications using a file explorer. The "Browse for file" and "Save as" dialogs are also available to webAppOS applications. Thus, OWLGrEd/webAppOS provides the same end user experience as the classical desktop-based OWLGrEd.

Finally, since webAppOS is able to synchronize web memory between multiple clients, additional clients (e.g., a debugger) can be attached to OWLGrEd. These clients can be used to manipulate OWLGrEd diagrams programmatically from the outside.

---

[7] http://owlgred.lumii.lv/.

[8] http://www.luaj.org/luaj.html.

[9] https://dojotoolkit.org/.

[10] http://www.gwtproject.org/.

### 4.3  DataGalaxies

The DataGalaxies tool provides a common space where different types of data transformations and visualizations can be joined together to perform manipulations on data and obtain the desired result. The flow of manipulations is represented graphically as a graph.

Unlike OWLGrEd, the DataGalaxies tool was initially created as a web application. However, it stored all data at the server side. Thus, when some data manipulation had to be performed at the client side, one or more round-trips were required to fetch the data from the server. When client-side code had to invoke some server-side data transformation, DataGalaxies relied on the Direct Web Remoting library, DWR[11]. The library provided a reverse AJAX implementation, which, in essence, was a patch to the HTTP protocol. The code was not elegant, but it worked.

When migrating DataGalaxies to webAppOS, we removed the DWR library and moved into web memory server-side data that had to be accessed from both the server and the browser. As a result, these data are now synchronized by webAppOS automatically via web sockets; thus, we avoid unnecessary round-trips and send data more efficiently. Besides, we removed the code that fetched data from the server. Now, data can be accessed from the client-side replica of web memory directly. As a result, the code became more elegant and more readable. We realize that if we had to develop the DataGalaxy tool from scratch, it would be much easier to implement it using webAppOS as the underlying platform. Furthermore, webAppOS applications benefit from many features available "for free" such as the default dialogs and the convenient built-in user authentication mechanism.

## 5  Implementation

### 5.1  Main Design Choices

Java is the primary language for server-side code. Since Java is platform-independent, webAppOS can be launched on a wide range of platforms. Another argument in favor of Java is that Java does not suffer from attacks based on buffer overflow. Finally, other languages can be invoked from Java using Java Native Interface, JNI, or various inter-process communication techniques.

Client-side webAppOS code is written in JavaScript as it is the de facto language for the code within the web browser. However, webAppOS does not prohibit to use other client-side technologies, which can be invoked from JavaScript[12].

---

[11] http://directwebremoting.org/.

[12] For instance, Java applets, VisualBasic, and ActiveX scripts can be launched by appending the appropriate tag (<script>, <object>, or <applet>) to the DOM; WebAssembly code can be launched by invoking WebAssembly.instantiate/instantiateStreaming, etc.

We use Jetty[13] as a Java-based out-of-the-box web server. At the client side, virtually any modern browser supporting JavaScript and web sockets can be used.

## 5.2   Implementing the Main Components

*Web Memory.* We use our efficient model repository AR for implementing web memory (one repository per slot) [7,8]. AR is able to use OS-managed memory-mapped files; thus, thousands of concurrent users can be served even on low-memory systems. Besides, AR uses an efficient encoding of models that resembles Kolmogorov complexity and is suitable for direct synchronization via web sockets.

*The Code Space.* The code space is represented by the *apps* directory at the server side. It contains subdirectories corresponding to webAppOS applications, web libraries, and services. Each subdirectory can contain *.webcalls* files containing declarations of web calls (their implementations are located in further subdirectories, e.g., *bin* for server-side Java code or *web-root* for client-side JavaScript code). Besides, there is a properties file describing how webAppOS should load, attach, and display the corresponding web application, web library, or service. Based on the data from the properties file, webAppOS finds the corresponding web application or web service adapter and registers URL paths such as /apps/myapp or /services/myservice. Web libraries are not registered, but they are loaded by webAppOS when they are required by some web application.

Client-side code is delivered according to the application or service adapter. Some adapters serve the *web-root* subdirectory; some implement redirects to local services; others implement Java servlets that generate HTTP responses on-the-fly.

*Web Processors.* Server-side and remote web processors are launched as separate OS processes via the corresponding *web processor adapters*. The adapters launch (or connect to) web processors and provide access to web memory. When a web processor crashes or freezes (e.g., due to some unhandled exception or an infinite cycle in a web call), the corresponding adapter can terminate and re-launch it. However, after re-launching a web processor, the underlying web memory slot is invalidated and re-loaded from the last saved state.

Typically, server-side local web processors are instances of the default web processor implemented in Java. This web processor is able to invoke web calls via the out-of-the-box web calls adapters for various programming languages such as Java and Lua.

There is only one default client-side web processor implemented in JavaScript, which relies on client-side web calls adapters for launching different types of client-side code.

*Web I/O Devices.* Non-standardized web I/O devices can be accessed from web calls (in the code space) via specific native APIs. However, for the standardized

---

[13] https://www.eclipse.org/jetty/.

web I/O devices, webAppOS scopes drivers have to be created (refer to Sect. 3.2). Scopes drivers should also contain standardized web I/O device drivers implementing the corresponding webAppOS API in Java and/or JavaScript. For the serverfull mode, only server-side web I/O device drivers are required. To support the serverless mode as well, the scopes driver should also provide an independent client-side implementation of device drivers.

After requesting and authenticating a scope, the corresponding access tokens are stored (e.g., in webAppOS registry or within client-side cookies) and can be used to access web I/O devices in that scope. Typically, these tokens are used by web I/O device drivers, which are then used internally by webAppOS to provide seamless access to the scope. However, the tokens can also be used by web calls that are able to access the scope directly.

*Bridges.* Both the client and the server have an internal component called a *bridge*. Bridges are responsible for:

- initializing and synchronizing web memory; the server-side bridge also manages web memory slots for different active projects;
- managing ingoing and outgoing web calls (web calls are either executed at the same side of forwarded to the other side);
- managing web processors at the corresponding network node[14].

The server-side bridge is implemented in Java as a web socket adapter for Jetty; it serves web sockets and implements server-side threads for synchronizing web memory and web calls. The client-side bridge, in its turn, is implemented via a *WebSocket* object in JavaScript.

When multiple clients are connected, the server-side bridge usually forwards client-side web calls to all of them. However, some client-side web calls can be marked as *single*. In this case, the web call will be passed only to one client, which issued the "parent" (previous) web call.

## 5.3   Implementing Communication Between Components

webAppOS components use several communication channels. If the communication is performed via the network or inter-process communication techniques, the corresponding channels are called *buses*. There are four main buses:

- *HTTP/AJAX Bus* is used to deliver client-side code and user interface (HTML/CSS/JavaScript) to the web browser; the bus is also used to access HTTP-based web services (including out-of-the-box services for file upload and download);
- *Web Socket Bus* is a web socket-based channel used by bridges for synchronizing web memory and forwarding web calls (when they have to be executed on the other node);

---

[14] Since currently there is only one client-side web processor, no manager is needed there.

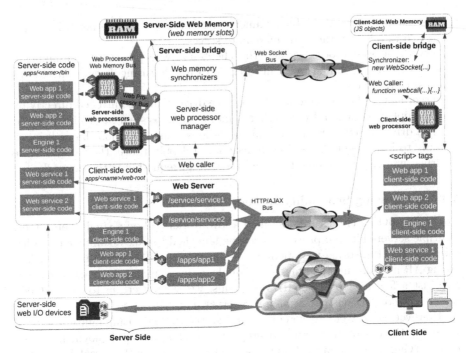

**Fig. 1.** Implementation of the web computer architecture (image adapted from the initial paper on webAppOS [9]). In-place communication is represented by think arrows, while buses are depicted by thick arrows. Cubes "P" and "C" stand for web processor and web call adapters, "S" and "A" for service and application adapters, "Sc" and "FS" for scopes and file system drivers.

- *Web Processor/Web Memory Bus* is used by server-side web processors (which are separate OS processes) to access web memory; the bus relies on memory-mapped files used by the AR repository;
- *Web Processor Bus* is a communication channel between the server-side bridge and server-side/remote web processors; implemented via Java RMI [13].

In-process communication is implemented via ordinary function calls or using threads. We list some examples.

- The web-server and the server-side bridge run in the same Java process; thus, they share the same memory and communicate directly. The same process is also responsible for initializing web memory slots.
- The server-side bridge also communicates directly to web processor adapters, which are implemented in Java ("P" in Fig. 1). These adapters launch (or connect to) web processors and provide them with the means to access Web Processor Bus and Web Processor/Web Memory Bus.
- The web server (Jetty) communicates directly to application and service adapters ("A" and "S" in Fig. 1). These adapters can either attach Java mod-

ules (e.g., servlets) directly or launch (or connect to) some other third-party service running on the same or remote server.

- Server-side web processors and the client-side web processor communicate with the corresponding web calls adapters directly (using Java or JavaScript calls, respectively).
- Server-side and client-side web I/O device drivers are also invoked directly by webAppOS on demand (e.g., when a mounted file system has to be accessed via a driver). However, drivers can use various communication channels internally to implement the desired functionality. For instance, the Google Drive driver will rely on Google Drive API and send requests via the network.

## 5.4    Addressing Scalability Issues

The webAppOS architecture described above works well on a single web server. Multiple server-side web processors can be launched to take advantage of multicore systems. Regarding web memory, we have tested 10,000 web memory slots (using AR memory-mapped files) on a single node assuming that each slot occupies just a few megabytes of RAM[15]. Thus, we are targetting to serve 10,000 concurrent connections per webAppOS server node [5].

However, to serve more concurrent users, we advise creating multiple virtual servers in the cloud. To be able to support such cloud-based deployments (each node serving approximately 10,000 users), webAppOS must be scalable. Below we explain how different parts of webAppOS can be scaled.

- Since the code space remains static for the most of time (excluding occasional configuration changes and updates), it can be shared among all webAppOS nodes as a network drive or replicated. That can be done using existing technologies (such as NFS or *rsync*).
- The server-side file system, which stores user home directories, can be shared or replicated in the same way as the code space.
- webAppOS registry can be configured to use the CouchDB no-SQL database, which has the built-in replication feature. Alternatively, the registry can be launched on a dedicated server accessible from all webAppOS nodes.
- E-mail sender (one of the server-side web I/O devices used by webAppOS itself) is specified by its URL and credentials. It can be an external server having its own load balancer, or there can be multiple local e-mail senders configured for each node individually.
- There is no need to support scalability for client-side web I/O devices since each user already has a dedicated browser instance relying on the client-side resources controlled by the user.
- We assume that one web memory slot entirely belongs to one webAppOS node. It is the responsibility of the load balancer to route web socket connections between multiple clients and multiple webAppOS nodes in a way that respects our assumption.

---

[15] Web-based Microsoft Office imposes the 5MiB restriction on files being edited online. Similarly, our web-based tools OWLGrEd/webAppOS and DataGalaxies normally require just a few megabytes of RAM per project.

- Adapters for stateless web applications and web services that do not require access to web memory (such as adapters serving static files or generating HTTP responses that do not depend on data from web memory) can be launched on each webAppOS node. The load balancer can switch between them randomly.
- For each stateful web application or service, only one instance will be launched on some webAppOS node. Other webAppOS nodes will redirect queries to that instance.
- For web applications and services requiring web memory, the adapters will be launched on each webAppOS node. If the request comes to the node having the required web memory slot, that node executes the request. Otherwise, the node redirects the request to the correct one.

## 6    Related Work

The end user experience with webAppOS resembles existing cloud-based application platforms such as iCloud, Microsoft Office Online, and Google Docs. An alternative way to communicate with the end user is the out-of-the-box webAppOS Desktop application, which provides the feeling of a classical desktop. Such web-based desktops are sometimes called "web operating systems", webOSes [10]. The term is applied mostly to client-side window managers such as Os.js[16], WebDesktop.biz[17], and AaronOS[18]. Unfortunately, they are not widely used; some of them have been discontinued (e.g., eyeOS, ZeroPC). Thus, we do not expect wide popularity of the built-in webAppOS Desktop application. Nevertheless, we can say that webAppOS is also a webOS, which goes a step further – it provides not only the client-side window manager but also the server-side environment and communication mechanisms.

There is a plethora of client-side libraries for creating rich HTML-based and single-page web applications, including AngularJS and Angular 2+[19], Dojo Toolkit and Dojo2[20], React[21], Aurelia[22], Ember[23], Vue[24], Backbone.js[25], Bootstrap[26], D3[27] as well as classical jQuery[28] and jQueryUI[29]. All they can be used

---

[16] https://www.os-js.org/.
[17] http://webdesktop.biz/.
[18] https://aaron-os-mineandcraft12.c9.io/aosBeta.php.
[19] https://angularjs.org/, https://angular.io/.
[20] https://dojotoolkit.org/, https://dojo.io/.
[21] https://reactjs.org/.
[22] https://aurelia.io/.
[23] https://emberjs.com/.
[24] https://vuejs.org/.
[25] https://backbonejs.org/.
[26] https://getbootstrap.com/.
[27] https://d3js.org/.
[28] https://jquery.com/.
[29] https://jqueryui.com/.

at the client-side in webAppOS (in both serverfull and serverless web applications). Different techniques to port existing non-JavaScript code to implement client-side web calls can also be used. They include Google Web Toolkit (for porting Java code)[30], Blazor (for compiling C# code to WebAssembly)[31], and others.

Popular environments that provide both client-side and server-side functionality are Node.js[32] and Meteor[33]. Unlike Node.js, webAppOS allows developers to use virtually any programming language available at the server or client side, not just JavaScript. Meteor is built on Node.js, but has a built-in client-server data synchronization mechanism, which resembles webAppOS web memory. However, Meteor uses MongoDB, a no-SQL database, which is optimized for fast queries, but not for fast writes. Besides, Meteor is also tied to JavaScript and requires to write explicit listeners in code to synchronize data, while webAppOS synchronizes web memory automatically.

Google Apps Script[34] is a platform for developing web applications based on Google services. This is an excellent choice if Google service are sufficient for the task. However, if specific server-side functionality is required, it has to be integrated manually. With webAppOS, such integration becomes easier.

CloudRail Unified APIs[35] was an initiative to provide universal APIs for various cloud services. It resembled standardized APIs for scopes and webAppOS web I/O device drivers. Regretfully, the unified API branch was discontinued by CloudRail on March 1, 2019. We hope that webAppOS devices can take over the baton by providing free and open-source APIs and implementations of the corresponding drivers for different cloud service providers.

An interesting approach for bringing traditional desktop applications to the web is via cloud platforms such as RollApp and AlwaysOnPC, where windows of classical applications are forwarded to the web browser[36]. Open-source libraries such as Gnome Broadway[37] and xpra[38] as well as commercial Citrix Virtual Apps[39] use a similar approach. The same approach can be introduced in webAppOS. However, it would require a dedicated web processor and more RAM for each running application; thus, the number of concurrent users that can be served simultaneously would decrease significantly.

Although we rely on our model repository AR to implement web memory, linked data and semantic web technologies such as RDF and OWL could also be used for that [18–21]. Semantic reasoners can even be viewed as specific instruction sets for web processors [3].

---

[30] http://www.gwtproject.org/.
[31] https://blazor.net/.
[32] https://nodejs.org/.
[33] https://www.meteor.com/.
[34] https://www.google.com/script/start/.
[35] https://cloudrail.com/.
[36] https://www.rollapp.com, http://www.alwaysonpc.com/.
[37] https://developer.gnome.org/gtk3/stable/gtk-broadway.html.
[38] https://xpra.org.
[39] https://www.citrix.com/products/citrix-virtual-apps-and-desktops/.

The Electron[40] framework is intended to simplify the development of cross-platform desktop applications using web technologies. That resembles how webAppOS is intended to support multiple target environments (web, desktop, and mobile), but without the requirement to use JavaScript for all the code.

There is an interesting relation between the web computer and the architecture of classical computers. If we re-arrange main elements from Fig. 1, we come up with Fig. 2(a), where we can notice a similarity with the typical motherboard layout (Fig. 2(b)).

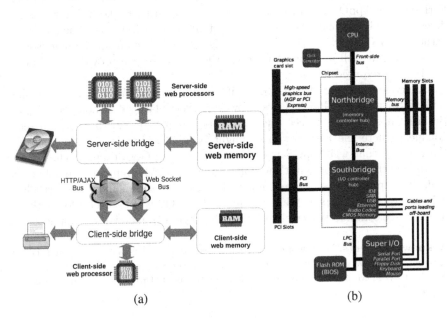

**Fig. 2.** (a) The overall webAppOS architecture. (b) A typical layout of the north and south bridges (image by Gribeco and Moxfyre, CC BY-SA 3.0).

## 7  Conclusion

The main advantage of using webAppOS to develop web applications is the illusion of a single target computer. This illusion corresponds to the physiology of the human brain; thus, web applications can be created faster and at a higher level of abstraction, where the network is factored out. The webAppOS learning curve is also very straightforward. Another benefit is that webAppOS provides common grounds for virtually all types of web applications and services. By using the appropriate adapters and drivers, different parts of the web application can be written using different technologies and programming languages. Since

---

[40] https://electronjs.org/.

webAppOS is open-source[41], it facilitates the usage of private web servers, where the users have more control over their data [15].

Technical strengths of webAppOS are the presence of automatically and transparently synchronized web memory and the ability to invoke code via web calls in an implementation-agnostic way. Synchronization is very fast. It bases on web sockets and efficient model encoding provided by the AR repository.

Alan Kay, a Computer Science pioneer, once said that the web browser acts as a mini-operating system. We would say that webAppOS is a step further; it is a superstructure over *both*, the server-side OS and the client-side web browser. Perhaps, webAppOS can eventually become standardized "kernel" for existing diversified web applications and services, similarly how Linux became a *de facto* kernel for GNU software [17]. However, significant efforts from the open-source community, as well as support from existing cloud service providers and other parties, are required for that.

Someone may ask: Why Google will not do the same? In fact, Google has a platform used by Google Docs. However, their platform is not open-source. Besides, most cloud services (including Google) rely on existing, proven technologies, where the learning curve might be longer, but is more predictable. We can say that webAppOS is the inversion of the Google approach. On the one hand, the web computer metaphor is closer to the human brain, but the underlying platform is new and not widely used at the moment. Nevertheless, it is innovative and open. We hope that webAppOS will be useful for both the open-source community as well as for developers of commercial web applications.

**Acknowledgments.** The work has been supported by European Regional Development Fund within the project #1.1.1.2/16/I/001, application #1.1.1.2/VI-AA/1/16/214 "Model-Based Web Application Infrastructure with Cloud Technology Support".

# References

1. Andrews, M., Whittaker, J.A.: How to Break Web Software: Functional and Security Testing of Web Applications and Web Services. Addison-Wesley Professional, Boston (2006)
2. Barzdins, J., Barzdins, G., Cerans, K., Liepins, R., Sprogis, A.: OWLGrEd: a UML style graphical notation and editor for OWL 2. In: Proceedings of OWLED 2010 (2010)
3. Corno, F., Farinetti, L.: Logic and reasoning in the semantic web (Part II - OWL). Materials for the "1LHVIU - Semantic Web: Technologies, Tools, Applications" course at Politecnico di Torino, Dipartimento di Automatica e Informatica (2012). http://elite.polito.it/files/courses/01LHV/2012/7-OWLreasoning.pdf
4. Dudáš, M., Lohmann, S., Svátek, V., Pavlov, D.: Ontology visualization methods and tools: a survey of the state of the art. Knowl. Eng. Rev. **33**, e10 (2018). https://doi.org/10.1017/S0269888918000073
5. Kegel, D.: The C10K problem. http://www.kegel.com/c10k.html

---

[41] http://webappos.org.

6. Kozlovics, S.: Calculating the layout for dialog windows specified as models. In: Scientific Papers, University of Latvia, vol. 787, pp. 106–124 (2012)
7. Kozlovičs, S.: Efficient model repository for web applications. In: Lupeikiene, A., Vasilecas, O., Dzemyda, G. (eds.) DB&IS 2018. CCIS, vol. 838, pp. 216–230. Springer, Cham (2018). https://doi.org/10.1007/978-3-319-97571-9_18
8. Kozlovičs, S.: Fast model repository as memory for web applications. Databases Inf. Syst. X **315**, 176–191 (2019)
9. Kozlovičs, S.: The web computer and its operating system: a new approach for creating web applications. In: Proceedings of the 15th International Conference on Web Information Systems and Technologies (2019). https://doi.org/10.5220/0008053800460057
10. Lawton, G.: Moving the OS to the web. Computer **41**(3), 16–19 (2008). https://doi.org/10.1109/MC.2008.94
11. Object Management Group: OMG Meta Object Facility (MOF) Core Specification Version 2.4.1 (2011)
12. Ovčinnikova, J., Čerāns, K.: Advanced UML style visualization of OWL ontologies. In: Proceedings of the Second International Workshop on Visualization and Interaction for Ontologies and Linked Data co-located with the 15th International Semantic Web Conference (ISWC 2016) CEUR 1704, pp. 136–142 (2016)
13. Pitt, E., McNiff, K.: Java.Rmi: The Remote Method Invocation Guide. Addison-Wesley Longman Publishing Co., Inc., Boston (2001)
14. Sprogis, A.: ajoo: WEB based framework for domain specific modeling tools. In: Frontiers in Artificial Intelligence and Applications Volume 291: Databases and Information Systems IX (2016)
15. Stallman, R.: Who does that server really serve? (2010). http://www.bostonreview.net/richard-stallman-free-software-DRM
16. Steinberg, D., Budinsky, F., Paternostro, M., Merks, E.: EMF: Eclipse Modeling Framework, 2nd edn. Addison-Wesley, Boston (2008)
17. Tozzi, C.: For Fun and Profit: A History of the Free and Open Source Software Revolution. The MIT Press, Cambridge (2017)
18. W3C: OWL Web Ontology Language reference (2004). http://www.w3.org/TR/owl-ref/
19. W3C: OWL 2 Web Ontology Language Document Overview, 2nd edn. (2012). http://www.w3.org/TR/owl2-overview/
20. W3C: RDF Vocabulary Description Language 1.0: RDF Schema (2014). http://www.w3.org/TR/rdf-schema/
21. W3C: Resource Description Framework (2014). http://www.w3.org/RDF/

# Digital Services Based on Vehicle Usage Data: The Underlying Vehicle Data Value Chain

Christian Kaiser[1,3]([⊠]), Andreas Festl[1], Gernot Pucher[2], Michael Fellmann[3], and Alexander Stocker[1]

[1] Virtual Vehicle Research GmbH, Inffeldgasse 21a, Graz 8010, Austria
{christian.kaiser,andreas.festl,alexander.stocker}@v2c2.at
[2] TraffiCon – Traffic Consultants GmbH, Strubergasse 26, Salzburg, Austria
pucher@trafficon.eu
[3] University of Rostock, Albert-Einstein-Straße 22, Rostock, Germany
michael.fellmann@uni-rostock.de

**Abstract.** The quantify-everything trend has reached the automotive sector while digitalization is a still the major driver of innovation. New digital services based on vehicle usage data are being created for different actors and purposes, e.g. for individual drivers who want to know about their own driving style and behavior or for fleet managers who want to find out about their fleet. As a side effect, a growing number of ICT start-ups from outside Europe have entered the automotive market to work on innovative use cases. Their digital services are based on the availability of vehicle data on a large scale. To better understand and capture this ongoing digital change in the automotive sector, we present an extended version of the Vehicle Data Value Chain (VDVC) originally published in Kaiser et al. (2019a) and use it as a model for better structuring, describing and testing digital services based on vehicle usage data. We classify digital services of two projects by using the VDVC in our paper, an intermodal mobility service and a pothole and driving style detection service. Thus, we evaluate the VDVC and show its general applicability and usefulness in a practical context.

**Keywords:** Big data · Big Data Value Chain · Vehicle Data Value Chain · Digital services based on vehicle usage data · Connected services · Crowdsourcing of data

## 1 Introduction and Motivation

Modern mobility is an important driver of our increasingly global economy: raw materials are transported around the globe and processed into products in value-added processes until they finally find their way to the customer via many intermediate stations. Passenger cars and trucks are assembled in a complex supply chain consisting of many small parts and components and finally manufactured in several value-added steps on a production line before they are delivered to customers. This basic business principle was very successful in many domains for a long time, until digitalization added another business aspect, which is becoming an important driver and has even become the decisive

A. Bozzon et al. (Eds.): WEBIST 2019, LNBIP 399, pp. 22–43, 2020.
https://doi.org/10.1007/978-3-030-61750-9_2

criterion in many sectors, including the automotive industry (Accenture 2016). Similar to smartphones, where the focus is no longer on the original innovation, i.e. telephoning, but on digital apps, it is becoming increasingly important for vehicles, too, which digital functionalities they offer - from the Bluetooth connectivity with smartphones to Vehicle-to-Infrastructure (V2I) and Vehicle-to-Vehicle (V2V) services or to third-party services that someone can install. And in the context of vehicle use, services based on vehicle usage data have the potential to go beyond the usual application focus of quantified self-applications, namely self-optimization, learning about oneself, social comparison and interaction or gaming, as they can even be extended in a life-saving manner. Driving style analysis, for example, is able to detect driver fatigue and distraction (Lechner et al. 2019), two of the most common causes of accidents. Thus, it is crucial for research to explore how digital services based on vehicle data can improve the practice of driving or enable novel applications for other stakeholders and other markets outside the automotive domain (Stocker et al. 2017).

The basis for digitalization in the automotive domain are the ever-increasing amount of vehicle usage data generated (e.g. modern vehicles are increasingly equipped with radar, lidar and video to support ADAS functionalities) and the ever-increasing capacity of information and communication technologies (ICT) to convert this data into business value for different stakeholder groups. These may include individual stakeholders (e.g. vehicle drivers) as well as organizational stakeholders (e.g. car manufacturers, fleet managers, infrastructure maintainers, or traffic planners). Utilizing "up to one hundred on board control units that constantly communicate with each other" (VDA 2016), modern vehicles are already generating big data using in-vehicle sensors. Certain parts of this data are safety-critical and must therefore not leave the car, while the rest can and will be used for the establishment of novel digital services based on vehicle usage data, which can go far beyond ensuring driving functionality and safety and opens up a multitude of possibilities.

As IT companies enter the automotive market with their services, the balance of power between the players in the automotive industry may also change. IT start-ups have already created several interesting digital services based on data from the vehicle's on-board diagnostic (OBD) interface or from the driver's smartphone (Kaiser et al. 2017). This has led to the emergence of new business models in the automotive sector and has even attracted the attention of car manufacturers already. A prominent example is BMW i Ventures and its recent investments in start-ups such as Nauto (improving the safety of commercial fleets, investment made in 2017) and Zūm (providing technologies for reliable child transportation, investment made in 2019). We have now reached the point where it is decided how to go on: Either the large vehicle manufacturers will buy in/redevelop the most promising digital services of the start-ups, or, to the vehicle could merely become an exchangeable device/platform on which digital services run, similar to the smartphone.

Digital services based on vehicle usage data are data processing services which, among other things, work with data related to vehicle driving and can offer added value to users. In this context, the term 'service' can be viewed from two different angles: On the one hand, a 'service' is understood as a piece of software applying approaches from computer science to transform and merge different sources of data (be it raw data or pre-processed data) into new, enriched forms of aggregated data (Lechner et al. 2019). When performed correctly, the value of these enriched data is inherently higher than the sum of values of the single datasets which were combined in the process. On the other hand, a 'service' is understood as something of economic relevance, providing an added value as a service offering to one or more stakeholder groups.

However, the market entry of start-ups has already created a new *data-driven service ecosystem* in the automotive sector, leading to new data flows and collaborations in service development, as Kaiser et al. (2019b) describes. In the high-level view of this empirically obtained ecosystem with experts from the field, there is a data flow from data providers to service providers, who offer services on the market that are consumed by service consumers at the end of the value chain. On closer inspection, for example, there are five ways in which a service provider can already obtain relevant data on a car trip, i) from a market place (e.g. otonomo.io), ii) directly from the car manufacturer (e.g. BMW), iii) from data intermediaries (e.g. HERE Technologies, which has a close relationship to BMW and Daimler), iv) from the results of other service providers and v) from external data sources (e.g. weather services, congestion warnings).

The enormous amount of data available today makes the creation of valid digital services possible in the first place, but also poses a major challenge with regard to data processing (Xu et al. 2017). To create value, data must be acquired, transformed, anonymized, annotated, cleaned, normalized, aggregated, analyzed, appropriately stored and finally presented to the end user in a meaningful way. This implies that an entire data value chain must be created, implemented and monitored. With this in mind, Kaiser et al. (2019a) derived the *Vehicle Data Value Chain (VDVC)* from the Big Data Value Chain as described by Curry (2016) and a literature review on relevant concepts for digital services based on vehicle usage data, including Quantified Self, Big Data, and the Internet of Things. This VDVC is intended to provide a structure and a framework allowing to systematically describe the transformation of data into valuable services, to compare existing digital vehicle services with each other and to understand and explain the data-related challenges associated with them. Hence, the VDVC was used to analyze, summarize and provide insights into existing start-up and vehicle manufacturer initiatives on the market. As a result, we decided to apply the VDVC in the development of services in two case studies, the intermodal mobility service MoveBW (case A) and a pothole and driving style detection service (case B). Finally, this paper is an extended version of Kaiser et al. (2019a), elaborating the VDVC and using another case study of a digital service based on vehicle data for evaluating the improved VDVC.

During the development of digital services based on vehicle data it will always be necessary to obtain an overview of certain characteristics of the individual data value chain steps, e.g. the scope of each step, the input data received in a particular step, the output data generated in a step, typical actors involved, typical architectures that are relevant, relevant trends and tools and, finally, the contribution of a particular step to value creation. For this reason, we subsequently extend the VDVC presented in Kaiser et al. (2019) by adding relevant characteristics to each data value chain step and thus aim to answer the following research question: *What are the relevant steps in developing digital vehicle services that should be part of a data value chain and how can the contribution to value creation be described with characteristics?*

After this introduction and motivation in Sect. 1, our paper continues with a review of background information in Sect. 2. In Sect. 3, we present and describe the extension of the Vehicle Data Value Chain. We then apply this value chain to analyze the intermodal mobility service MoveBW (case A) as well as a pothole and driving style detection service (case B) in Sect. 4. Finally, we draw a conclusion and an outlook of the paper in Sect. 5.

## 2 Background

### 2.1 Data as Business Enabler

Tim O'Reilly formulated his extensively quoted principles of Web 2.0 (O'Reilly 2005) including one about the emerging value of data more than a decade ago. Since then, the hype on how to generate added value from all kinds of available data has continued to grow. Data has become the new buzzword. A book by Mayer-Schoenberger and Cukier (2013) on how Big Data is changing our world has become an international bestseller and been cited by researchers more than 5360 times according to Google Scholar. Big Data has received considerable attention from multiple disciplines, including information systems research (Abbasi et al. 2016) and database management (Batini et al. 2015), to name but two.

Due to the exponential growth in the amount of data, for example, an amount of 16 ZB (16 trillion GB) of useful data is expected in 2020 (Turner et al. 2014). It is just a logical consequence that data generation, data analysis, data usage – and the new business models associated with it – have found their way into all areas of life. Homes are increasingly equipped with smart meters, a replacement for mechanic measurement of electricity usage, enabling the emergence of digital services to assist home monitoring and to optimize electricity usage. Smartwatches can track the wearer's movements and, create behavioral data and calculate periodic statistics such as daily, weekly, or monthly walking distances including burned calories per day, week, or month. Many people use their smartphones when exercising to gather extra information on their workout effectivity.

Smartphone apps such as Runtastic (2017a) and Strava (2017) help to monitor how and where people run or cycle, automatically calculating route, pace and periodic statistics including mean speed, time per kilometer, and calories burned. These apps even allow sharing the aggregated data via social networks, thus enabling benchmarking with peers and increasing the joy of exercise. The pattern of collecting, analyzing, and sharing data constitutes the baseline for individual improvements. Instantly calculated and visualized behavioral statistics are easy to compare or share with peers on social media. The collected information per se is not new to these communities. For instance, experienced runners started comparing their real and average time per kilometer using stopwatches a long time ago. However, the simplicity of digital services and the fact that many friends on social media regularly post about their exercising routine has motivated a whole digital generation to track themselves, as 300 million downloads of the Runtastic app (recently renamed to Adidas running) demonstrate (Runtastic 2020). 30 million app sessions per month in Europe produce a reasonable amount of big movement data, which is sufficient for performing representative data analyses and have led to an acquisition by the sports clothing company Adidas. To summarize, digitalization has greatly simplified data collection and analysis methods which used to be too complex and/or only available to experts. Hence, more and more people are joining the self-tracking movement and, in turn, produce more and more data which can be exploited using novel digital services.

## 2.2 A Value Chain for Big Data

In contrast to all previous technical or organizational innovations, the Internet age has made it possible for data volumes to reach undreamt-of dimensions. Big Data refers to the current conglomerate of newly developed methods and information technologies to capture, store and analyze large and expandable volumes of differently structured data. In a definition by Demchenko et al. (2013), the defining properties of Big Data are Value, Variety, Velocity, Veracity and Volume as shown in Fig. 1. Exploiting the new flows of data can even improve the performance of companies, if the decision-making culture is appropriate (McAfee and Brynolfsson 2012).

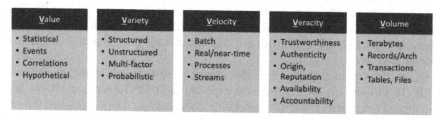

**Fig. 1.** The 5 vs of big data (Demchenko et al. 2013).

It seems that smart things are increasingly based on big data analysis, which makes it possible to speak of an intimate relationship between those two. While in the Web 2.0 era data was mainly generated by humans sharing user-generated content on portals including YouTube, Wikipedia, or Facebook, the Internet of Things has led to new patterns of data generation driven by machines. Smart, connected objects equipped with all kinds of sensors have now taken over this task (Porter and Heppelmann 2014 and 2015). The Quantified Self phenomenon is making use of these data generated by things (Swan 2009, 2015). Quantified Self refers to the intention to collect any data about the self that can be tracked, including biological, physical, behavioral, and environmental information. Making use of these data to establish applications and services has become a major creator of value. This value is created through multiple activities which are chained together, while the value of the output is steadily increasing.

A company's activities to create and build value were once described by Porter and Millar (1985) with the so-called concept of the value chain. However, this value chain concept can be applied to the data domain to describe activities ranging from data generation to the usage of data in data-driven services for the customer. Data value chains are a model to describe data flows as a series of steps, each of them transforming the value of data. Recently, Åkerman et al. (2018) described a data value chain in the context of production, where data analytics leads to regulations of a production system like in a closed loop control system. Furthermore, the concept of data value chains has been used to describe the value of Linked Data (Latif et al. 2009) and Big Data (Curry et al. 2014) as illustrated in Fig. 2. As modern vehicles are likely to produce big data (e.g. from and for (semi-)automated vehicles), the Big Data Value Chain including several steps of Big Data transformation in the process of generating the data-driven result with the maximum business value is of high relevance to the automotive sector (Xu et al. 2017).

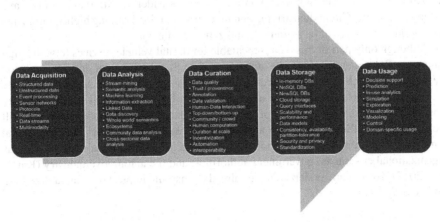

**Fig. 2.** The big data value chain of Curry et al. (2014)/Curry (2016).

## 2.3 Big Data Based on Vehicle Usage Data

The automotive industry is also constantly finding innovations for its vehicles as a result of electrification and comfort requirements. For example, mechanical components such as hand brakes or window lifters are increasingly being changed to electronic versions, such as the electric hand brake and electric window lifters. The status (handbrake is applied or released) and its process status (handbrake is applying/releasing) can be captured and used as input for vehicle safety checks and other features. An applied handbrake will automatically be released if the driver starts driving to prevent damage. The data generated through all these vehicle functions can be captured and used within other scenarios, e.g. to create statistics on how often a window is opened/closed or how often somebody is wedged in.

Also due to the common practice of vehicle development to purchase many components from suppliers, many vehicle sensors have so far only been used to provide and support a specific functionality and to increase comfort and safety, although these vehicle sensor data may also be interesting for third parties. As sensors and car features may widely differ from manufacturer to manufacturer and even per car variant, there is not only one single truth about how much data is effectively generated by a modern vehicle today. For instance, the participants from the European research project AutoMat state in a deliverable (Automat 2018) that about 4000 CAN bus signals (one signal could be one measurement value) per second create up to 1 GB of data per CAN bus (without mentioning a sample rate). According to Pillmann et al. (2017), there are "usually 4–12

CAN busses in one car" (with varying amounts of input signals). This clearly shows the high amount of data generated as a by-product during vehicle use.

For highly automated driving, several camera, radar and LiDAR (Light Detection and Ranging) systems are currently being implemented in the vehicles to cover every corner of the vehicle environment. Autonomous vehicles may be forced to exchange information with other vehicles (V2V) and with the infrastructure (V2I), which will boost the amount of available vehicle data enormously in the future. Considering different countries and different patterns of individual driving and mobility behavior, bringing highly automated driving into practice will be a grand digitalization challenge.

Although only part of this data is available for digital vehicle services (e.g. the high sampling rates generate such large amounts of data that the limits of data transmission are exceeded, which would require re-sampling at a lower rate or some signals are simply not relevant) and while only a portion of these data will be made accessible due to safety reasons (EU 2013), the remainder of accessible sensor data from modern vehicles will most likely be sufficient to design and develop a reasonable number of novel digital vehicle services for various stakeholder groups, including individual drivers, various organizational customers, government authorities, and the automotive industry (Kaiser et al. 2017). To sum up, modern vehicles already constitute impressive generators of big vehicle usage data.

## 3   A Value Chain for Vehicle Usage Data

### 3.1   Quantified-Self

Digital natives like to have access to services anytime and anywhere and are therefore willing to let their mobile devices such as smartphones and smart watches generate data around the clock. Increasing the knowledge about oneself and eventually enabling new discoveries while performing physical activities including running or cycling has turned into a business-relevant phenomenon. The behavior of turning collected data about oneself into actionable knowledge and insight which is valuable for other stakeholders, too, has been termed Quantified Self. Interestingly, the quantified self-phenomenon has recently been successfully transferred to the automotive industry by US-based start-ups. In this sense and quite analogously, Quantified Vehicles (Stocker et al. 2017) imply a successful transformation of data from different kinds of sensors related to the vehicle (in-vehicle sensors, smartphone and wearable sensors used by the driver) into actionable knowledge, e.g. on the behavior of the vehicle. This way, they generate value for different kinds of stakeholders that are part of digital vehicle data service ecosystems such as insurance or fleet management providers, finally resulting in novel digital services based on vehicle data in various domains (Kaiser et al. 2018b, 2019b).

Self-tracking with consumer devices, as shown in the example of Runtastic (Adidas running), can also be transferred to vehicles: Vehicles already collect a large amount of operating data via sensors and control units that ensure the functionality of the vehicle. However, these big vehicle data could be used to enable a series of apps and services for different customer groups. The market value for vehicle usage data is considered to be even higher than for other markets due to the importance of vehicles in first world countries. A number of US-based ICT start-ups seized this opportunity, now offering smartphone and web applications providing insights into vehicle-generated data, after they received up to €25 million of funding from investors (Stocker et al. 2017). Interestingly, while some car manufacturers and suppliers (e.g. Magna International, Continental ITS, and BMW i Ventures) are among the investors, forming strategic partnerships with start-ups, others participate in research projects and try to keep data-related business in their own area of influence. This holds for Volkswagen, for example, which coordinates the EU project AutoMat to develop a marketplace for vehicle lifecycle data (Stocker and Kaiser 2016). Furthermore, recent reports from the German automotive industry association (VDA) suggest that car manufacturers "have to hold a stronger position in the future and may limit the capabilities of third parties to freely access car data." To summarize, the potential of vehicle usage data seems to be such that it has become a battle worth fighting (Kaiser et al. 2017). How vehicle usage data generates value leads us to the next section in which we describe the Vehicle Data Value Chain.

## 3.2   The Vehicle Data Value Chain (VDVC)

To systematically describe the transformation of data into valuable services, the concept of value chain can create a suitable structure and framework. In this regard, we propose the Vehicle Data Value Chain (VDVC) as a lightweight model. We derived the VDVC from the Big Data Value Chain (Curry 2016, illustrated in Fig. 2). We adapted Curry's value chain regarding the name, number and order of stages to reflect our experiences from research projects in the automotive domain. The stage of *Generation* (of vehicle usage data) was added as a separate stage to explicitly reflect the origin of the data (e.g. in-vehicle or related sensors). The stage *Acquisition* (of vehicle usage data) corresponds to Curry's Data Acquisition. Moreover, we have changed the order of Curry's stages of analysis and curation since we interpret the terminology differently. For example, Curry seems to include normalization procedures implicitly within machine learning in the stage of Data Analysis, whereas we consider this as an important separate pre-processing step which correlates with Curry's stage of Data Curation. Hence, we have re-named Curry's stage of Data Curation, *Pre-processing*, which is followed by the stages *Analysis*, *Storage*, and *Usage* (in each case: of vehicle usage data), as visualized in Fig. 3. As the result of the processing could be the input for further analysis, an arrow back to Acquisition indicates the possible a circular path.

Furthermore, to compare digital services based on vehicle data and to understand and explain the data-related challenges associated with them, we added eight characteristics to each value chain step: *i) Description/Scope* to describe the scope of the step, *ii) Input examples* and *iii) Output examples* to name possible inputs and outputs per step, *iv) Actor examples* to name relevant actors in this step, *v) Architecture examples* to describe which architecture usually is used in a specific step, *vi) Trend examples* to name current trends in the specific value chain step, *vii) Tool examples* to name possible tools and *viii) Contribution to value creation* to summarize the contribution of this step to value creation. The single value chain steps are shown in Fig. 4 and are described in the following subsections.

**Generation (of Vehicle Usage Data).** This step has the scope of generating measurements through any sensors which can capture condition data directly (engine RPM or

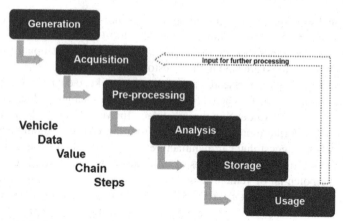

**Fig. 3.** The vehicle data value chain derived from Curry (2016) and based on Kaiser et al. (2018b) and Kaiser et al. (2019a).

vehicle speed) or indirectly (road surface). In the case of direct influence, we see three main data sources: In-vehicle sensors, smartphone sensors and sensors in individual user devices (e.g. a pulse watch). An indirect data sources can be literally any data source that provides information on the state of a vehicle, its driver or surroundings; an example could be a road operator camera to display traffic flow. This process step is essential for the vehicle data value chain, since the data origin determines the reliability and the type of influence (direct, indirect). The current trend to equip modern vehicles with ADAS functionalities (e.g. through the use of radar and lidar sensors for better detection of the driving environment) increases the amount of data generated and the possibilities for use cases once more.

**Acquisition (of Vehicle Usage Data).** This step describes the process of collecting the generated data. In-vehicle sensor data is not directly accessible as it is secured in order to safeguard vehicle functionality and is therefore only exchanged between the various electronic control units via one of the vehicle's internal bus systems, e.g. CAN bus. However, a filtered quantity of this sensor data is accessible via the On-board diagnostic (OBD) interface (Turker and Kutlu 2015), which is intended to be used by service staff to read out the generated error messages. It is therefore possible to develop plug-in devices with an internet connection, thereby effectively using the OBD-port as a source of sensor data. There are already some professional solutions with data acquisition devices built into the vehicle, which read signals directly from the CAN bus in an unfiltered way. To meet the requirements of the EU Directive 2010/40/EU – establishing inter alia the costless provision of universal, road safety-related minimum traffic information (EU 2013) - a standardized interface would be feasible sooner or later. Data from smartphone sensors is acquired using specific applications, capable of gathering and transmitting data. In the case of external data sources, the main issues are the varying availability and quality levels of the data. For example, APIs usually limit the number of requests allowed per time interval, so the acquisition process must be adapted to meet these thresholds.

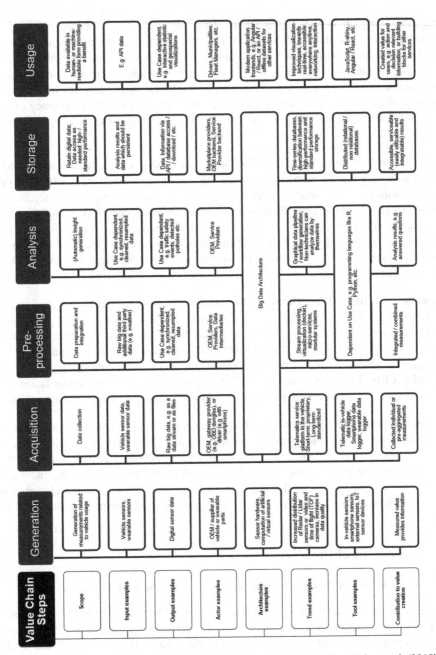

**Fig. 4.** The vehicle data value chain derived from Curry (2016) and based on Kaiser et al. (2018b) and Kaiser et al. (2019a) extended with characteristics.

Gathered data is stored for further processing; the chosen storage and format heavily depend on the subsequent processing steps.

**Pre-processing (of Vehicle Usage Data).** This step consists of the process of data preparation and integration. It is the sum of any anonymization, annotation, cleansing and normalization activities before any data analysis is conducted. Sensor values including private user information, erroneous sensor readings, different sensor sampling frequencies or unsynchronized data are examples of issues addressed in this stage. Data quality has a high impact on service quality. For instance, if the accuracy of the GNSS signal is low, a trip may not be linked to the correct road and may lead to wrong conclusions.

**Analysis (of Vehicle Usage Data).** This step is the process of automatic insight generation, with the purpose of extracting useful hidden information. This involves linking data from different data sources, exploring the data, performing statistical analyses and using machine learning algorithms to detect latent information hidden in the data. For instance, weather data can be linked to vehicle speed on a particular road to determine whether the driver is driving differently in wet or icy conditions. Weather data can be linked to acceleration data to determine whether a driver is driving aggressively in bad weather conditions.

**Storage (of Vehicle Usage Data).** In this step of the value chain, proper data access is established. It is already defined in the Big Data Value Chain as "the persistence and management of data in a scalable way that satisfies the needs of applications that require fast access to the data" (Curry 2016). In the case of vehicle sensor data, persistent storage is usually achieved by using a combination of classical relational databases (for metadata), Big Data file systems (for raw input data) and so called "time series databases" to store data that changes with time, which allow fast analyses on the stored contents.

**Usage (of Vehicle Usage Data).** The final step deals with making the data available in human- or machine-readable form (or both, as required). It includes all kinds of user or software interaction with the collected data and any conclusions derived from it in the above-mentioned process. The retrieved data could either be regarded as the end result of the process, being presented more or less directly to end users, or it could serve as input for further processing steps, thus forming a circular path in the processing chain.

## 4    Evaluation of the VDVC

### 4.1    Case A: Description of the Intermodal Mobility Service MoveBW

A regional, intermodal mobility service called MoveBW helps to increase the compliance rate of transport users (e.g. the percentage of people using a park and ride option) in relation to the current transport strategy of the region. The strategy offered by an European industry consortium mainly aims at meeting air quality targets and reducing traffic jams all over the federal province of Baden-Württemberg (Germany), including its provincial capital Stuttgart.

Geographically situated in a valley basin, Stuttgart, like all cities in valley basins (e.g. Graz), struggles with air pollution through fine dust. Thus, the city of Stuttgart continuously develops transport strategies to better comply with air quality regulations. In the past, these strategies were communicated to the public using radio traffic messages or electric traffic signs only. However, the compliance rate and thus success were comparably low. The MoveBW mobility service smartphone application aims to increase said compliance rate, especially that of visitors new to the region. It does so by including easy-to-use routing functionalities which are connected to rewards: Bonus points are granted if a user follows the recommended route. Collected bonus points can later be exchanged for immaterial or monetary values.

The intermodal journey planner allows users of the MoveBW smartphone application to plan their trips in advance. They can pick their preferred combination of transport modes from different options suggested to them. Additional information is displayed, not only showing travel time, but also eco-friendliness, travel costs and incentives gained (e.g. public transport vouchers and $CO_2$ savings). Moreover, it is possible to directly book tickets for the different modes of transport included in their preferred journey and yet to receive only one bill. In this way, transport services such as public transportation, car sharing, bike sharing, and parking space management are integrated conveniently, encouraging users to make efficient use of all modes of transport. The application also provides on-trip navigation and information on traffic obstructions such as construction works or accidents.

The MoveBW services are currently being monitored and evaluated in an extensive test phase. Based on the findings, both the digital service and traffic control strategies will be revised, aiming to maximize favored effects on the individual mobility behaviors of traffic participants, for example by applying different strategies for daily commuters and visitors. The smartphone application is planned to be released in the first quarter of 2019. Mock-ups of the current design are shown in Fig. 5.

**Fig. 5.** The MoveBW smartphone application provides functions for intermodal journey planning, traffic information, ticketing and on-trip navigation. (Source: https://www.altoros.com/blog/mobile-devices-are-propelling-industrial-iot-scenarios/).

A special challenge regarding data management is the multitude of data sources for the intermodal routing algorithms in the MoveBW App. The Vehicle Data Value Chain introduced in Sect. 3 helps to provide a clearer view. Its application to the underlying data transformation process, from Data Generation to Data Usage, is shown in Table 1.

**Table 1.** An overview of the MoveBW-Service. (Source: Kaiser et al. 2019a).

| VDVC step | Description of MoveBW-service |
|---|---|
| Data generation | Various sensor data and basic reference data is considered, e.g.<br>– floating car data: average mean travel time per road segment based on anonymized GNSS data of vehicles,<br>– stationary traffic measurement: rate of flow for single measurement locations,<br>– public transport: schedule and sometimes occupancy rate,<br>– car park interfaces: occupancy rate,<br>– park & ride interfaces: occupancy rate,<br>– air quality measurement units: air quality measurements and forecast (includes weather forecast); |
| Data acquisition | Querying web APIs from the various data sources. Additionally, the smartphone App which is described in Data Usage provides GNSS information, which is used for on-trip routing and to detect which means of transport the user actually uses to be able to reward them if the recommended option is used |
| Data pre-processing | Annotation, normalization and semantic extraction of data. Transformation of data to meet a common reference basis (in this case a public transport grid, no typical geo-coordinates). Furthermore, GNSS data from the smartphone App is anonymized (start- and end-trajectories are truncated). In this step the data is hosted in a distributed database system (e.g. PostgreSQL cluster) |
| Data analysis | A dynamic routing algorithm which also takes the provided intermodal transport strategy, $CO_2$ savings, and personal preferences into account. A self-developed algorithm which utilizes pgRouting (an open source project to extend PostGIS/PostgreSQL to provide geospatial routing functionality) and the popular Dijkstra algorithm (to find the shortest path between nodes). Provision of routing recommendations (weightings for routes) through this algorithm |
| Data storage | A distributed database system, e.g. a PostgreSQL cluster |
| Data usage | The MoveBW App currently being developed should help the commuter to choose a mode of transport and guides the commuter to the selected destination in compliance with environmentally-oriented traffic management strategies |

In case of MoveBW, where all steps of the MoveBW service are known to the authors, the VDVC provides a framework to describe the service layer by layer and thus also helps others to understand the service and its underlying value chain.

In the next section, the development of a pothole and driving style detection service is described using the VDVC.

## 4.2 Case B: Description of a Pothole and Driving Style Detection Service

Generating value out of vehicle data is a challenging task: For this purpose, vehicle data analytics has become an important technique in identifying the value of generated vehicle data. However, to exploit this value in products and services, several steps must be performed, and several (not only technical) challenges have to be solved. In the beginning, an appropriate analytics question must be identified such as e.g. identify the driving style of the driver from vehicle data, detect the road surface quality, identify potholes on roads, or predict the engine's wear.

Then, vehicle data must be captured: Three different approaches for data capturing are possible: the installation/use of own sensors within the vehicle to record vehicle movements and other contextual information, the connection of a vehicle data logger to the vehicle's on board diagnostic (OBD) interface to capture vehicle data such as vehicle speed or RPM, or the installation of a professional Controller Area Network (CAN) logger to obtain even more vehicle data from the vehicle's CPUs such as for example the state of vehicle assistance systems or the steering wheel angle. While the first option is probably the simplest one, it can only record contextual data and track the movement of the vehicle, but it does not allow access to vehicle sensors. The second option can provide already access to some vehicle sensor data such as vehicle speed or engine temperature, which is relevant for testing whether the vehicle's emissions are still within tolerance. The third option in theory provides access to all vehicle sensor signals, but only if the device listening to the CAN bus can decode the streamed raw CAN bus data to readable data, requiring either the vehicle manufacturer or the respective vehicle CPU manufacturer to provide the necessary decoding information (usually referred to as CAN-DBC files) (Fig. 6).

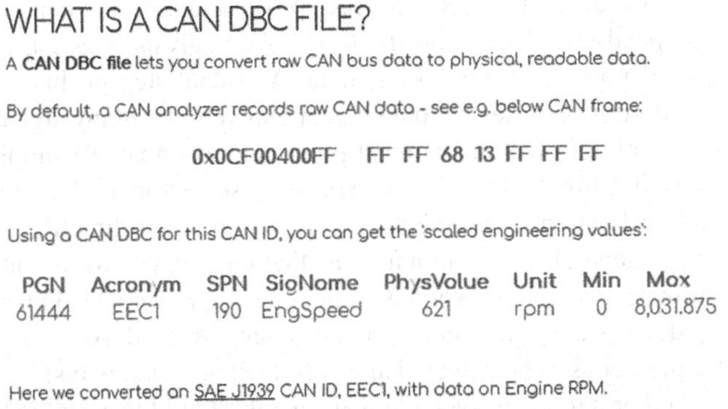

## WHAT IS A CAN DBC FILE?

A **CAN DBC file** lets you convert raw CAN bus data to physical, readable data.

By default, a CAN analyzer records raw CAN data - see e.g. below CAN frame:

0x0CF00400FF    FF FF 68 13 FF FF FF

Using a CAN DBC for this CAN ID, you can get the 'scaled engineering values':

| PGN | Acronym | SPN | SigName | PhysValue | Unit | Min | Max |
|-----|---------|-----|---------|-----------|------|-----|-----|
| 61444 | EEC1 | 190 | EngSpeed | 621 | rpm | 0 | 8,031.875 |

Here we converted an SAE J1939 CAN ID, EEC1, with data on Engine RPM.

**Fig. 6.** CAN DBC files. Source: CSS electronics (2020).

Different data loggers may store the data in different formats. Typically, they can collect multiple signals at once, which are all transmitted on the same wire. Thus, the logger needs to know and save at least three different properties of the data: What was measured, what was its value and when was it measured. This naturally leads to a tabular format very similar to the example depicted in Table 2.

**Table 2.** Vehicle raw data structure (example).

| Timestamp | Signal name | Signal value |
|---|---|---|
| 2019-9-13 5:28:36.206089 | RPM | 1500 |
| 2019-9-13 5:28:36.226331 | Acceleration-X | 0.476 |
| 2019-9-13 5:28:36.245312 | Vehicle Speed | 39 |
| 2019-9-13 5:28:36.268915 | Engine oil temperature | 90 |
| .. | .. | .. |

While this format is convenient for the logger to store data, it is much less suited for a statistical analyses or automated processing of the data. There are three main difficulties: First, several signals are mixed together in one column, creating the need for grouping and filtering even before very simple operations. Second, there can be multiple signals that were measured at the same time, requiring the analyst to investigate multiple rows at once to check a single instance in time. The third difficulty lies in the varying sampling rates of the signals. Each signal may have been captured with a different rate and even within a single signal, smaller deviations of the sampling rate are possible and common. Clearly pre-processing of the captured vehicle data is needed to make it better explorable for data analysts.

After the required vehicle data is stored, a series of further steps must be performed to prepare the data for analysis. This data (pre-)processing process can be quite comprehensive and depends very much on the respective analysis question to be solved, e.g. the detection of potholes from vehicle data. A crucial step in this process is the alignment of the coordinate system of data logger and vehicle. Many signals are vector valued, with acceleration as the maybe most prominent example. To simplify analyses and interpretations, it is highly desirable to express these vectors in the reference frame of the car, i.e. x-Acceleration should be the component in the x-direction of the car/the driving direction. In general, one cannot assume that the logger was mounted such that its internal coordinate system corresponds to the one of the vehicle. This is especially true when cheap devices that are mounted by end-users are used. Any misalignment of the reference frames needs to be detected and corrected prior to analysis.

As with most other data types, vehicle data signals should be searched for missing values, wrong values, and outliers and these should be removed. Some signals may contain a lot of noise and must be smoothed. To separate the signals into different columns the data should be transformed using the 'signal name' as pivot. Simultaneously, it makes sense to resample each signal to a common sampling rate from the analysis' viewpoint. The "right" sampling rate again depends on the question the be answered. The result is than in a similar form as depicted in Table 3. Now each row corresponds exactly to a point in time and the time interval between the rows is constant, in this example 0.1 s/10 Hz.

**Table 3.** Structure of pre-processed vehicle usage data (example).

| Timestamp | Engine speed | Acceleration-X | Vehicle speed | .. |
|---|---|---|---|---|
| 2019-9-13 5:28:36.20000 | 1500 | 0.477 | 39 | |
| 2019-9-13 5:28:36.30000 | 1501 | 0.479 | 40 | |
| 2019-9-13 5:28:36.40000 | .. | .. | .. | |

The data prepared in this way can now be used to work on the vehicle data analysis question and/or to search for interesting events (such as potholes for example). Depending on the type of event, multiple signals can be relevant. Events should usually be post-processed to combine separate events, which are only divided by a short-time interruption, into a single event. The recorded events may be linked with weather and position data, so that for each event the time and place of occurrence as well as the prevailing weather is known.

For different types of events, different detection methods need to be employed. One can detect a pothole event (driving over a pothole) by investigating acceleration values and rotation rates as follows: Consider the acceleration normal to the road, as well as the vehicle's rotation around its lateral axis ('pitch') The acceleration readings will exhibit a distinct spike, while a certain pattern is simultaneously visible in the rotation rate: When the front tires are in the pothole, the front of the vehicle is lower than the rear, if the rear tires are in the pothole, it is vice versa, causing a rotation around the lateral axis. This results in a typical "pitch" movement that can be detected. In a last step, the results of the analysis - in this case the detected potholes - can be visualized on a map. In our case this supports drivers in not choosing bad roads, or support road operators in better maintaining roads.

To detect strong acceleration and braking events, the signals vehicle speed, acceleration in the direction of travel and rotation around the lateral axis ("pitching") are particularly suitable. The "pitching" is caused by the change in weight distribution when the speed changes: when a vehicle is accelerating, more weight moves to the rear axle - the rear drops and the front rises. When a vehicle is braking, the opposite is true. These movements can be detected. However, since detection using only a single signal can be prone to error, we always use several signals in our algorithm, which must all deflect simultaneously to trigger detection.

The driving styles of drivers can differ in many facets (e.g.: comfort level, gear choice, aggressiveness). Depending on the type of vehicle the driving style may have a large influence on fuel/power consumption, component-wear and road safety. In an attempt to quantify this influence, we use all calculated events to calculate a 'risk score' that indicates how unsafe a single trip was. The more safety-related events per time unit occurred in a trip, the higher the value. Furthermore, we consider the influence of environmental conditions in our calculations. For example, heavy braking in rain will result in a higher risk than the same braking on a dry road. To make the risk score interpretable, we normalize it using the scores from all available trips as a basis. We then present the value as statistical rank, for example a value of 56.72% means that this trip is safer than 56.72% of all trips in the database. In a map visualization, the driver is presented the trip with markers indicating start and stop positions, as well as locations for safety-relevant events.

Based on this methodology, a smartphone application, shown in Fig. 7, has been developed for drivers interested in monitoring their driving style.

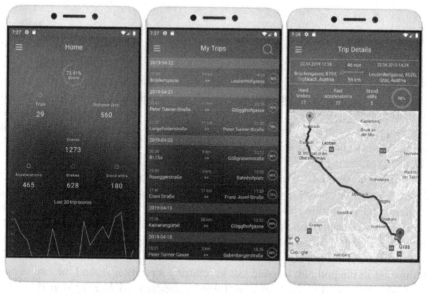

**Fig. 7.** A smartphone application for driving style detection.

On the left screen named *Home*, the driver has an overview of his trips. In the presented figure, his overall score is 73.41%; he has 29 trips with a total distance of 560 km. In these trips 1273 events have been detected, which are composed of 465 acceleration events, 628 brake events and 180 stand-still events. On a second screen named *My Trips,* which is displayed in the center, a list of the most recent trips, grouped by date, is shown. For each trip, the information on which location and at which time the trip started and ended is displayed together with the trip score and the trip distance. Selecting one of the trips opens a third screen named *Trip Details*, where additionally the events are decomposed into categories and the trip is visualized on a map.

Now that we have described the idea of this service, we want to show in the following table how clear and comparable the service becomes by using the VDVC (Table 4).

**Table 4.** An overview of the pothole and driving style detection service.

| VDVC step | Description of pothole and driving style detection service |
|---|---|
| Data generation | Vehicles are equipped with data loggers that record the signals required for pothole and driving style detection (e.g. speed, acceleration, rotation, position, etc.). These data loggers are connected to the on-board diagnostic interface of the vehicle and additionally generate acceleration, rotation and GPS data |
| Data acquisition | Vehicle movement data including OBD measurements as well as acceleration, rotation and position measurements is periodically recorded and imported as raw vehicle data into a local PostgreSQL database on the data logger. The collected data is made available as a data stream or as manually exported files in a PostgreSQL database running in the cloud |
| Data pre-processing | The pre-processing of the vehicle data includes the alignment of the datalogger's coordinate axis with the trajectories of the vehicle, the search for missing and incorrect values and outliers and their elimination, the smoothing of the signals to reduce noise and the interpolation of all signals to a useful sampling rate. Additionally, contextual weather data is integrated |
| Data analysis | For pothole detection, the acceleration perpendicular to the road and the "pitching" of the vehicle (i.e. the rotation around the transverse axis) are used. If these exceed certain threshold values, a pothole event is generated. In comparison, vehicle speed, acceleration in the direction of travel and rotation around the transverse axis ("nodding") are used to detect events relevant to driving safety, such as strong acceleration, braking and cornering maneuvers. If these exceed certain threshold values, a harsh acceleration, braking and cornering event occurs |
| Data storage | The events calculated in the analysis phase (harsh acceleration, braking, cornering as well as potholes) are stored in the PostgreSQL database together with their GPS locations and the corresponding weather information to visualize them on maps and perform additional statistical analyses, such as calculating a risk score for a single trip, taking into account the amount and severity of detected events per trip length as well as the respective weather conditions and a cumulative risk score for a driver |
| Data usage | Drivers should be provided with information to improve their driving. The application shown in the figure above should help the driver to monitor his own driving and compare it with the driving of other drivers in order to improve driving safety. Finally, the application can visualize detected potholes so that the driver can avoid driving into these potholes |

## 5   Conclusion and Outlook

An increasing number of digital services based on vehicle usage data are offered on the market and are increasingly used and demanded by users. Digitalization has not only become an important driver of innovation in the automotive sector, but may also change the balance of power in the automotive sector in the long term. With the background that our society is strongly driven by mobility, it is almost our duty to examine the emergence of digital services based on vehicle usage data more closely. Consequently, in our paper we have looked at a way of better describing and structuring digital services based on vehicle usage data. After a comprehensive analysis of related work, we have reviewed two different digital services by using the VDVC for a better structured description of how value is created. Using the VDVC model, we explicitly describe which activities must be carried out in the individual steps of the value chain in order to finally enable these two services.

As an outlook, it should be mentioned that digital vehicle services and the required technological infrastructure to facilitate data acquisition, pre-processing, analysis and storage, are currently a hot topic in the automotive domain. There are already ideas for using blockchain technology and brokers to make data sharing more transparent and secure, as described in Kaiser et al. (2019). Yet, while some car manufacturers invest in start-ups, others limit access to data via the OBD interface, arguing that they are not suitable for digital vehicle services (VDA 2016; ACEA 2016). In contrast, the European Automobile Manufacturers Association ACEA promotes car data sharing (ACEA 2017).

Regulation (EU) No. 886/2013 (concerning the Directive 2010/40/EU on Intelligent Transport Systems ITS), published by the European Commission, has actually been regulating the provision of universal, road-safety relevant minimum traffic information to users free of charge for years and calls on car manufacturers to make safety-relevant data available to the public via national contact points (EU 2013). While the vehicle manufacturers have long referred to the no longer up-to-date transmission standard based on WLAN technology (e.g. G5), several EU-wide initiatives (such as the C-ROADS initiative) have not given up, extending the development to telecommunications technologies (e.g. 4G, 5G) and presenting a concrete implementation plan for C-ITS services with Day 1 Applications. Since the end of 2019, the latest Volkswagen Golf is the first series-production vehicle on the market to use this data exchange standard. The C-ROADS initiative of several EU member states and road operators aims to use C-ITS services to enable the transmission of infrastructure information (e.g. roadside units) to the vehicle cockpit, e.g. to inform about dangerous situations, e.g. a vehicle backing out or pedestrians in the crosswalk behind the next bend. (C-ROADS 2017).

At the same time the International Organisation for Standardisation (ISO 2017) has set up a standardization work group titled *ISO/TC 22/SC 31/WG 6 Extended Vehicle/Remote diagnostics* to inter alia define access, content, control and security mechanisms for the provision of vehicle data for web services (VDA 2016).

Additionally, current EU-funded projects such as EVOLVE are developing solutions to ease the integration and fusion of multiple data sources for the purpose of service and business development using Linked Data (EVOLVE 2019; Latif et al. 2009). "Linked data is a lightweight practice for exposing and connecting pieces of data, information, or knowledge using basic web standards. It promises to open up siloed data ownership and is already an enabler of open data and data sharing" (Rusitschka and Curry 2016).

To conclude, we expect the market of digital services based on vehicle usage data to grow tremendously in the future, as the combination of vehicle data with data from external sources (e.g. weather data, traffic data, open data) will enable new scenarios for digital vehicle services.

**Acknowledgement** The EVOLVE project (www.evolve-h2020.eu) has received funding from  the European Union's Horizon 2020 research and innovation program under grant agreement No 825061. The document reflects only the author's views and the Commission is not responsible for any use that may be made of information contained therein .

# References

Abbasi, A., Sarker, S., Chiang, R.H.: Big data research in information systems: toward an inclusive research agenda. J. Assoc. Inf. Syst. **17**(2) (2016). http://ahmedabbasi.com/wp-content/uploads/J/AbbasiSarkerChiang_BigData_JAIS_2016.pdf

Accenture, Digital Transformation of Industries: Automotive Industry (2016). https://www.accenture.com/t20170116T084448__w__/us-en/_acnmedia/Accenture/Conversion-Assets/WEF/PDF/Accenture-Automotive-Industry.pdf. Accessed 08 Jan 2020

ACEA (European Automobile Manufacturers Association): ACEA Position Paper: Access to vehicle data for third-party services (2016)

ACEA (European Automobile Manufacturers Association) (2017). http://cardatafacts.eu/. Accessed 08 Jan 2020

AutoMat. http://automat-project.eu/. Accessed 08 Jan 2020

AutoMat. AutoMat Deliverable D5.3: Full Prototype of Cross-Sectorial Vehicle Data Services (2018)

Åkerman, M., et al.: Challenges building a data value chain to enable data-driven decisions: a predictive maintenance case in 5G-enabled manufacturing. Procedia Manuf. **17**, 411–418 (2018)

Batini, C., Rula, A., Scannapieco, M., Viscusi, G.: From data quality to big data quality. J. Database Manag. **26**(1), 60–82 (2015)

Curry, E., Ngonga, A., Domingue, J., Freitas, A., Strohbach, M., Becker, T.: D2.2.2. Final version of the technical white paper. Public deliverable of the EU-Project BIG (318062; ICT-2011.4.4) (2014)

CSS electronics (2020). https://www.csselectronics.com/screen/page/dbc-database-can-bus-conversion-wireshark-j1939-example/language/en. Accessed 16 Jan 2020

Curry, E.: The big data value chain: definitions, concepts, and theoretical approaches. In: Cavanillas, J.M., Curry, E., Wahlster, W. (eds.) New Horizons for a Data-Driven Economy, pp. 29–37. Springer, Cham (2016). https://doi.org/10.1007/978-3-319-21569-3_3

C-ROADS. Detailed pilot overview report (2017). https://www.c-roads.eu/fileadmin/user_upload/media/Dokumente/Detailed_pilot_overview_report_v1.0.pdf. Accessed 08 Jan 2020

Demchenko, Y., Grosso, P., de Laat, C., Membrey P.: Addressing big data issues in scientific data infrastructure. In: 2013 International Conference on Collaboration Technologies and Systems (CTS), San Diego, CA, pp. 48–55 (2013). https://doi.org/10.1109/cts.2013.6567203

EVOLVE (2019). https://www.evolve-h2020.eu/. Accessed 08 Jan 2020

EU (2013). https://eur-lex.europa.eu/legal-content/EN/TXT/?uri=CELEX:32013R0886. Accessed 08 Jan 2020

ISO (2017). https://www.iso.org/committee/5383568.html. Accessed 08 Jan 2020

Kaiser, C., Festl, A., Pucher, G., Fellmann, M., Stocker, A.: The vehicle data value chain as a lightweight model to describe digital vehicle services. In: 15th International Conference on Web Information Systems and Technologies (2019a)

Kaiser, C., Stocker, A., Viscusi, G., Festl, A., Moertl, P., Glitzner, M.: Quantified cars: an exploration of the position of ICT start-ups vs. car manufacturers towards digital car services and sustainable business models. In: Proceedings of 2nd International Conference on New Business Models, pp. 336–350 (2017)

Kaiser, C., Steger, M., Dorri, A., Festl, A., Stocker, A., Fellmann, M., Kanhere, S.: Towards a privacy-preserving way of vehicle data sharing – a case for blockchain technology? In: Dubbert, J., Müller, B., Meyer, G. (eds.) AMAA 2018. LNM, pp. 111–122. Springer, Cham (2019). https://doi.org/10.1007/978-3-319-99762-9_10

Kaiser, C., Stocker, A., Festl, A., Lechner, G., Fellmann, M.: A research agenda for vehicle information systems. In: Proceedings of European Conference on Information Systems (ECIS) 2018 (2018b)

Kaiser, C., Stocker, A., Fellmann, M.: Understanding data-driven service ecosystems in the automotive domain. In: Proceedings of Americas Conference on Information Systems (AMCIS 2019) (2019b)

Latif, A., Saeed, A.U., Hoefler, P., Stocker, A., Wagner, C.: The linked data value chain: a lightweight model for business engineers. In: Proceedings of I-Semantics 2009. 5th International Conference on Semantic Systems, pp. 568–577 (2009). Journal of Universal Computer Science

Lechner, G., Fellmann, M., Festl, A., Kaiser, C., Kalayci, T.E., Spitzer, M., Stocker, A.: A lightweight framework for multi-device integration and multi-sensor fusion to explore driver distraction. In: Giorgini, P., Weber, B. (eds.) CAiSE 2019. LNCS, vol. 11483, pp. 80–95. Springer, Cham (2019). https://doi.org/10.1007/978-3-030-21290-2_6

Mayer-Schoenberger, V., Cukier, K.: Big Data: A Revolution That Will Transform How We Live, Work, and Think. Houghton Mifflin Harcourt, Boston (2013). ISBN 0544002695 9780544002692

McAfee, A., Brynjolfsson, E.: Big data: the management revolution. Harv. Bus. Rev. **90**, 60–68 (2012)

Nauto. https://www.nauto.com/. Accessed 08 Jan 2020

O'Reilly, T.: What is web 2.0. O'Reilly Media, Sebastopol (2005)

Pillmann, J., Sliwa, B., Schmutzler, J., Ide, C., Wietfeld, C.: Car-to-cloud communication traffic analysis based on the common vehicle information model. In: IEEE Vehicular Technology Conference (VTC-Spring) Workshop on Wireless Access Technologies and Architectures for Internet of Things (IoT) Applications (2017)

Porter, M.E., Millar, V.E.: How information gives you competitive advantage (1985)

Porter, M., Heppelmann, J.E.: How smart, connected products are transforming competition. Harv. Bus. Rev. **92**, 64–88 (2014)

Porter M., Heppelmann J.E.: How smart, connected products are transforming companies. Harv. Bus. Rev. **93**, 96–114 (2015)

Runtastic (2017a). https://www.runtastic.com/en. Accessed 08 Jan 2020

Runtastic (2020). https://www.runtastic.com/career/facts-about-runtastic/. Accessed 19 Jan 2020

Rusitschka, S., Curry, E.: Big data in the energy and transport sectors. In: Cavanillas, J.M., Curry, E., Wahlster, W. (eds.) New Horizons for a Data-Driven Economy, pp. 225–244. Springer, Cham (2016). https://doi.org/10.1007/978-3-319-21569-3_13

Stocker, A., Kaiser, C.: Quantified car: potentials, business models and digital ecosystems. E & i Elektrotechnik und Informationstechnik **133**(7), 334–340 (2016)

Stocker, A., Kaiser, C., Fellmann, M.: Quantified vehicles. Bus. Inf. Syst. Eng. **59**(2), 125–130 (2017)

Strava (2017). https://www.strava.com. Accessed 08 Jan 2020

Swan, M.: Emerging patient-driven health care models: an examination of health social networks, consumer personalized medicine and quantified self-tracking. Int. J. Environ. Res. Public Health **6**(2), 492–525 (2009). https://doi.org/10.3390/ijerph6020492

Swan, M.: Connected car: quantified self becomes quantified car. J. Sens. Actuator Netw. 4(1), 2–29 (2015)

Turker, G.F., Kutlu, A.: Methods of monitoring vehicle's CAN data with mobile devices. Glob. J. Comput. Sci. 5(1), 36–42 (2015). http://dx.doi.org/10.18844/gjcs.v5i1.31

Turner, V., Gantz, J.F., Reinsel, D., Minton, S.: The digital universe of opportunities: rich data and the increasing value of the internet of things. Rep. from IDC EMC (2014)

VDA: Access to the vehicle (and vehicle generated data) (2016). https://www.vda.de/en/topics/innovation-and-technology/network/access-to-the-vehicle.html. Accessed 08 Jan 2020

Xu, W., Zhou, H., Cheng, N., Lyu, F., Shi, W., Chen, J., Shen, X.: Internet of vehicles in big data era. IEEE/CAA J. Autom. Sin. 5(1), 19–35 (2017)

# Optimized Coordination and Simulation for Industrial Human Robot Collaborations

André Antakli[✉], Torsten Spieldenner, Marcel Köster, Julian Groß,
Erik Herrmann, Dmitri Rubinstein, Daniel Spieldenner, and Ingo Zinnikus

German Research Centre for Artificial Intelligence (DFKI),
Campus D3 2, 66123 Saarbruecken, Germany
{andre.antakli,torsten.spieldenner,marcel.koester,julian.gross,
erik.herrmann,dmitri.rubinstein,daniel.spieldenner,ingo.zinnikus}@dfki.de
http://www.dfki.de

**Abstract.** For years, the manufacturing industry has been investing substantial amounts of research and development work for the implementation of hybrid teams of human workers and robotic units. The composition of hybrid teams requires an optimal coordination of individual players with fundamentally different characteristics and skills. In this paper, we present a highly configurable simulation environment supporting end-users, e.g. manufacturing planners, to optimally prepare, evaluate and improve the collaboration of hybrid teams in the scope of production lines. For generating the optimal task assignment, a GPU-based high-performance optimizer is introduced into the simulation environment. The framework is embedded in a web-based distributed infrastructure that models and provides the involved components (digital human models, robots, visualization environment) as resources. We illustrate the approach with a use case originating from the aircraft industry.

**Keywords:** Human robot collaboration · Multi-agent systems · Linked Data · 3D simulation

## 1 Introduction

For years, the manufacturing industry has been investing substantial amounts of research and development work for the implementation of hybrid teams that consist of human workers and robotic units. The collaboration between humans and robots (HRC) is expected to increase the degree of automation in many areas. The main aim of these efforts is to relieve the strain on people in production lines, but also to combine the strengths of the involved hybrid team members.

The composition of hybrid teams requires an optimal coordination of individual players with fundamentally different characteristics and skills. On the one hand, human workers have a certain degree of independence, dexterity and

© Springer Nature Switzerland AG 2020
A. Bozzon et al. (Eds.): WEBIST 2019, LNBIP 399, pp. 44–68, 2020.
https://doi.org/10.1007/978-3-030-61750-9_3

flexibility in the execution of a task. On the other hand, robots require detailed instructions for the task at hand. Coordinating hybrid teams at execution time requires ad hoc and context-aware task assignment for human workers as well as scheduling for robots. In order to ensure operational readiness and reliability, as well as effective operations, scenarios and situations with various coordinated team activities must be evaluated. For these reasons, a highly configurable simulation environment is needed to model and validate such configurations.

In the following, we present our approach to a highly configurable simulation environment supporting end-users, such as manufacturing planners, to optimally prepare, evaluate and improve the collaboration of hybrid teams in the scope of production lines. We propose a web-based infrastructure, in which the components are represented as resources. The resource-oriented infrastructure can be used to integrate simulation subsystems. Furthermore, it can also be used during the manufacturing process to exchange information between production control, robots and sensor/actuator systems. Our framework consists of a visualization environment, in which end-users can flexibly manipulate the scenery objects at run-time and validate time constraints. To enable intuitive modeling of agent behavior for orchestration and control of simulated hybrid teams, we have integrated several concepts that can dynamically generate human motions based on captured data. The integration of the components is based on Web technology and standards which provide an abstraction layer for the communication and data exchange between the subsystems.

The paper is structured as follows. Section 2 presents our framework and the interplay of the different components. Section 3 describes the web-based communication layer. Section 4 introduces the general optimization concept for on-the-fly scheduling. In Sect. 5, we introduce the AJAN agent service and in Sect. 6 our visualization environment with the motion synthesis system. In Sect. 7, a use-case scenario in the context of hybrid teams in manufacturing is presented. Finally, we discuss open issues in Sect. 8, related work in Sect. 9 and conclude in Sect. 10.

This paper is a thoroughly revised and considerably extended version of [3], introducing in particular the heuristic optimizer and its integration into the simulation framework. A novel use case with specific challenges for optimization and coordination is used for illustrating the interaction of the components.

## 2   Simulation Framework Overview

In this section, we present the overall architecture of the simulation framework. With the proposed framework, we provide a simulation environment for a manufacturing planner, in which assembly processes of hybrid teams can be simulated in three-dimensional space. The main purpose is the optimization of the workflow itself. However, it is also designed to explore suitable setups of the real assembly environment to meet spatial and time constraints. To achieve these goals, an environment is needed in which the actors of a hybrid team can be visualized as realistically as possible and controlled in a way that is as close as possible to the real behavior and motions of the individual team members. Figure 1 shows the components basically required for this.

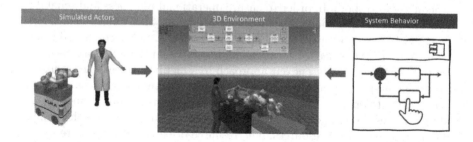

**Fig. 1.** Main approach with simulated actors, 3D environment and system behavior.

Consequentially, a 3D visualization of a real manufacturing site with its actors is the central point to give the manufacturing planner the possibility to display intuitively the circumstances of the environment and to adjust them manually according to the identified restrictions. The motions of the visualized actors must be realized by components that come as close as possible to reality so that the planned processes can also be implemented in the real environment. In the case of a real cobot, its control system should also be used in virtual space. Here it must be ensured that the physical conditions and sensors of such a cobot are properly simulated. When simulating the human workers, real motions should be used as far as possible. Obviously, motion capture data are suitable for this. When it comes to the actual process to be planned, the planner should be provided with a tool that makes it as easy as possible to implement it. Since we are talking about autonomous team members, an approach should be used that is able to represent exactly this autonomy. In addition, tools should be available in which the planned process can be further optimized.

The required components must be interconnected in a suitable form so that individual components can be used in and are conform to the real environment. In addition, depending on the use case, further approaches need to be integrated in order to offer the manufacturing planner the best possible support.

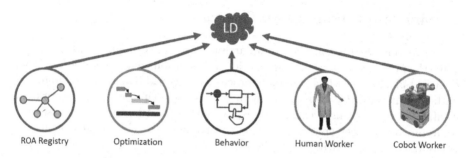

**Fig. 2.** Framework Overview with Linked Data (LD) as communication layer.

The primary task is to realize an extendable architecture that allows to integrate and orchestrate all necessary components for the simulation of human and cobot workers. Moreover, the framework needs to follow a modular approach to ensure that it can be used in the scope of a real production environment. The realized framework consists of multiple components (see Fig. 2). The integration of these subsystems is realized based on standard Web technologies, enhanced with semantic features, establishing a *resource-oriented architecture* (see Sect. 3). One component which we integrated in that way is used to compute optimized schedules of high-level assembly tasks and to distribute them among the actors in hybrid teams (see Sect. 4). For modeling and executing the autonomous behavior of workers in simulated assembly scenarios to fulfill these scheduled high-level tasks, we are using the multi-agent system AJAN (see Sect. 5). For simulating the human and cobot workers, we use a component for generating human worker motions using motion captured data (see Sect. 6) and the cobot control component *Robot Operating System* (ROS) [37] with an integrated simulation unit (Gazebo) [23]. The simulation of the actors is visualized in Unity3D[1], a widely-used game engine. The 3D scene modeled with Unity3D also represents the real task environment. Accordingly, it makes the virtual environment available to the other components.

## 3  Resource-Oriented Linked Data Integration Layer

As depicted in Fig. 2, the nature of software, their data sources and provided network interfaces, differ widely, ranging from robotic operation systems, over highly dynamic data stores, to 3D game engines for interactive simulation and visualization. This variation calls for an integration layer to achieve *structural interoperability*, if not even *semantic interoperability* [40] between the different components, meaning that applications are not only using structural compatible data layouts, but data can be mutually exchanged and understood between applications.

Particularly in the domain of IoT, the W3C Web of Things Working Group[2] proposes to use the Web as convergence and integration platform. The so emerging *Web of Things (WoT)* [15] defines a web-based abstraction layer for IoT platforms, protocols, data models and communication patterns. To unleash its full potential, the emerging WoT is expected to evolve into a Semantic Web of Things (SWoT) [36]. The SWoT will heavily rely on Linked Data (LD) principles [16] to semantically describe IoT entities in terms of their actions, properties, events and metadata [39] independent of the underlying IoT platform.

This vision extends also to server-client communication. Verborgh et al. claim that for clients to act as *intelligent agents*, it must be given that client applications are able to explore and understand server functionality and data autonomously [43]. In this respect, providing server data as HTTP resources that fulfill Fielding's *hypermedia constraints* [9], and with this, comply to a level

---

[1] Unity3D: https://unity3d.com.

[2] https://www.w3.org/WoT/WG/.

3 Richardson maturity model [33], has been found a suitable way to match the requirements identified by Verborgh et al.

In the following, we outline how we achieve to lift the software components indicated in Fig. 2 to a LD representation to achieve a *Resource Oriented Architecture (ROA)* for the framework toolchain. The LD layer of the resulting architecture ensures structural interoperability of the different tools' runtime data. By ensuring Level 3 Richardson Maturity Model compliance, we ensure more over that data can be autonomously explored and interpreted by AJAN agents, which are describe in Sect. 5 in more detail.

### 3.1   Data Publication

We employ *ECA2LD* [41] to lift the stand-alone World server, as well as Unity3D, to RDF[3]. ECA2LD performs an automatic structural mapping from Entity-Component-Attribute (ECA) based runtimes, as it is the case for Unity3D and the standalone worldserver, to a Linked-Data representation in compliance with the Linked Data Platform W3C recommendation[4].

As result of the mapping, Entities (resp. *game objects* in Unity3D), attached Components, and selected Attributes that model relevant information, such as 3D position in space, sensor data, and others, are all represented by individual resources with an HTTP endpoint. Relevant information about the resources is provided by RDF triples that describe the structure and type of data. Relations between resources, such as Entity-Component relations, are established as links between resources. Being provided with an arbitrary resource as entry point, clients are by this able to autonomously explore the provided server data by following the established links. Moreover, the RDF description of provided data enables clients to identify subsets of resources of interest for their interaction via a SPARQL Query interface[5].

Using the above mentioned methodologies for data publication on a common Web layer, we achieve a unified, mutually understood data representation. Independent of the underlying application, clients are able to explore data by following links, also between applications. By this, we achieve full structural and data interoperability on the Web as integration layer.

**Interfaces to Data Resources:** The originally published version of the ECA2LD lifting library [41] provides the following HTTP operations on created resources: GET, to read out resource information; PUT, to update resource information; POST, to create a resource; and DELETE, to delete the resource. Information about further interaction possibilities with the resource can be obtained by using the HTTP OPTIONS operation.

In addition to Entity, Component and Attribute resources, as described in the original papers [3,41], we create an additional resource endpoint that emits

---

[3] https://www.w3.org/RDF/.
[4] https://www.w3.org/TR/ldp/.
[5] https://www.w3.org/TR/rdf-sparql-query/.

the *Attribute Value* of an Attribute under a fresh IRI $\nu(v_a)$; $\nu(\cdot) : \Sigma^+ \to \text{IRI}$ denotes a function that mints fresh IRIs for Attributes and Attribute Values, based on the name of Attribute $v_a$. This resource is linked to the respective Attribute endpoint by the RDF predicate `rdf:value` (see Fig. 3, 1).

In addition to the usual HTTP operations, Attribute Value endpoints provide subscription mechanisms, using either HTTP Webhooks, or Websocket endpoints. Those are advertised as part of the response to an OPTIONS request as RDF triple set as shown in Fig. 3, 2.

$$
(1) \quad \frac{\forall \textbf{Attribute}\, n_a}{\nu(n_a)\ \texttt{rdf:value}\ \nu(v_a)} \qquad (2) \quad \frac{\forall \textbf{AttributeValue}\, v_a,\ \textbf{Protocol}\, p}{\begin{array}{l} \nu(v_a)\ \texttt{sub:endpoint}\ \sigma(v_a)\,. \\ \sigma(v_a)\ \texttt{sub:protocol}\ p. \\ \sigma(v_a)\ \texttt{rdf:format}\ f. \end{array}}
$$

**Fig. 3.** Triples generated to link Attribute Value resources to Attributes (1), and to describe available subscription protocols and formats on Attribute Value resources (2).

We link subscription endpoints $\sigma(v_a)$, $\sigma(\cdot)$ being a function that mints a fresh IRI for a subscription endpoint, to their respective Attribute Value endpoint $\nu(v_a)$ using predicate `sub:endpoint`. The protocol by which $\sigma(v_a)$ communicates is given in RDF compliant description $p$, linked by predicate `sub:protocol`. Finally, using predicate `rdf:format`, we link an RDF-based data sheet $f$ describing the transferred data model as emitted by resource $\sigma(v_a)$.

From the data provided, clients can infer self-drivenly the most suitable channels for subscription based on locally implemented capabilities.

**Entity Collections and Cross-referencing Distributed Data Sets:** The original paper in which the ECA2LD mapping algorithm is described only maps the ECA data on Entity, Component, and Attribute level. We have extended this mapping to take into account the distributed nature of the scenario with its various data providers.

$$
(3) \quad \frac{\forall\ \textbf{EntityCollection}\, \textbf{E},\ \forall\ (n_e, \textbf{C}_e) \in \textbf{E}}{\begin{array}{l} \nu(n_\textbf{E})\ \texttt{rdf:type}\ \texttt{ldp:BasicContainer}\,. \\ \nu(n_\textbf{E})\ \texttt{ldp:contains}\ \nu(n_e)\,. \end{array}}
$$

**Fig. 4.** Triples produced for an Entity Collection **E** to link contained entities to the respective collection.

In the presented architecture, different runtimes (Unity 3D, ROS operation system, and others) all provide their own, locally maintained subset of Entities. Employing again minting functions $\nu(\cdot) : \Sigma^+ \to \text{IRI}$ for minting a fresh IRI from a given name of a resource, we create resources for each of the collections.

For each Entity Collection **E** being assigned a unique name $n_E$, we produce sets of triples as shown in Fig. 4.

In addition to the usual HTTP methods as described above, HTTP routes for Entity Collections provide a SPARQL query interfaces by query via GET as specified by the SPARQL 1.1 Protocol specification [45]. The respective query is executed over the RDF graph that conveys information about the collection resource itself, as well as all contained Entity resources along with their attached Components and Attributes.

Using HTTP POST operations, Entity Collections accept as added data triples of the form $[\sigma(n_E),$ `ldp:contains`, $\nu(n_e)]$, with $\sigma(n_E)$ being the IRI of a remote Entity Collection with name $n_E$, and $\nu(n_e)$ the IRI of an entity contained in Entity Collection **E**, and notions of IRI minting functions $\nu(\cdot)$ and $\sigma(\cdot)$ as introduced above. Upon receiving a triple of above form, the receiving entity collection **U** with name $n_U$ and IRI $\sigma(n_U)$ adds to its local graph representation the triples

$[\sigma(n_U),$ `rdfs:seeAlso`, $\sigma(n_E)]$, and
$[\sigma(n_U),$ `foaf:knows`, $\nu(n_e)]$.

An example of a resulting graph for an Entity Collection with a set of locally hosted entities ("`ldp:contains`") and reference to externally managed resources ("`rdfs:seeAlso`" and "`foaf:knows`") is shown in Fig. 5.

```
<http://127.0.0.1:12345/world/>
    a ldp:BasicContainer;
    ldp:contains <http://127.0.0.1:12345/world/robot/>,
        <http://127.0.0.1:12345/world/tool/>,
        <http://127.0.0.1:12345/world/workbench/>,
        <http://127.0.0.1:12345/world/worker/>;

    rdfs:seeAlso <http://localhost:54321/unity/>,
        <http://vm-host:9997/ros/>.

    foaf:knows <http://localhost:54321/unity/eca2ld/worker>,
        <http://vm-host:9997/ros/mobi-pick>,
        <http://vm-host:9997/ros/mobi-pick/gripper>,
        <http://vm-host:9997/ros/mobi-pick/platform>.
```

**Fig. 5.** Example of the RDF graph representation of an Entity Collection resource with knowledge of and links to external Entity Collections.

By performing all steps above, machine clients gain knowledge about and can self-drivenly explore the structure of the data by the taken means for *Data Publication*. Clients gain knowledge about and may self-drivenly explore interfaces and protocols to interact with data by the taken means for the proper description of *Interfaces to Data Resources*. And last, clients gain knowledge about and may self-drivenly explore distributed sets of data by the newly implemented means for *cross-referencing Entity Collections*, and the provided SPARQL query endpoints over Entity Collection datasets.

## 3.2 Interfaces to Robot Control and Simulation

Following, we show how we employ the aforementioned Linked Data integration layer to connect robotic systems to the simulation environment, as presented in [3]. In this implementation, we use ROS [37], a popular open-source robotics middleware, to communicate between simulation runtimes and robotic systems (see also Sect. 2). ROS implements many robotic components and algorithms like *navigation stacks* (e.g. SLAM navigation) and *motion planning* (e.g. MoveIt). For details on how we employ ROS in the presented system, we refer to the aforementioned conference paper on which this article is based [3].

The robotic systems, driven by the ROS operation system, are embedded into our architecture by a RESTful layer that complies to the *Linked Robotic Things* model, presented by Schubotz et al. [39]. Comparable to the Linked Data Platform representation that is generated from ECA based runtimes by ECA2LD (cf. Sect. 3.1), the Linked Robotic Thing defines a Web model for robotic data that fulfills level 3 Richardson Maturity Model. In short, with the Linked Robotic Things model, we are able to semantically describe ROS robots in terms of components (such as sensors, joints) and actions, and provide associated LD-compliant APIs. Each of these concepts is provided with an individual HTTP resource that, in addition to the standard HTTP verbs, offers subscription mechanisms to constantly read and write data from and into the robotic application. This data may include, but is not limited to, streaming data from robotic sensors, reading or writing joint values, or sending commands to the robotic execution system.

For lifting robotic systems to the Linked Robotics Thing specification, we modeled the respective robotic properties and actions in terms of Entity Components and Attributes, and used the ECA2LD lifting approach to lift the resulting model to a Linked Data Web-layer. Interaction via HTTP endpoints and subscriptions as specified by the Linked Robotic Thing model are then provided by the respective modes of interaction as offered by the ECA2LD resources.

The endpoints are moreover wired to the ROS action and subscription endpoints, and by this allow to directly access the robotic systems. Consequently, this access is now provided transparently over the unified shared Linked Data integration layer of the resource oriented architecture.

Furthermore, ROS supports robot simulation by integrating the *Gazebo Robot Simulator* [23] which provides Gazebo services by exposing them as ROS services. In order to use the robot simulation, we configure ROS to use Gazebo instead of a real robot. This guarantees that the robot behavior in the simulation is at least close to the 'real' robot behavior. For controlling the robot commands can be sent via the ROA to navigation planning, movement planning and picking components.

# 4    High Performance Online Scheduling of Workers

Solving scheduling problems has been well known in the field of computer science and mathematics for decades. However, many approaches focus on the optimality of the solutions instead of the required computing time. Especially traditional approaches based on general problem descriptions require long computation times – even for the first available solution that satisfies all constraints. Therefore, parallel constraint solvers/optimizers have been created in the past to overcome these limitations [1,6]. In our context, external timing requirements are most important similar to simulations that require a very low latency [14,26]. This has a significant influence on the optimization strategy being used. Recent advances in the direction of highly-parallel optimization [24,25] offer the opportunity to solve sophisticated optimization problems heuristically on GPUs in a fast and efficient way. These approaches do not guarantee an optimal solution; however, this is typically not required. As previously mentioned, our domain prefers response times over all other requirements. This is caused by the primarily targeted use cases, in which the environmental conditions dynamically change over time. An optimal solution (that was computed in several minutes) cannot reflect the environment any more and is obsolete by construction. Moreover, expressing domain knowledge allows us to significantly enhance convergence of the optimizer. This is a well known strategy from the field of high-performance computing/compiler construction/parallel programming [7,27]. The same strategy can be applied to the domain of optimization in the scope of domain-specific problem descriptions that exploit special properties of the problem being solved.

In order to circumvent these issues and to realize an online scheduling of workers and robots, we leverage the most recent approaches from the field of high-performance optimization. For this reason, our proposed optimization model is completely GPU based and is able to deliver a *potentially good* solution in approx. less than 100 ms on average. The proposed model is stateless: It does not remember any environment-specific settings for the next optimization run. In contrast to classical approaches from the domain of *automated planning* and *operations research* we do not perform a *re-planning* using adjusted parameters. Instead, we compute a completely new plan from scratch, which can be performed considerably faster. A downside of this general method is the issue that previously assigned actions will not be taken into account automatically. Therefore, a new plan can be incompatible to an already created plan in terms of different assignments. Consider a simple scenario with a single actor $X$. $X$ receives an assignment in time step $t$ which recommends him to move to position $P1$. Assume a new optimization run that is triggered after several seconds due to some external conditions. The result of this run determines a new action for $X$: move to position $P2$. Unfortunately, $X$ is still moving to position $P1$, which may cause confusion or can lead to never ending re-assignments. To avoid such situations, we integrated additional restrictions into the internal decision-making process of the optimizer. This allows us to fix the current assignment of an actor with respect to the next decision. Once the current action has been finished, we release this binding to enable further assignments.

The optimizer itself is implemented as a REST-based service environment that can be called to compute the next *good* assignment for every actor involved. Since the optimizer is stateless, we require a *complete world model* for every execution run (see Fig. 6). Constraints and time-dependent actions are modeled via *components* (or rules), as described in [25]. Every component has a particular purpose (like moving an actor). It checks its pre-conditions (whether a rule can be applied) and adapts the current optimization state accordingly. Applying all rules one after another realizes an abstract simulation of the whole domain over time. Once a variable in the scope of a single state (in this case: an actor) requires a new assignment, the optimizer switches from the simulation to a heuristically-based assignment mode. During assignments, we generate (potentially) multiple successor states to explore the search space. We follow the GPU-based method from [24] to realize successor-state generation in a highly efficient way.

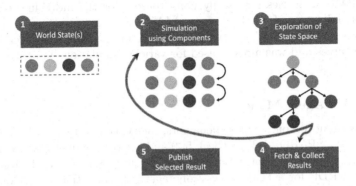

**Fig. 6.** The conceptional high-level optimizer workflow. First, we receive at least a single input world state. Afterwards (Step 2) we perform a simulation using a component-based model to approximate and estimate how every state might behave in the future. In Step 3, the optimizer explores the state space by creating and expanding successor states. After several iterations (see Step 2), we fetch and collect the resulting states to compute the best decision. This information will be propagated to other services afterwards.

## 5   Distributed Control with AJAN

The *Heuristic Optimizer* works on a high-level task basis which corresponds to the level in manufacturing planning. The worker assigned to a given task must decide for himself how to subdivide it into individual actions in order to accomplish the task with his individual abilities. Thus, the worker acts autonomously depending on given constraints.

Besides the implementation of autonomous worker behavior, the individual components of the presented distributed system must be orchestrated. The multi-agent system (MAS) paradigm has already proven that it can be used to realize autonomous entities, but also advanced distributed applications in environments with a high diversity like IoT or LD domains, see [5,8,11,22,48]. Individual agents of a MAS are autonomous, interconnected and to a certain extent intelligent units, which perceive their environment and decide independently how to interact with it. The MAS paradigm is predestined to implement a higher value 'intelligent' functionality of semantically described heterogeneous domains on application level, while hiding the deployment context from the user. This paradigm is also suitable to implement autonomous behavior of simulated entities, like three dimensional human or cobot workers.

AJAN (Accessible Java Agent Nucleus) is an agent system designed to interact with LD domains. SPARQL enhanced Behavior Trees (BT), so called SPARQL-BTs, are used as an agent behavior model to dynamically explore such domains and to query and orchestrate LD resources. For an intuitive modeling of AJAN agents a standalone web editor is provided. It offers a graphical user interface to model agent behavior via drag'n'drop and provides a view to hide native SPARQL queries for use by non-experts. For the individual control of the simulated actors of a hybrid team, AJAN agents are used in our approach. AJAN is a multi-agent Web service developed for the intelligent orchestration of LD resources and was already used for various simulations in 3D worlds, see [2,3,49].

## 5.1   AJAN Agent Model

An AJAN agent has one or more behaviors, each executed in a single thread and consisting of a SPARQL-BT (see Sect. 5.2) and a corresponding execution knowledge (EK), which stores inter-behavior knowledge (e.g. procedural variables) in memory as RDF for a faster access; one agent specific RDF based knowledge base (KB), storing inter-agent knowledge (e.g. the agent status), which can be accessed by all agent behaviors[6]; one or more events, each holding RDF data in the form of named graphs for behaviors; and one or more HTTP endpoints. These endpoints are the agent's interfaces to its LD-domain and forward incoming RDF messages as named graphs in form of events. Behaviors can be linked to these events. If an event occurs, the behaviors linked to it are executed. While executing a SPARQL-BT, it can access special incoming event data by querying its named graph. Each Behavior can also create events to trigger other behaviors. In addition, the agent state can be checked and manipulated during execution, as well as interacting with LD resources.

By using the AJAN plug-in system, AI methods can be integrated as behavior primitives for behavioral modeling. For example, a SPARQL-BT can be synthesized during GraphPlan-based [29] action planning, or by using the SPIN-rule engine[7] or ASP solver[8], the agent KB can be extended (Fig. 7).

---

[6] Not like EKs, where only the corresponding agent behaviors has access to.

[7] Reasoning and Validation with SPIN: https://rdf4j.org/documentation/program ming/spin/.

[8] We are using the clingo solver from the Potsdam Answer Set Solving Collection: https://potassco.org/. To translate the RDF based AJAN knowledge base of an agent into ASP rules, we are using the approach of [20].

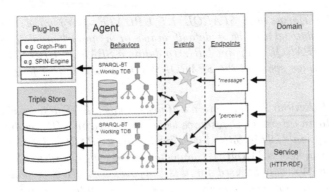

**Fig. 7.** AJAN-Agent model overview (Image source [3]).

## 5.2  AJAN Behavior Model

For modeling agent behavior in LD domains, AJAN uses the SPARQL-BT (SBT in short) approach, an extension of the well known Behavior Trees (BT) paradigm, which is widely used in industry and robotics (see [28,31,34]). SBT, as one might expect, is a combination of the BT paradigm with SPARQL, which is first mentioned in [38]. Basically, BTs are used in AJAN to perform contextual SPARQL queries for state checking, updating, constructing RDF data used for action executions, or to control the internal execution of a AJAN agent behavior. Furthermore, SBTs are defined in RDF, whereby a semantic description of the behaviors they implement is available and to meet the requirements of the LD paradigm. SBTs use standard BT composite and decorator nodes and are processed like typical BTs[9], but this approach defines five main new node types to work on RDF-based datasets and resources using SPARQL queries. Thus, a SBT can always access one or more triplestores via SPARQL endpoints that follow the SPARQL protocol [45]. In addition to the SBT nodes presented below, further nodes are available, e.g. to dynamically choose and execute AJAN behaviors or to interact with LD-resources like AJAN-agents, using HTTP methods like GET, POST or DELETE.

SPARQL-BT Condition: *A SBT Condition is a BT leaf node that makes a binary statement about the presence of a graph-pattern in an RDF dataset. It returns two states after execution: SUCCEEDED and FAILED and can be used to formulate state conditions of an agent. Thereby, it performs one SPARQL 1.1 ASK query on a defined RDF dataset. The dataset can be a default graph or a named graph and is represented by its SPARQL endpoint URI. To define a SPARQL ASK query, the complete language space of the SPARQL 1.1 language with regard to ASK operations in [46] can be used.*

SPARQL-BT Update: *This leaf node returns two states after execution: SUCCEEDED and FAILED and can be used to create, delete or update RDF data.*

---

[9] Used BT lib.: https://github.com/libgdx/gdx-ai/wiki/Behavior-Trees.

*Thereby, it performs one SPARQL 1.1 UPDATE query on a defined RDF dataset. The dataset can be a default graph or a named graph and is represented by its SPARQL endpoint URI. To define a SPARQL UPDATE query, the complete language space of the SPARQL 1.1 UPDATE language in [47] can be used.*

**SPARQL-BT Action:** *A SBT Action leaf node sends a RDF dataset via HTTP or WebSocket to an external LD-resource which is defined by a URI endpoint and an action description[10]. This dataset is defined using a SPARQL 1.1 CONSTRUCT query. The complete SPARQL 1.1 language space with regard to CONSTRUCT operations in [46] can be used for this purpose. The RDF response resulting from the executed external resource is then inserted into a named graph of the agents knowledge base. In this context, named graphs define the source of the received result. A SBT Action node returns three states as comparable action nodes of other BT implementations, SUCCEEDED, FAILED and RUNNING. Actions that do not immediately receive a result from executed LD resources, are so-called asynchronous actions.*

**SPARQL-BT Executor:** *A SBT Executor composite node can have multiple child nodes, where only one child node is executed per Executor call, depending on the agent knowledge. The selection of the next child node to execute is done by a SPARQL 1.1 SELECT query. The complete SPARQL 1.1 language space with regard to SELECT operations in [46] can be used for this purpose. Here an integer value representing the position or index of the respective child, starting with 0, is defined through the WHERE clause of the query and bound to a specified SPARQL 1.1 variable (?intValue). If multiple values are bound to this variable, one is selected randomly. A SBT Executor node returns the status of the executed child node (SUCCEEDED, FAILED or RUNNING) or FAILED if the selected child node does not exist.*

**SPARQL-BT Repeater:** *The SBT repeater decorator node can have only one child node. This child node is executed several times per repeater call, depending on the agent knowledge. The definition of the iterations is done by a SPARQL 1.1 SELECT query. The complete SPARQL 1.1 language space with regard to SELECT operations in [46] can be used for this purpose. A specified SPARQL 1.1 variable (?intValue) is used to bind a positive integer value, defined by the WHERE clause of the query, that represents the number of rounds, starting with 0. If multiple values are bound to this variable, one is selected randomly. A SBT Repeater node returns three states after execution: SUCCEEDED, if all iterations are executed; FAILED if a malformed iteration number is defined; and RUNNING while the decorator is running.*

**SPARQL-BT Plug-In Node:** *The functionality of the SBT approach can be extended within AJAN via so-called plug-ins. This is useful if you want to use domain-specific algorithms within a SPARQL-BT without having to implement*

---

[10] The description of resource actions respectively affordances is oriented to the action language *A* defined in [12].

*an external service. A SBT Plug-In node has full access to the local agent knowledge that runs this BT. All SPARQL 1.1 query forms can be used for this. Depending on the implemented logic such a node can have all typical BT states.*

## 5.3   AJAN Editor

The AJAN Editor is a standalone web-editor to model agents with its behaviors and actions. It is implemented among others with Node.js[11] and Cytoscape[12]. To establish a connection to a AJAN instance the user can enter the URI to the corresponding RDF triplestore, where all agent related definitions are stored. Figure 8 shows the main window of the editor, in which agent behaviors can be modeled. The canvas where SBTs are modeled by connecting and positioning SBT primitives or nodes, is placed in the middle of the window. Primitives instead are offered as a list on the left side of the window. Supported by graphical elements like icons, color and shape, the different node types can be distinguished and their purpose can be easily communicated. To define those node attributes and to map their node properties to the corresponding RDF definitions, a editor specific vocabulary is available. The displayed SBT in Fig. 8, is executed from left to right and from top to bottom. The turquoise colored nodes are Pluig-In nodes, the blue colored are conditions, the green one is a update and the yellow ones are actions. On the right side, node properties can be edited, such as SPARQL queries. To allow the user a more intuitive and faster modeling of SPARQL queries, several functionalities have been implemented.

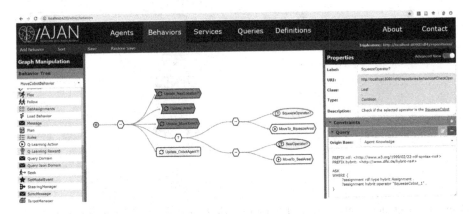

**Fig. 8.** AJAN Editor for modeling SPARQL-BTs.

---

[11] Node.js: https://nodejs.org/en/.
[12] Cytoscape: https://cytoscape.org/.

## 5.4    AJAN Application Plug-Ins

For the application presented in the scope of this work, we extended AJAN with several Plug-In nodes, as already viewed in Fig. 8 or presented in [3] for the AJAN-ECA2LD communication. For the interaction between AJAN and the *Heuristic Optimizer* from Sect. 4 a thin communication layer has been realized as a SBT leaf node. This layer uses the SPARQL 1.1 query interfaces offered by the ECA2LD based data providers to gather information as expected by the optimizer as input.

The queries are written such that they return as result the IRIs to resources of interest in the world model. This applies in particular to Attribute Value HTTP endpoints and their respective subscription channels as advertised by HTTP OPTIONS request. Retrieving the reference to Attribute Value endpoint URIs instead of the Attribute Value raw data allows to maintain the local data representation entirely by storing references to the relevant resource endpoints. Thus, requesting relevant resource endpoints via potentially computationally costy SPARQL queries needs to be done only once during system initialisation.

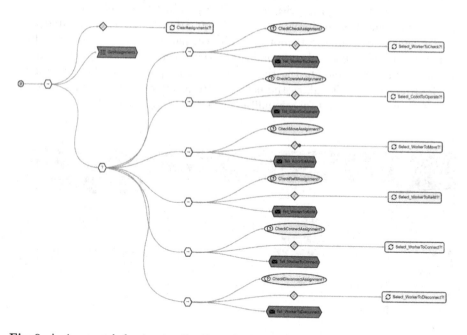

**Fig. 9.** Assignment behavior: to distribute high-level task assignments from the optimizer to the specified hybrid team actors.

When subsequently calling the optimizer HTTP API for a fresh set of production steps, the current world status is retrieved via HTTP GET from the stored references, and serialized to a single JSON object as expected by the optimizer. Finally, the response that is sent by the optimizer is deserialized into tasks that are consumed by AJAN and assigned to the particular agents in further SBT steps, as you can see in Fig. 9.

**Offering Plug-In Functionality as SPARQL-BT Node:** As mentioned before, SBTs are described in RDF. To add new node types into a SBT a new RDF vocabulary has been defined, as it is needed for the presented application. Here the node type and dynamic parameters such as the endpoints to the ECA2LD and the optimizer environment are described as RDF statements. While initiating the agent behavior, its RDF representation is mapped via RDF-Beans[13] to the corresponding JAVA based implementation. Thus, also Plug-Ins for AJAN using this library and are integrated into the agent framework via pf4j[14].

## 6   3D Scene Simulation Environment

The frameworks as used according to Sect. 3.2 so far only cover robotic components and plan execution. We maintain and simulate additional objects and entities which are not part of the robotic world in an interactive 3D run-time environment in the Unity3D[15] game engine. This allows for including avatars of human workers, as well as rigid bodies for tools and working material that is crucial for completion of the modelled task, but not directly linked to any robotic system. The simulated three-dimensional environment is visualized in a planning-editor and contains all objects to be displayed with their respective states. The editor interface provides means to the end-user to manipulate 3D objects and properties of the production units at run-time.

We implemented a set of Unity3D scripts that use *ECA2LD* (cf. Sect. 3.1) to publish data of Unity3D game objects directly in terms of Linked Data Platform resources. This way, connected applications can retrieve simulation relevant data, i.e. states of simulated objects, via a Web based LD integration layer, that complies to the concepts described in [41].

As previously mentioned in Sect. 3.2, we are using ROS and Gazebo to perform the actual simulation of robotic actors of hybrid teams. Therefore, in order to use Unity3D as visualization environment, we synchronize the commands executed by ROS in the Gazebo simulator also with a robot model in Unity3D. For this purpose, ROS#[16] is used to import URDF (Unified Robot Description Format) models into Unity3D and to synchronize the simulated robotic motions with the corresponding 3D representation in Unity3D. To ensure that the Gazebo simulation is correct, we also stream back scene changes from Unity3D via ROS# (e.g. worker movements).

To generate realistic human animations for the workers in our simulation, we use machine learning models created based on motion capture data. Depending on the type of action, we either apply generative statistical motion models [30]

---

[13] RDFBeans is an object-RDF mapping framework for Java: https://rdfbeans.github.io.

[14] Plugin Framework for Java (PF4J): http://www.pf4j.org.

[15] Unity: https://unity3d.com.

[16] Open Source C# library for communicating with ROS: https://github.com/siemens/ros-sharp.

or phase-functioned neural networks [19] to generate the motions. For walking motions, we use a phase-functioned neural network which produces a sequence of poses of arbitrary length given a target walk path. However, for manipulation actions with constraints on the hands, such as picking of objects, fastening of screws or actions involving tools, we apply the statistical motion synthesis in combination with inverse kinematics to produce motion clips. To accelerate the statistical motion synthesis for the real-time application, we prepare a search data structure for each model that enables a fast look up of a motion example given constraints before it is further optimized [18].

The human motion synthesis functionality is integrated into Unity3D via a network connection to an external server that controls the state of the human workers in the simulation by sending a continuous stream of poses. For this purpose, either a TCP or a WebSocket connection can be used, depending on whether the web browser is the target platform of the Unity3D application.

To control the worker motions, the motion synthesis service provides a REST interface that takes a custom JSON format describing a sequence of actions, each with a set of spatial constraints. We realized a Linked Data interface in a Unity3D script that translates the behavior defined by AJAN into the custom input format and derives the spatial constraints automatically from the 3D environment based on annotated scene objects and standard path planning functionality of the game engine.

Given a set of motion constraints, the service will start a separate motion synthesis thread to generate a constrained motion ahead of time and store the result in a pose queue that is used to synchronize the worker state with Unity3D. As soon as the pose queue is empty, the motion synthesis service will notify AJAN via the LD interface that the action was completed and start looping an idle motion until the next action is specified. In case that the worker needs to react to environmental changes, such as on object in the walk path, the pose queue can be emptied earlier by specifying a new action before the current action is complete.

## 7   Application Scenario

The collaboration between numerous workers and cobots during the process of the semi-hull construction of a commercial airplane demonstrates the challenge

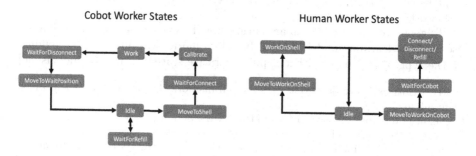

**Fig. 10.** Work states for cobot and human workers to complete their tasks.

of finding an optimal coordination of individual steps taken by each actor of a hybrid team.

## 7.1 Scenario Overview

The task that serves as evaluation use case consists of preparing a number of fixation rivets, which are used to attach fortification stringers to the semi-hull, for final sealing, check for faulty rivets before the sealant is applied, and finally perform the sealing. The task is carried out by a team consisting of two human workers and two cobot units. One cobot takes care of preparing the rivets for sealing by squeezing off excess collar parts. The other applies the sealant to readily prepared rivets. The human workers carry out their routines until they are specifically requested by the cobots to perform quality checks on the finished cobot tasks, or attach or detach power- and material-supply connections at a cobot's work position (see also Fig. 10).

The purpose is the optimization of production cycle times w.r.t. minimizing idle times of individual worker units, while avoiding frequent interruption of human worker tasks. This is particularly important since we do not want to reduce a worker's freedom in the scope of a currently active task. As outlined in Sect. 4, the optimizer is stateless and needs up-to-date environmental information from the real world. This representation contains all required properties, as well as their current values, that have been resolved from the surrounding framework. The set of properties include information related to the current tasks, the positions and other state-dependent properties of all actors. However, this set is not limited to actors as the required tools and manufacturing settings have to be transferred as well.

## 7.2 Scenario Realization

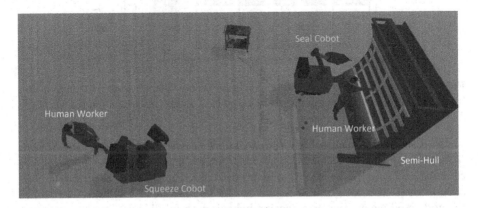

**Fig. 11.** Assembly scenario visualization in Unity3D.

The scenario is visualized using Unity3D (see Fig. 11) and using our out-of-the-box web-communication utility to integrate our systems. As described in Sect. 3.2 and discussed in [3], we have integrated the cobots for sealing and squeezing into the simulation framework. The workers are animated using motions synthesized by machine learning models and provided by our *Motion Synthesis* service described in Sect. 6. For each possible action of the workers in the scenario, a specific motion model has been created based on motion capture data. This ensures that all the worker movements are reasonable and can be performed by a living human being in a real world scenario. For details on the motion data used and a description of the preprocessing, see [17].

Workers and cobots are modeled as individual assignable variables in the scope of the optimization model. Individual properties and constraints (like the remaining time until the sealing liquid cannot be used any more) are added via components to the optimizer. The designed heuristics try to minimize all idle times while paying special attention to other time-critical requirements. In order to ensure low response times (including data pre- and postprocessing of less than 100ms) we have selected a number of states that provides good results while not exceeding the overall timing requirements. *Good results* refer to solutions that will not become significantly better by increasing the number of states or the processing time.

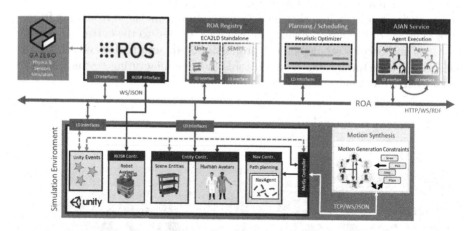

**Fig. 12.** Architecture of the proposed simulation framework. The different components from the heterogeneous software pool are linked by a unified resource-oriented LD layer.

To assign and execute high-level tasks which were defined by the *Heuristic Optimizer* an AJAN agent, the assignment agent, is used to perform the *SPARQL-BTs* (SBT in short) described in Sect. 5.4. After reading the new assignments, each assignment is sent to the defined worker agent. Afterwards, the addressed agents perform specific behaviors to fulfill the assigned high-level task. Instead of depicting all possible actions and processes in the optimizer, an abstraction layer was introduced in which we realize the autonomy of the actors to be simulated. In addition, it allows us to use the AJAN to more flexibly modify the low-level behaviors of each worker and adapt them to the distributed environment (Fig. 12).

The behavior of each human and cobot worker is modeled as SBT using the AJAN editor. This not only creates a blueprint for the task at hand to realize the worker states shown in Fig. 10, but also allows each actor to react to changes in the environment in real time when executing these behaviors. Every actor in the scene shares common knowledge synchronized via the ROA, and each change in the world state is considered there as well. For this purpose each actor applies the same SBT to explore the ROA and to subscribe to resource changes. The underlying information comes from various resources that the agent collects, and makes them available through its KB for behavioral execution. For example, the status information or the position of a rivet originates from the Unity3D environment. All subscribed resource endpoints were referenced from the previously explored ECA2LD-based ROA. These endpoints can also be used to manipulate the resources, e.g. to change a rivet status.

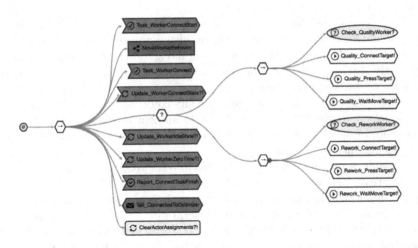

**Fig. 13.** SPARQL-BT perform a connection task by a simulated human worker.

While executing a specific behavior, resources as well as states of working areas, workers and tasks have been updated in the ECA2LD environment through the corresponding endpoints. As an example a connection behavior is shown in Fig. 13. This SBT will be executed by a human worker agent if a cobot needs to be connected to a working area. With the turquoise colored leaf nodes the ECA2LD world model is updated, instead the yellow nodes performs actions realized with the *Motion Synthesis*. After a high-level task is completed, the assignment agent is put into a new state (by a completion message, see purple node) in which the agent is able to receive new assignments from the optimizer.

# 8   Findings and Key Results in Application Scenario

Given a specified team behavior with roles and individual tasks assigned, several aspects of the team performance can be simulated and evaluated. Evaluation criteria are e.g. time to fulfill a specific task sequence, reachability of positions and objects, or ergonomic assessment of poses based on visual appearance with respect to different body sizes. In the application scenario presented above, a number of observations and experiences have been made:

- in certain configurations and job assignments, the robot is often slowed down since trajectories of workers and robot interfere. A deliberate change of the assignments helps to reduce certain interferences;
- the robot can grasp a tool from a specified position but the ensuing grasp pose leads to a frequent slip of the tool in the gripper. To cope with this, a worker has to correct the grip or take over the tool immediately;
- depending on a position assigned or calculated, the robot is supposed to grasp a tool from a commissioning area which cannot be reached. Changing the position increases the success rate;
- in some cases, the same issue occurred for human workers. In this scope, ergonomic aspects are assessed based on visual appearance;
- the robot might damage the wing during navigation, if the robot arm is not properly stored for driving. For this reason, we introduced a safe area, which cannot be entered by a robot;
- we discovered that certain task assignments could be improved based on the information resolved from the ROA. A prominent example in this case is a scenario, in which it is better to assign a task to a worker instead of a robot due to distance constraints;
- if available, sensor information can be fed into the ROA to evaluate the impact on the team behavior;
- when simulating human behavior to evaluate hybrid teams, the unpredictability of human behavior is a problem. Several intended human responses may be uncritical, but in some situations a safety-critical moment may occur. One possible way to take this into account is to randomize human behavior and generate a variety of actions to test effects on robot behavior;
- finally, it is possible to take the context into account: is the configuration of team tasks able to deal with e.g. a change in the clock rate or problems due to missing supplies.

# 9   Related Work

In a recent survey on HRC, [44] distinguish basic *safety measures*, human-robot *coexistence* and human-robot *collaboration*. In coexistence, humans and robots share a common workspace, but have possibly independent goals. In collaboration, at least parts of the actions of the individual team members are coordinated towards reaching a shared goal, such as e.g. lifting and mounting heavy parts together in an assembly line. Fundamental for both, coexistence and collaboration, are in fact safety mechanisms which guarantee that collisions are avoided or as harmless as possible.

Several approaches focus on risk assessment in HRC scenarios based on built-in safety measures to reduce hazards. [35] and [13] consider HRC mainly from the robot-oriented perspective of collision avoidance. [4] presents a design method for facilitating and automating risk assessment in HRC scenarios. Although risk assessment is an important aspect of HRC, especially in industrial contexts, it is rather a prerequisite for designing adaptable HRC workspaces. Given safety measures on the robotic side, the question still remains which impact these measures have on the coordination and collaboration of workers and robots in flexible environments.

Several commercial systems allowing the configuration and 3D simulation of target processes in production environments in the shop-floor context, e.g. Tecnomatix[17], FlexSim[18], visTABLEtouch[19] or SIMUL8[20]. DELMIA[21] for example, is a tool which allows additionally the validation of 'produced' products and the evaluation of manufacturing processes. DELMIA is also used in [21] for prototyping CPPS environments. [32] present an extension of the IMMA tool for ergonomic assessment of HRC scenarios. [10] describes EMA, a tool for ergonomic assessment of worker behavior which has recently been extended with robotic capabilities to simulate collaborations. The main deficit of these industrial frameworks is the limited support for specifying dynamical and mutual dependencies between the actors which is required for evaluating team-oriented behavior especially in critical situations [42].

## 10   Conclusion

We presented a novel framework for 3D simulation of hybrid teams in production scenarios. The web- and RDF-based architecture allows the integration of external services (e.g. ROS-based robot control software) to ensure an adequate simulation of the robot behavior. The optimal coordination of team members is generated by an high-performance heuristic optimizer which computes task assignments for actors in a given scenario. With the help of RDF and based on the task assignments, the agent system AJAN is able to control the behavior of different actor types in the simulation environment. To demonstrate the effectiveness of the new concept, we have successfully realized an application case in the context of an aircraft assembly line.

**Acknowledgements.** The work described in this paper has been funded by the ITEA 3 project MOSIM (grant no. 01IS18060C) as well as by the German Federal Ministry of Education and Research (BMBF) through the projects Hybr-iT (grant no. 01IS16026A) and REACT (grant no. 01/W17003).

---

[17] Tecnomatix: plm.automation.siemens.com/Tecnomatix.

[18] FlexSim: www.FlexSim.com/FlexSim.

[19] visTABLEtouch: www.vistable.de/visTABLEtouch-software.

[20] SIMUL8: www.SIMUL8.com.

[21] DELMIA: www.transcat-plm.com/software/ds-software/delmia.

# References

1. Abdelkafi, O., Chebil, K., Khemakhem, M.: Parallel local search on GPU and CPU with OpenCL Language. In: Proceedings of the First International Conference on Reasoning and Optimization in Information Systems. IEEE (2013)
2. Antakli, A., Hermann, E., Zinnikus, I., Du, H., Fischer, K.: Intelligent distributed human motion simulation in human-robot collaboration environments. In: Proceedings of the 18th International Conference oh Intelligent Virtual Agents, pp. 319–324. ACM (2018)
3. Antakli, A., et al.: Agent-based web supported simulation of human-robot collaboration. In: Proceedings of the 15th International Conference on Web Information Systems and Technologies (WEBIST), pp. 88–99 (2019)
4. Awad, R., Fechter, M., van Heerden, J.: Integrated risk assessment and safety consideration during design of HRC workplaces. In: 2017 22nd IEEE International Conference on Emerging Technologies and Factory Automation (ETFA), pp. 1–10. IEEE (2017)
5. Bosse, S.: Mobile multi-agent systems for the internet-of-things and clouds using the javascript agent machine platform and machine learning as a service. In: 2016 IEEE 4th International Conference on Future Internet of Things and Cloud (FiCloud), pp. 244–253. IEEE (2016)
6. Campeotto, F., Dovier, A., Fioretto, F., Pontelli, E.: A GPU implementation of large neighborhood search for solving constraint optimization problems. In: Proceedings of the Twenty-first European Conference on Artificial Intelligence (2014)
7. Danilewski, P., Köster, M., Leißa, R., Membarth, R., Slusallek, P.: Specialization through dynamic staging. In: Proceedings of the 13th International Conference on Generative Programming: Concepts & Experiences (GPCE), pp. 103–112. ACM (2014)
8. Diaconescu, I.M., Wagner, G.: Modeling and simulation of web-of-things systems as multi-agent systems. In: Müller, J.P., Ketter, W., Kaminka, G., Wagner, G., Bulling, N. (eds.) MATES 2015. LNCS (LNAI), vol. 9433, pp. 137–153. Springer, Cham (2015). https://doi.org/10.1007/978-3-319-27343-3_8
9. Fielding, R.T., Taylor, R.N.: Principled design of the modern web architecture. ACM Trans. Internet Technol. (TOIT) **2**(2), 115–150 (2002)
10. Fritzsche, L., Schönherr, R., Illmann, B.: Interactive simulation and ergonomics assessment of manual work with EMA - applications in product development and production planning. In: Advances in Applied Digital Human Modeling, pp. 49–58. AHFE (2014)
11. Garcia-Sanchez, F., Fernández-Breis, J.T., Valencia-Garcia, R., Gómez, J.M., Martinez-Béjar, R.: Combining semantic web technologies with multi-agent systems for integrated access to biological resources. J. Biomed. Inform. **41**(5), 848–859 (2008). https://doi.org/10.1016/j.jbi.2008.05.007
12. Gelfond, M., Lifschitz, V.: Action languages. Electron. Trans. AI **3**(16) (1998). https://ep.liu.se/ea/cis/1998/016/index.html
13. Gopinath, V., Johansen, K.: Risk assessment process for collaborative assembly-a job safety analysis approach. Procedia CIRP **44**, 199–203 (2016)
14. Groß, J., Köster, M., Krüger, A.: Fast and efficient nearest neighbor search for particle simulations. In: Computer Graphics & Visual Computing (CGVC). The Eurographics Association (2019)
15. Guinard, D., Trifa, V.: Towards the web of things: web mashups for embedded devices. In: Workshop on Mashups, Enterprise Mashups and Lightweight Composition on the Web (MEM), vol. 15 (2009)

16. Heath, T., Bizer, C.: Linked data: Evolving the web into a global data space. Synth. Lect. Semant. Web Theory Technol. **1**(1), 1–136 (2011)
17. Herrmann, E., et al.: Motion data and model management for applied statistical motion synthesis. In: Smart Tools and Apps for Graphics. The Eurographics Association (2019)
18. Herrmann, E., Manns, M., Du, H., Hosseini, S., Fischer, K.: Accelerating statistical human motion synthesis using space partitioning data structures. Comput. Animat. Virtual Worlds **28**(3–4), e1780 (2017)
19. Holden, D., Komura, T., Saito, J.: Phase-functioned neural networks for character control. ACM Trans. Graph. (TOG) **36**(4), 42 (2017)
20. Ianni, G., Martello, A., Panetta, C., Terracina, G.: Efficiently querying RDF (S) ontologies with answer set programming. J. Log. Comput. **19**(4), 671–695 (2008)
21. Kashevnik, A., Teslya, N., Yablochnikov, E., Arckhipov, V., Kipriianov, K.: Development of a prototype cyber physical production system with help of smart-M3. In: IECON 2016–42nd Annual Conference of the IEEE Industrial Electronics Society, pp. 4890–4895. IEEE (2016)
22. Khriyenko, O., Nagy, M.: Semantic web-driven agent-based ecosystem for linked data and services. In: Proceedings of the Third International Conferences on Advanced Service Computing, pp. 25–30 (2011)
23. Koenig, N., Howard, A.: Design and use paradigms for gazebo, an open-source multi-robot simulator. In: 2004 IEEE/RSJ International Conference on Intelligent Robots and Systems (IROS), vol. 3, pp. 2149–2154. IEEE (2004)
24. Köster, M., Groß, J., Krüger, A.: FANG: fast and efficient successor-state generation for heuristic optimization on GPUs. In: Wen, S., Zomaya, A., Yang, L.T. (eds.) ICA3PP 2019. LNCS, vol. 11944, pp. 223–241. Springer, Cham (2020). https://doi.org/10.1007/978-3-030-38991-8_15
25. Köster, M., Groß, J., Krüger, A.: Parallel tracking and reconstruction of states in heuristic optimization systems on GPUs. In: Parallel and Distributed Computing, Applications and Technologies. International Conference on Parallel and Distributed Computing, Applications and Technologies. Springer (2019)
26. Köster, M., Krüger, A.: Adaptive position-based fluids: Improving performance of fluid simulations for real-time applications. Int. J. Comput. Graph. Animat. (IJCGA) **6**(3), 1–16 (2016)
27. Köster, M., Leißa, R., Hack, S., Membarth, R., Slusallek, P.: Platform-specific optimization and mapping of stencil codes through refinement. In: Proceedings of the First International Workshop on High-Performance Stencil Computations, pp. 1–6 (2014)
28. Marzinotto, A., Colledanchise, M., Smith, C., Ögren, P.: Towards a unified behavior trees framework for robot control. In: 2014 IEEE International Conference on Robotics and Automation (ICRA), pp. 5420–5427. IEEE (2014)
29. Meneguzzi, F.R., Zorzo, A.F., da Costa Móra, M.: Propositional planning in BDI agents. In: Proceedings of the 2004 ACM Symposium on Applied Computing, SAC 2004, pp. 58–63. ACM (2004)
30. Min, J., Chai, J.: Motion graphs++: a compact generative model for semantic motion analysis and synthesis. ACM Trans. Graph. (TOG) **31**(6), 153 (2012)
31. Nguyen, H., Ciocarlie, M.T., Hsiao, K., Kemp, C.C.: ROS commander (ROSCo): behavior creation for home robots. In: 2013 IEEE International Conference on Robotics and Automation, pp. 467–474 (2013)
32. Ore, F., Hanson, L., Delfs, N., Wiktorsson, M.: Virtual evaluation of industrial human-robot cooperation: an automotive case study. In: 3rd International Digital Human Modeling Symposium. Elsevier (2014)

33. Parastatidis, S., Webber, J., Silveira, G., Robinson, I.S.: The role of hyperme-dia in distributed system development. In: Proceedings of the First International Workshop on RESTful Design, pp. 16–22. ACM (2010)
34. Paxton, C., Hundt, A., Jonathan, F., Guerin, K., Hager, G.D.: CoSTAR: instruct-ing collaborative robots with behavior trees and vision. In: 2017 IEEE International Conference on Robotics and Automation (ICRA), pp. 564–571. IEEE (2017)
35. Pedrocchi, N., Vicentini, F., Matteo, M., Tosatti, L.M.: Safe human-robot cooper-ation in an industrial environment. Int. J. Adv. Robot. Syst. (2013)
36. Pfisterer, D., et al.: SPITFIRE: toward a semantic web of things. IEEE Commun. Mag. **49**(11), 40–48 (2011). https://doi.org/10.1109/MCOM.2011.6069708
37. Quigley, M., e al.: ROS: an open-source robot operating system. In: ICRA Work-shop on Open Source Software, Kobe, Japan, vol. 3, p. 5 (2009)
38. Schreiber, W., Zürl, K., Zimmermann, P. (eds.): Web-basierte Anwendun-gen Virtueller Techniken: Das ARVIDA-Projekt - Dienste-basierte Software-Architektur und Anwendungsszenarien für die Industrie. Springer, Heidelberg (2017). https://doi.org/10.1007/978-3-662-52956-0
39. Schubotz, R., Vogelgesang, C., Antakli, A., Rubinstein, D., Spieldenner, T.: Requirements and specifications for robots, linked data and all the REST. In: Proceedings of Workshop on Linked Data in Robotics and Industry 4.0 (LIDARI). CEUR (2017)
40. Sheth, A.P.: Changing focus on interoperability in information systems: from sys-tem, syntax, structure to semantics. In: Goodchild, M., Egenhofer, M., Fegeas, R., Kottman, C. (eds.) Interoperating Geographic Information Systems. The Springer International Series in Engineering and Computer Science, vol. 495, pp. 5–29. Springer, Boston (1999). https://doi.org/10.1007/978-1-4615-5189-8_2
41. Spieldenner, T., Schubotz, R., Guldner, M.: ECA2LD: from entity-component-attribute runtimes to linked data applications. In: Proceedings of the International Workshop on Semantic Web of Things for Industry 4.0. Springer (2018)
42. Tsarouchi, P., Makris, S., Chryssolouris, G.: Human-robot interaction review and challenges on task planning and programming. Int. J. Comput. Integr. Manuf. **29**(8), 916–931 (2016)
43. Verborgh, R., Steiner, T., Van Deursen, D., Van de Walle, R., Valles, J.G.: Efficient runtime service discovery and consumption with hyperlinked RESTdesc. In: 2011 7th International Conference on Next Generation Web Services Practices, pp. 373–379. IEEE (2011)
44. Villani, V., Pini, F., Leali, F., Secchi, C.: Survey on human-robot collaboration in industrial settings: safety, intuitive interfaces and applications. Mechatronics **55**, 248–266 (2018)
45. W3C: SPARQL 1.1 Protocol (2008). https://www.w3.org/TR/sparql11-protocol/. Accessed 16 Jan 2020
46. W3C: SPARQL 1.1 Query Language. https://www.w3.org/TR/2013/REC-sparql11-query-20130321/ (2013). Accessed 16 Jan 2020
47. W3C: SPARQL 1.1 Update. https://www.w3.org/TR/sparql11-update/ (2013). Accessed 16 Jan 2020
48. Xu, X., Bessis, N., Cao, J.: An autonomic agent trust model for IoT systems. Procedia Comput. Sci. **21**, 107–113 (2013)
49. Zinnikus, I., et al.: Integrated semantic fault analysis and worker support for cyber-physical production systems. In: 2017 IEEE 19th Conference on Business Informat-ics (CBI), vol. 1, pp. 207–216. IEEE (2017)

# Text Web Templates Considered Harmful

Fernando Miguel Carvalho[1($\boxtimes$)] ⓘ, Luis Duarte[1] ⓘ, and Julien Gouesse[2]

[1] ADEETC, ISEL, Polytechnic Institute of Lisbon, Lisbon, Portugal
{mcarvalho,lcduarte}@cc.isel.ipl.pt
[2] Orange, Paris, France
gouessej@orange.fr

**Abstract.** For the last decades text-based templates have been the primary option to build dynamic web pages. Until today, no other alternative has rebutted this approach. Yet, using text-based templates has several drawbacks including: 1. blocking resolution, 2. programming languages heterogeneity, 3. limited set of templating features and 4. opinionated idioms. In this paper we show how a domain specific language (DSL) for HTML (such as HtmlFlow, Kotlinx.html or React JSX) can suppress the text-based templates limitations and outperform state-of-the-art template engines (such as JSP, Handlebars, Thymeleaf, and others) in well known benchmarks. To that end, we use the Spring Framework and the sample application PetClinic to show how a DSL for HTML provides unopinionated web templates with boundless resolving features only ruled by the host programming language (such as Java, Kotlin or JavaScript).

**Keywords:** Web templates · Dynamic web pages · Domain specific languages · Web application · HTML

## 1 Introduction

Web templates (such as JSP, Handlebars or Thymeleaf) are based in HTML documents, which are augmented with template specific markers (e.g. <%, {{}} or ${}) representing *dynamic* information that can be replaced at runtime by the results of corresponding computations to produce a *view* [1,16]. The parsing and markers replacement process (i.e. *resolution*) is the main role of the *template engine* [31]. Even for those engines providing markers extensibility, these markers obey to a set of rules that restrict access to the host programming language features (e.g. Java) from the template. Thus, web templates development is dictated by the engine guidelines that force programmers to follow a set of given idioms and practices, i.e. *opinionated* [30].

In Listing 1.1 we show a sample Thymeleaf template [15] of a Spring web application [23] (part of the owner details view of the PetClinic web application [11]). This template builds a dynamic table containing a description list on each table row. In this case, the template receives a data model object **owner** with a **pets** property (line 2) and for each pet it generates a table row (**tr** in line

© Springer Nature Switzerland AG 2020
A. Bozzon et al. (Eds.): WEBIST 2019, LNBIP 399, pp. 69–95, 2020.
https://doi.org/10.1007/978-3-030-61750-9_4

2) containing a description list (dl in line 4) with the pet's name (line 6) and its birthdate (line 9). This Listing highlights the *heterogeneity* resulting from the technological mix of the HTML language with Thymeleaf template dialects (i.e. attributes beginning with th) and also the web framework programming language (i.e. Java) that is used, for example, on the auxiliary function call of line 9: temporals.format(pet.birthDate,'yyyy-MM-dd').

**Listing 1.1:** Thymeleaf template for owner details view of PetClinic web application.

```
1   <table class="table_table-striped">
2     <tr th:each="pet_:_${owner.pets}">
3       <td valign="top">
4         <dl class="dl-horizontal">
5           <dt>Name</dt>
6           <dd th:text="${pet.name}"></dd>
7           <dt>Birth Date</dt>
8           <dd
9             th:text="${#temporals.format(pet.birth,_'yyyy-MM-dd
               ')}">
10          </dd>
11        </dl>
12      </td>
13    </tr>
14  </table>
```

Template engines distinguish themselves by the idiom and subset of available markers to control the dynamic content. But generally, all engines provide the same set of core templating features through specific dialects such as those used in the example of Listing 1.1 that we may group in the following categories:

1. *text replacement* – all expressions denoted with ${...} markers in lines 2, 6 and 9.
2. *variables* – in line 2 we declare an auxiliary variable pet.
3. *control flow* such as conditional evaluation and loops – th:each *loop* in line 2.
4. *utility functions* – there is a set of built-in Thymeleaf utility objects available through the marker #, such as #temporals in line 9.
5. *partial views* or *fragments* inclusion (i.e. transclusion [35]) – in Sect. 4.
6. *data binding* [29] – property pets of the owner *data model* [13], in line 2.

These dialects lead web frameworks to encompass at least 3 distinct programming languages on web development: 1) a high-level programming language used, for example, to gather data and build a *data model*, 2) HTML to build the skeleton of the web template and 3) template specific markers to manage the dynamic content of the web page. From these observations we argue that text-based templates, such as Thymeleaf templates incur in the following drawbacks:

1. no compile time validation;
2. require keen understanding of a diversity of technologies including the web framework host language (e.g. Java), HTML and the template engine dialects;

3. intricate definition from mixing idioms between HTML, template dialects and high-level programming language (e.g. line 9 of Listing 1.1);
4. restricted set of control flow features enforced by template dialects, such as th:each.

In this paper we state that an internal domain specific language (DSL) for HTML, such as HtmlFlow [8], KotlinX.html [27] or React JSX [37], can mitigate all pointed disadvantages and still provide the core templating features. These DSLs avoid specific dialects and give programmers all the freedom of the core programming language (Java, Kotlin or JavaScript). They let programmers interleave fluently HTML building blocks with any available construction of the host programming language. Thus, programmers may choose the most convenient idiom to write the template's control flow according to their preferences

In [10] we show how a *higher-order template* (HoT) does not block the template resolution and *pushes* the resulting HTML to the response stream as its content is being resolved [22,28]. Rather than *pulling* data from a source and fully complete markers of a template, HoT reacts to data and *push* the resulting HTML as it is being resolved. This approach provides better user experience keeping the browser responsive, even on presence of large data sets, and presents better rendering performance, in comparison to state of the art template engines, such as Handlebars and React, as shown in performance benchmarks [10,32]

To prove the effectiveness of HtmlFlow even for developing complex web applications we have replaced Thymeleaf templates of the Spring PetClinic [11] web application by HtmlFlow based templates. Spring PetClinic is an open-source Java application commonly used to demonstrate different design patterns and concepts, which was inspired by PetStore [34] that illustrates the use of J2EE to develop an eCommerce web application. Our work demonstrates how HtmlFlow simplifies several template idioms and still preserves the web templates role through HoT. Finally, we use the same approach with alternative DSLs for HTML namely j2Html [2], KotlinX.html and React, where HtmlFlow outperforms the competition in well-known benchmarks [10,32].

For the remainder of this paper we present in the next section state of the art solutions that deal with web templates and domain specific languages. Then in Sect. 3 we compare different alternative DSLs for HTML. In Sect. 4 we revisit the concept of *higher-order templates* (HoT) provided in HtmlFlow. After that in Sect. 5, we present the implementation of the most used template idioms with Thymeleaf and HtmlFlow in the PetClinic web application. In Sect. 6, we present a performance evaluation. Finally, in Sect. 7 we conclude and discuss some future work.

## 2   State of the Art

In this section we discuss related work in web templates and domain specific languages field. We first address in Subsect. 2.1 the main properties that dictates the design of web template engines. After that, in Subsect. 2.2, we present background work on domain specific languages and their main characteristics.

## 2.1   Web Templates

Web template engines deal with data models as their *inputs* to produce HTML as *output* [16]. Martin Fowler distinguishes between two possible approaches followed by view engines: 1) *template view* and 2) *transform view*. The former is HTML centric and thus oriented to the *output*. In this case, the view is written in the structure of the HTML document and embed markers to indicate where data model properties need to go. Since the seminal technologies JSP, ASP and PHP appeared with the *template view* pattern, many other alternatives emerged along the last two decades[1], turning this pattern into one of the most used approaches in web applications development.

On the other hand, the *transform view* is oriented to the *input* and how each part of the input is directly transformed into HTML. XSLT is maybe one of the most well-known programming languages to specify transformations around XML data. In this case the XML data takes the place of the *input* that is transformed by the XSLT to another format (e.g. HTML). Also, the functional nature of the transform view pattern enables its *composition* in a pipeline of transformations where each stage takes the result of the previous transformation as input and produces a new output that is passed to the next transformation. For example, the Cocoon Java library [7] provides a framework for building pipelines of XML transformations steps specified in XSLT.

The *transform view* pattern has similarities with the *higher-order templates* [10] approach of HtmlFlow where a view is a first-class function that takes an object model as parameter and applies transformations over its properties. The object model has the role of the *input* (e.g. XML data) and the HTML domain-specific language is the idiom used to transform the model into HTML.

## 2.2   Domain Specific Languages

The idea of domain-specific languages (DSL) was first approached by Landin [25], which introduces a framework that dictates the design of a specific language restricted by a domain. A DSL is a programming language specialized to a particular *application domain* [14]. This is in contrast to general-purpose languages, which are broadly applicable across domains.

DSLs can be divided in two types: *external* or *internal* [17]. *External* DSLs are languages created without any affiliation to a concrete programming language. An example of an external DSL is the regular expressions search pattern [36], since it defines its own syntax without any dependency of programming languages. Furthermore, regular expressions are easier to use and manipulate by experts than implementing the same set of verification rules through control flow instructions, such as `if/else` and `String` operations. Writing in Java programming language an equivalent validation to that one presented in Listing 2.1 would require more than a single line of code to verify if a string is in 12-h format with optional leading 0.

---

[1] wikipedia.org/Comparison_of_web_template_engines.

**Listing 2.1:** Regular expression for time in 12-hour format with optional leading 0.

```
(0?[0-9]|1[0-1]):([0-5][0-9])
```

On the other hand an *internal* DSL is defined within a host programming language as a library and tends to be limited to the syntax of the host language, such as Java. For that reason, internal DSLs can also be referred as *embedded* DSLs since they are embedded in the programming language where they are used.

JQuery [33] is one of the most well-known examples of an internal DSL in Javascript, designed to simplify HTML DOM [21] tree traversal and manipulation. In the data structures field the Language Integrated Query (LINQ) [20] is an example of an internal DSL that enables querying of any kind of collection. An idea that is heavily inspired by the concept of *lazy lists*, also known as *streams*, first described in 1965 by Landin [24].

Another example of an internal DSL is jMock [18], which is a Java library that provides tools for test-driven development. In Listing 2.2 we can see that jMock uses a DSL to create expectations. In the concrete example it obtains the value of a property `Greeting` (`getGreeting()` in line 5), and asserts if it matches the expected value, which is `Good afternoon` in line 6. In this case the semantics of the methods used by jMock aim to simplify the programmer's understanding of the tests that are being performed.

**Listing 2.2:** jMock example.

```
1  final GreetingTime gt = context.mock(GreetingTime.class);
2  (new Greeting()).setGreetingTime(gt);
3
4  context.checking(new Expectations(){{
5    one(gt).getGreeting();
6    will(returnValue("Good_afternoon"));
7  }});
```

In common all internal DSLs, such as JQuery, LINQ or jMock, use functions to define their languages. According to [17] we may identify three different patterns of combining functions to make a DSL: 1) *function sequence*; 2) *method chaining*, and 3) *nested function*.

A *function sequence* is about a combination of function calls as a sequence of statements. Consider for example the following set of functions: `html()`, `head()`, `body()`, `title()`, `div()` and `p()`, each one responsible for creating the corresponding HTML element with the same name of the function. So, the HTML document in Listing 2.4 could be the result of the execution of the corresponding Java program in Listing 2.3.

**Listing 2.3:** Function sequence based DSL for HTML.

```
html();
  head();
    title();
      p("My title");
  body();
    div();
      p("A statement.");
```

**Listing 2.4:** Resulting HTML of 2.3.

```
<html>
  <head>
    <title>
      <p>My title</p>
    </title>
  </head>
  <body>
    <div>
      <p>A statement</p>
    ...
```

As we can see in Listing 2.3, if we try to lay out and organize a function sequence in an appropriate way, we can read it clearly as the resulting output in HTML. The major problem regarding this approach is whichever way we use to define a function sequence we will always need auxiliary context variables in order to know where we are in the building process. Considering the calls to p(), the builder needs to know which element will contain the resulting paragraph element. So, it does that by keeping track of the current HTML element in a variable. If these functions are global, then the state will end up being global too.

*Method chaining* pattern avoids this problem, since it is based on methods instances calls, where the target object may track any necessary context. In this case, it uses a sequence of method calls where each call acts on the result of the previous call. Thus, the methods are composed by calling one on top of the other. Yet, we still need some kind of bare function to begin the chain, such as new Html() in Listing 2.5 that instantiates the target root.

**Listing 2.5:** Method chaining based DSL for HTML.

```
new Html()
  .head()
    .title()
      .p("My title")
  .body()
    .div()
      .p("A statement.")
```

**Listing 2.6:** Nested function based DSL for HTML.

```
html(
  head(
    title(
      p("My title")),
  body(
    div(
      p("A statement.")))));
```

*Nested function* combines functions by making function calls arguments in higher-level function calls. This approach eliminates the need for a context variable, as the arguments are all evaluated before a function is called. A simple sequence of nested functions ends up being evaluated backwards to the order they are written. This means that arguments are first evaluated before the function being invoked. In Listing 2.6 p() is first evaluated and its resulting paragraph will be the argument of the call to title(), which in turn will be the argument of head() and henceforward.

Yet, the nested function pattern incurs into the same problems of functions globalness as function sequence pattern.

# 3 Domain-Specific Languages for HTML

Given the DSL design alternatives presented in Sect. 2.1 we may describe DSLs for HTML according to the classification presented in the Table 1. For comparison we also include in Table 1 a non DSL-based engine, i.e. Thymeleaf, as the representative of most text-based templates such as JSP, Handlebars, Velocity and others. *Functional templates* regard the capacity of implementing Web templates as first-class functions, which is only possible with an internal DSL for HTML. The performance results in the Spring templates benchmark [32] are relatively to HtmlFlow, which is the most performant engine among these libraries. We are not considering React performance on these results, because this benchmark evaluates the performance of resolving HTML based templates in the web server, whereas React only resolves HTML within the browser and just receives plain JSON from the web server. Nevertheless, in [10] we have already compared the performance including all the processing pipeline from the web server to the browser, which shows that React is almost 4 times slower than the competition rendering HTML for a data source with 10000 items.

**Table 1.** Comparing Thymeleaf characteristics with DSLs for HTML.

| Library | DSL | Template dialect | Functional templates | HTML safety | Data structureless | Spring templates benchmark |
|---------|-----|------------------|----------------------|-------------|--------------------|-----------------------------|
| **Thymeleaf** | - | Thymeleaf | × | × | - | 32% |
| **j2html** | Internal | Java | ✓ | × | × | 26% |
| **kotlinX.html** | Internal | Kotlin | ✓ | ✓ | ✓ | 58% |
| **React** | External | JavaScript | ✓ | × | × | - |
| **HtmlFlow** | Internal | Java | ✓ | ✓ | ✓ | 100% |

In the following subsections we will describe each one of the DSLs for HTML and further properties: *HTML safety* and *data structureless*, which are an essential design key for the best performance presented by HtmlFlow.

## 3.1 j2Html

As other internal DSLs for HTML, j2html replaces the need of textual template files by templates defined within the Java language, which enables the use of all Java programming language features to control the flow of the dynamic parts. J2html uses a *nested function* approach where templates has a similar layout to that one presented in Listing 2.6. Thus, since arguments are first evaluated before the function being invoked, this technique does not allow the resulting

HTML to be emitted on demand according to functions calls order. Otherwise the HTML would be generated backwards.

So, the result of the execution of a j2Html template is a tree structure that compose Tag objects [19]. This template must be further resolved through the render() method to produce an HTML document.

Furthermore, the major handicap of j2html is the lack of *validation* of the HTML language rules either at compile time or at runtime. Hence, it does not provide HTML safety because it does not ensure that the resulting HTML is conforming a valid HTML document.

## 3.2   KotlinX.html

The KotlinX.html [27] is another popular DSL for HTML and it has been written in Kotlin programming language. One of the Kotlin design principles was to create an inter-operative language with Java. Although its syntax is not compatible with the standard Java syntax, both languages can coexist within the same program source code. Other main advantage of Kotlin is that it heavily reduces the amount of textual information needed to create code by using type inference and other techniques.

The KotlinX.html provides a fluent interface that mixes the three approaches of combining functions: function sequence, method chaining, and nested function. Yet, that mix is hidden when we are programming in Kotlin thanks to the mechanism of *function literals* (i.e. *lambdas*) with *receiver* [6].

Considering the use case of an internal DSL for HTML presented in Sect. 2.2, the corresponding version for Kotlin using *function literals with receiver* would be written according to Listing 3.1. The equivalent use in Java of this Kotlin DSL is presented in Listing 3.2. In truth, whenever we write in Kotlin a block {...} following a function name (e.g. head {...}), we are invoking that function with the block {...} as the the function's argument. To that end, the block {...} is passed as an anonymous function (or *lambda*) to the invoked function.

**Listing 3.1:** Kotlin type-safe builders for HTML.

```
html {
  head {
    title {
      p("My title")
    }
  }
  body {
    div {
      p("A statement.")
    }
  }
}
```

**Listing 3.2:** Kotlin type-safe builders for HTML invoked with Java code.

```
html(self -> {
  self.head(self ->
    self.title(self ->
      self.p("My title")
    )
  );
  self.body(self ->
    self.div(self ->
      self.p("A statement.")
    )
  );
} ;
```

Method calls to `head`, `title`, `p`, etc. in Listing 3.1 are equivalent to `this.head`, `this.title` and `this.p`. The `this` target is implicit and is the corresponding `self` lambda parameter of Listing 3.2. Declaring the `self` parameter as a *receiver* has the advantage of allowing the use of parameterless lambdas. In Kotlin, a parameterless lambda is denoted as {...} rather than {... -> ...}, which leads to the idiom expressed in the example of Listing 3.1.

As a result of using function arguments, it delays the evaluation of those functions and suppresses the backwards evaluation problem intrinsic to the *nested function* approach. So, the result of the execution of a KotlinX.html template does not require any auxiliary data structure and can be immediately emitted as functions are being invoked. Hence KotlinX.html templates resolution provides both modes: a DOM tree based and a *data structureless* mode that can be generated to an output stream.

Like HtmlFlow, the HTML fluent interface for KotlinX.Html is automatically built from the XSD definition of the HTML 5 language. Thus, the generated DSL ensures that each element only contains the elements and attributes stated in the HTML5 XSD document.

## 3.3  React

React introduces a syntax extension to JavaScript (JSX) that allows the use of plain HTML together with JavaScript. This means that you can use JSX inside of if statements and for loops, assign it to variables, accept it as arguments, and return it from functions.

As others internal DSLs for HTML, React allows programmers to use any valid JavaScript expression interleaved with the HTML template definition. JavaScript expressions should be wrapped in curly braces as denoted in line 6 of Listing 3.3.

**Listing 3.3:** Example of a React template defining an HTML divisory with current date.

```
1  class DateDiv extends React.Component {
2    render() {
3      return (
4        <div>
5          <h1>Date Time</h1>
6          <h2>It is {new Date().toLocaleTimeString()}.</h2>
7        </div>
8      }
9    }
10 }
```

Yet here, JSX behaves as an external DSL since HTML is a distinct idiom from JavaScript. After compilation, JSX expressions become regular JavaScript function calls and evaluate to JavaScript objects.

Moreover React templates result in a representation of the user-interface kept in memory to hold all information about the component tree. Although highly optimized this approach incurs in additional overheads of maintaining this auxiliary data structure.

## 3.4   HtmlFlow

The primary goal of HtmlFlow was to provide a DSL that helps developers to write safe HTML in Java programs. HtmlFlow distinguishes for providing:

1. *data structureless* – a key factor that contributes to achieve better performance than competition in several benchmarks;
2. *method chaining* that allows the calls to be chained together in a single statement (i.e. *method chaining*).
3. *HTML safety* ensuring that the resulting HTML is conforming to a valid HTML document.

**Data Structureless.** A distinct aspect of HtmlFlow in comparison to other DSLs is that it follows a *data structureless* approach. This means that invoking the HtmlFlow API does not instantiate any objects representing nodes or elements, and it neither stores or maintains such useless objects in memory. Instead HtmlFlow API methods emit HTML on demand as they are being invoked. This is one of the key aspects that makes HtmlFlow one of the most performant engines in a diversity of state of the art benchmarks [9, 10, 32].

This core characteristic is the result of the fluent API nature of HtmlFlow, which enforces methods to be invoked by the same order they are chained. We will put it clear after giving some details about the HtmlFlow API design in next section.

**Method Chaining.** Regarding the *method chaining* requirement we stated that every HTML element (i.e. instance of `Element`) returned by a method call should have methods to create the next inner HTML element, such as the following pipeline:

`div().table().tr()....`, which should create a `div` element containing a `table` that in turn will have a table row element `tr`. On the other hand, we would like to have an auxiliary method that allows to navigate back in the elements tree. So, all HtmlFlow elements have the `__()` method that returns the corresponding element's parent. Moreover, this method should return the parent element with the correct type. Regarding the previous example, this means that calling `__()` after `tr()` should return an instance of `Table` whereas calling `__()` after `table()` should return an instance of `Div`. When we navigate back to the parent element we would like to get a consistent route.

We tackle this issue through *generics* [26], which allow us to keep track of the tree structure of the elements that are being created and keep adding elements, or moving up in the tree structure without losing the type information of the parent. In Listing 3.4 we can observe how we can take advantage of the type arguments.

Listing 3.4: Explicit use of type arguments in the subtypes of Element.

```
Html<Element> html = new Html<>();
Body<Html<Element>> body = html.body();

P<Header<Body<Html<Element>>>> p1 = body.header().p();
P<Div<Body<Html<Element>>>> p2 =  body.div().p();

Header<Body<Html<Element>>> header =  p1.__();
Div<Body<Html<Element>>> div = p2.__();
```

When we create the Html element we should indicate that it has a parent, for consistency. Then, as we add elements, such as Body, we automatically return the recently created Body element, but with parent information that indicates that this Body instance is descendant of an Html element. After that, we create two distinct P elements, p1, which has an Header parent, and p2, which has a Div parent. This information is reflected in the type of both variables. Lastly, we can invoke the __() method, which returns the current element parent, and observe that each P instance returns its respective parent object, with the correct type.

In the example presented in Listing 3.4 the usage of the *fluent interface* might seem to be excessive verbose to define a simple HTML document. Yet, for most common purposes we can suppress the auxiliary variables and simplify its usage chaining method calls as we show in Listing 3.5.

Listing 3.5: Example of the implicit use of type arguments in HtmlFlow API.

```
Html<Element> html = new Html<>()
  .body()
    .header()
      .p().__()
    .__() // header
    .div()
      .p().__();
    .__() // div
  .__(); // body
```

**HTML Safety.** Finally, the invocation chain should produce valid HTML. This means that HtmlFlow should not allow statements like img().table(); since in HTML we may not include a table inside an image. To that end, every instance of Element returned by HtmlFlow only provides methods to create children elements conforming to HTML 5 rules. So, every concrete element is represented by a class extended from Element with a subset of methods that respects the kind of permitted children elements.

Following this idea we have developed the xmlet platform [12] that parses the XSD schema of HTML5 and automatically generates all elements classes and interfaces required by HtmlFlow. All the implementations of the Element interface corresponding to all kind of HTML elements available in HTML 5 are automatically built from the XSD definition of the HTML 5. These implementations are part of the **HtmlApi** auxiliary library used by the HtmlFlow as denoted in Fig. 1.

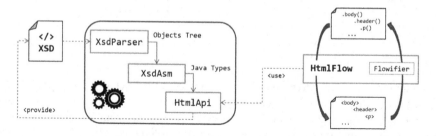

**Fig. 1.** xmlet framework build process and its organization in three main components: XsdParser, XsdAsm and HtmlApi.

In turn, the **HtmlApi** is built with the support of ASM [4] (bytecode instrumentation tool) implemented by the **XsdAsm** component, which consumes the information gathered and provided by the **XsdParser**.

The HtmlFlow also includes the **Flowifier** feature that allows to get an HtmlFlow template view definition from the corresponding HTML source. This feature was crucial to translate the PetClinic HTML views to the equivalent definition in HtmlFlow idiom.

## 4   HoT: Higher-Order Templates

A higher-order template (HoT) is an advanced technique for resolving a *template view* progressively as data from its *context object* is being available, rather than waiting for whole data and resolve the entire template. A higher-order template (HoT) defines a *template view* as a function and its *context object* as other function received by argument. Also, a higher-order template can receive other templates as parameters. In this case, these parameters play the role of *partial views*. Like a higher-order function may take one or more functions as arguments, a higher-order template may take one or more *templates views* as arguments. This compositional nature enables reusing template logic.

Templates in HtmlFlow are specified through Java functions, which can be defined as named or anonymous functions (i.e. *lambdas*) For example, the template of Listing 1.1 can be expressed in HtmlFlow with the **tracksTpl** function of Listing 4.1.

**Listing 4.1:** HtmlFlow template function for a division element with a dynamic unordered list.

```
HtmlTemplate<Stream<Track>> tracksTpl =   (view, tracks) ->
    view
    .div()
      .ul()
      .of(ul -> tracks.forEach (item -> ul
        .li().text(item.getName()).__() // li
    ))
      .__ () // ul
    .__(); // div
```

The `tracksTpl` function receives two parameters: an HtmlFlow view and a context object (e.g. `tracks`). The `view` parameter provides the HTML *fluent interface* [17] with methods corresponding to the name of HTML elements and two additional methods: 1) `__()` to close an HTML element tag, and 2) `of(elem -> ...)` useful to chain a statement that starts with an expression different from the previous element (i.e. `elem` in the lambda). The `tracks` parameter acts like the *model* in the *model-view-controller* pattern [13]. Here the `tracks` is a Java `Stream`, which is an abstraction over a lazy sequence of objects (i.e. instances of `Track`). Some may argument that a Java `Stream` is not a first-class function, such as we have claimed that a *context object* would be for a HoT. Yet, that is only a design choice of the Java environment, since in truth any sequence (such as `Stream`) can be implemented through a higher-order function [3]. Nevertheless, in this case, the `tracks` object is traversed in the `forEach` method call (i.e. `tracks.forEach(...)`) chained within the template definition.

Regarding a template with *partial views* then the corresponding function should receive a further argument for each partial view. For example, considering that the `tracksTpl` function takes an additional `footer` argument, then it can include this partial view through the method `addPartial()` that is available in all elements objects. We can chain the call to `addPartial()` in the template definition as depicted in the example of the Listing 4.2, that adds the `footer` after the definition of the unordered list.

**Listing 4.2:** HtmlFlow template with a partial view `footer`.

```
HtmlTemplate<Stream<Track>> tracksTpl = (v, trks, footer) ->
    v
    .div()
    ... // adds ul and an li for each track
    .of(div -> div.addPartial(footer));
    .__() // div
```

If a partial view has no context object and does not require model binding, then we can discard the template function and directly create that view from an expression, through the `view()` factory method of the class `StaticHtml`. For example, we may define a billboard division (i.e. `bbView`) as depicted in the following view definition:

```
HtmlView bbView = StaticHtml.view().div().text("Dummy billboard").__();
```

Another advantage of using views as first-class functions is to allow views composition. For example, if want to define a partial view (e.g. `footerView`) with a placeholder for another partial view (e.g. `banner`), then we may define a `footerView` method that takes an `HtmlView` as the `banner` parameter and returns a new `HtmlView` as depicted in Listing 4.3.

**Listing 4.3:** Partial view definition of a `footer` that takes another `banner` view as parameter.

```
HtmlView footerView(HtmlView banner) {
  return StaticHtml.view()
    .div()
      .of(div -> div.addPartial(banner))
      .p().text("Created_with_HtmFlow").__() // p
    .__(); // div
}
```

Thus, we may finally compose the `tracksTpl` template of Listing 4.2 with the `footerView`, which in turn will be filled with the `bbView`. This creates the following pipeline: `tracksTpl <- footerView <- bbView`.

For the `tracksTpl` function we can create a corresponding view (i.e. `tracksView`) through the `view()` factory method of the class `DynamicHtml` as depicted in line 2 of Listing 4.4. Finally, we may compose all the parts of the `tracksView` through the `render` method of `HtmlView`. For example, given a `tracks` stream, the `footerView` and the `bbView` we may resolve the `tracksView` as depicted in line 3 of Listing 4.4. Here we can observe the pipeline: `tracksView <- footerView <- bbView` with `tracksView` taking the `footerView` as argument, which in turn receives the `bbView` as argument.

**Listing 4.4:** Composing and resolving the `tracksView`.

```
Stream<Track> tracks = ...
HtmlView<Stream<Track>> tracksView = DynamicHtml.view(
    tracksTpl);
String html = tracksView.render(tracks, footerView(bbView));
```

Having all the compositional parts of a template view defined as first-class functions (the template itself, the context object and partial views) is a key feature to achieve the HtmlFlow compositional nature.

## 5    Templates Idioms

We will use the PetClinic Spring application [11] as a use case of web templates to compare several Thymeleaf dialects with the equivalent construction in a DSL for HTML. The templates are responsible for displaying a *data model* and performing any display logic that is particular to the type of view being rendered. In this, case we are going to analyze how the following templates patterns are solved through specific Thymeleaf dialects for each particular view:

1. variable assignment and conditional evaluation – `createOrUpdateOwnerForm.html` view using `th:with` and `th:text`.
2. switch statement – `inputField.html` view using `th:switch` and `th:case`.
3. if statement and iteration loop – `vetList.html` view using `th:if` and `th:each`.
4. binding inputs and preprocessing expression – `selectField.html` view using `th:field` and dialect `_${expression}_`
5. fragments and layouts – `layout.html` view using `th:fragment` and `th:replace`.

Here we are only illustrating a small subset of Thymleaf dialects including 10 different building blocks. We also highlight how a DSL for HTML can suppress the need of this auxiliary features giving examples of the same views built with HtmlFlow, KotlinX.html or React that does not require any auxiliary mechanism beyond their host programming language, i.e. Java, Kotlin or JavaScript.

## 5.1  Variable Assignment and Conditional Evaluation

**Thymeleaf.** The PetClinic application uses the same view to update or create an owner object. This view presents an HTML form with the submit button presented in Listing 5.1, which contains the label *'Add Owner'* or *'Update Owner'* depending on whether the view is returned from the `/owners/new` or `/owners/ownerId/edit` path.

Listing 5.1: Thymleaf template button to create or update owner.

```
1  <button
2      th:with="text=${owner.isNew()}_?_'Add_Owner'_:_'Update_
          Owner'"
3      class="btn_btn-default"
4      type="submit"
5      th:text="${text}">
6  </button>
```

To that end, the corresponding HTML button defines its text content through the Thymeleaf attribute `th:text`, i.e. line 5 of Listing 5.1. The value of this attribute is equals to result of the expression `${text}`, where `text` is a variable previously declared and assigned with attribute `th:with` in line 2 of Listing 5.1. In turn, the assignment statement of line 2 uses the Thymeleaf ternary operator to build an expression that results in *'Add Owner'* or *'Update Owner'* depending on whether the `owner` object has its property `isNew()` set to true, or not. Note, this statement uses a mix of Java to evaluate the property `isNew()` of the `owner` object and the Thymeleaf dialect to build the ternary expression. Thus, the resulting complexity comes from the use of the additional Thymeleaf dialect and two further attributes (`th:text` and `th:with`) to achieve the desired behavior.

**HtmlFlow.** In opposition, HtmlFlow let programmers interleave any kind of Java statements to achieve this goal. We may choose between a Java if statement or a ternary operator according to the developer programming stylistic preferences. In Listing 5.2 we present the equivalent HtmlFlow definition to the button of Listing 5.1. Note that we can discard the auxiliary variable **text** used in the Thymeleaf example, since we are customizing the button through a pure Java statement.

Listing 5.2: HtmlFlow template button to create or update owner.

```
1   .button()
2       .attrClass("btn_btn-default")
3       .attrType(EnumTypeButtonType.SUBMIT)
4       .text(owner.isNew() ? "Add_Owner" : "Update_Owner")
5   .__()
```

**Kotlinx.html.** Kotlinx.html shares the same expressiveness advantages of HtmlFlow: fluent and HTML safety. Despite the idiomatic and syntax differences between Java and Kotlin, the definition of Listing 5.2 share the same layout of Listing 5.3.

Listing 5.3: KotlinX.html template button to create or update owner.

```
1   button {
2       classes = setOf("btn_btn-default")
3       type = ButtonType.submit
4       text(if (owner.isNew) "Add_Owner" else "Update_Owner")
5   }
```

**ReactJS.** Similar to HtmlFlow and Kotlinx.html the React also allows the use of the core framework programming language (i.e. JavaScript) in its entire plenitude. Yet, since JSX is an external DSL mixed with pure JavaScript we must delimit JavaScript blocks with a special character, i.e. {...}. Due to the JSX dialect nature, some words are neither HTML nor JavaScript, such as **className** in line 2, of Listing 5.4. Nevertheless, the conditional evaluation stated with the JavaScript ternary operator in line 5 is analogous to the expression of the same line in Listing 5.2.

Listing 5.4: React template button to create or update owner.

```
1   <button
2     className='btn btn-default'
3     type='submit'
4     onClick={this.onSubmit}>
5       {owner.isNew ? 'Add Owner' : 'Update Owner'}
6   </button>
```

## 5.2 Switch Statement

Another way to display content conditionally is using the equivalent switch statement. The PetClinic application takes advantage of this construction to provide a single input control implementation with different behaviors according to the

type of data. To that end, it defines a Thymeleaf *fragment* that exports an HTML
div element with a label and an input elements. In Listing 5.5 we present a
simplified version of the inputField.html fragment that only includes the input
definition.

Listing 5.5: Thymleaf fragments inputField.html.

```
 1   <th:block th:fragment="input␣(label,␣value,␣type)">
 2     <div class="form-group">
 3       ...
 4       <div th:switch="${type}">
 5         <input th:case="'text'" type="text" value="{value}" />
 6         <input th:case="'date'" type="text" value="{value}"
 7           placeholder="YYYY-MM-DD"
 8           title="Enter␣a␣date␣in␣this␣format:␣YYYY-MM-DD"
 9           pattern="(?:19|20)[0-9]{2}-(?:(?:0[1-9]|1[0-2])-..."/
                 >
10       </div>
11     </div>
12   </th:block>
```

This fragment is defined with the tag th:block and attribute th:fragment
that we will describe ahead in Sect. 5.5. Note in Listing 5.5 that depending on the
parameter type (th:switch on line 4) this fragment will present a different kind
of input element that can be according a free input text or a date format. Yet,
part of the definition of this input is repeated in lines 5 and 6, because there are a
couple of attributes definitions shared in both cases, namely the attributes type
and value. On the other hand, the HtmlFlow template definition of Listing 5.6
does not need to repeat the assignment of the attributes type and value and
thus, it only includes a single use of these attributes (line 4).

Listing 5.6: HtmlFlow fragment InputField.

```
 1   HtmlView<LabelAndValue> view = DynamicHtml.view((v, model) -> v
 2     .div().attrClass("form-group")
 3       ...
 4       .input().attrType(TEXT).attrValue(model.value)
 5         .of(__ -> { if(model.value instanceof LocalDate)input
 6           .attrPlaceholder("YYYY-MM-DD")
 7           .attrTitle("Enter␣a␣date␣in␣this␣format:␣YYYY-MM-DD")
 8           .attrPattern("(?:19|20)[0-9]{2}-(?:(?:0[1-9]|..."));
 9         })
10       .__()
11     .__()
12   )
```

Thanks to the compositional nature of higher-order templates this fragment is defined with a first-class function as any other template view in HtmlFlow, avoiding specific markers such as Thymeleaf `<th:block th:fragment>`. Also this HtmlFlow partial view does not require the additional parameter `type` to check the class of the instance `value`. Instead, we can simply use the Java `instanceof` operator (line 5) to verify the type of the instance `value`.

## 5.3   If Statement and Iteration Loop

The `VetList` view aims to show a list of all veterinaries, where each row presents the veterinarian's full name and all its specialties concatenated in a single String. Yet, if a veterinary does not have any specialty then it should present the String `none`. To that end, the corresponding Thymeleaf template of Listing 5.7 takes advantage of the `th:each` to traverse the `vets.vetList` (line 2) and to join all specialties (line 6 and 7). On the other hand, it uses the `th:if` (line 9) to check whether the list is empty and present the String `none` if it is.

**Listing 5.7:** `vetList.html` Thymeleaf sample for displaying veterinaries.

```
1  <tbody>
2    <tr th:each="vet : ${vets.vetList}">
3      <td th:text="${vet.firstName + ' ' + vet.lastName}"></td>
4      <td>
5        <span
6          th:each="specialty : ${vet.specialties}"
7          th:text="${specialty.name + ' '}"
8        />
9        <span th:if="${vet.nrOfSpecialties == 0}">none</span>
10       </td>
11     </tr>
12  </tbody>
```

Again a DSL for HTML suppresses the use of additional dialects and may achieve the desired layout only with Java statements, such as the HtmlFlow sample presented in Listing 5.8. Here we are only taking advantage of the `forEach()` traversal method provided by the Java Stream API (line1) and a Java ternary operator (line 5).

**Listing 5.8:** `VetList` HtmlFlow sample for displaying veterinaries.

```
1  .tbody().of(tbody -> vets.forEach(v -> tbody
2    .tr()
3      .td().text(v.getFirstName() + " " + v.getLastName()).__()
4      .td().span()
5        .text(v.nrOfSpecs() == 0 ? "none" : join(" ", v.specs())))
6      .__().__()
7    .__() //tr
8  )).__() //tbody
```

## 5.4  Binding Inputs and Preprocessing Expression

The `select` HTML element has similar behavior to the well known drop-down component, also known as *combo box*. The `SelectField` view aims to bind all elements of an `items` list to a `select` element. Yet, it must also assign the HTML attribute `selected` of the corresponding `option` element that matches the `selected` parameter passed to this view. This is exactly the algorithm implemented by the HtmlFlow `SelectField` view that receives a `src` parameter with the `items` list and the `selected` object, as presented in Listing 5.9.

**Listing 5.9:** SelectField HtmlFlow partial view sample.

```
1   .select()
2     .of(select -> src.items.forEach(item -> select
3       .option().attrValue(item.toString()).of(opt -> {
4         if(src.selected.equals(item.toString()))
5           opt.attrSelected(true);
6         })
7         .text(item)
8       .__() //option
9     ))
10  .__() //select
```

In line 2 of Listing 5.9 we are traversing the `items` list through the `forEach()` method and in line 3 we are adding an HTML `option` element for each of those items. If an item is equal to the `selected` parameter (line 4) then we will add the attribute `selected` to the related `option` element (line 5). Finally in line 7 we include the `item` as the text of the `option` element.

The Thymeleaf corresponding version mitigates all the details of the algorithm expressed in Listing 5.9. Yet, it also requires keen knowledge of the Thymeleaf dialects able for preprocessing expressions as depicted in Listing 5.10.

**Listing 5.10:** selectField.html Thymeleaf partial view sample.

```
1   <select th:field="*{__${name}__}">
2     <option th:each="item : ${items}" th:value="${item}"
3       th:text="${item}">
4       dog
5     </option>
6   </select>
```

First the `th:field` attribute (line 1 of Listing 5.10) behaves differently depending on whether it is attached to an `input`, `select` or `textarea`. Then values for the `th:field` must be selection expressions denoted as *{...} because they will be evaluated on the form-backing bean and not on the context variables. And finally the --${...}-- is a *preprocessing expression*, which is an inner expression that is evaluated before the whole expression. This is the tricky part of the Thymeleaf dialect that will check the property identified by `name` in the `item` object (line 2) that may be selected, or not, in the corresponding option element.

## 5.5   Fragments and Layouts

Layouts aim to reuse a common structure (usually composed by header, footer and navigation bar) among different template views. To that end the PetClinic application defines a `layout.html` fragment parametrized with a `template` view that is included dynamically based on the inclusion of template fragments. In the sample of Listing 5.11 the line 2 defines the `layout` fragment and in line 5 it includes the `template` view embedding its content within the layout through the `th:block th:insert` tag.

Listing 5.11: `layout.html` view sample.

```
1  <!doctype html>
2  <html th:fragment="layout_(template)">
3    ...
4      <div class="container">
5        <th:block th:insert="${template}"/>
6    ...
7  </html>
```

On the other hand, each view inheriting the `layout.html` should specify the content that should be passed to the layout as the `template` parameter. In Listing 5.12 we present an example of how the PetClinic application includes a Thymeleaf template view within the `layout.html`. In line 2 it uses the `th:replace` to invoke the layout and pass the `body` element as argument. In turn, this `body` element includes all the content to be presented as the `VetList` web page.

Listing 5.12: `vetList.html` view inclusion in `layout.html`.

```
1  <html
2    th:replace="~{fragments/layout_::_layout_(~{::body},'vets')}">
3  <body>
4    <h2>Veterinarians</h2>
5    ...
6  </body>
```

Again HtmlFlow takes advantage of functions composition to define a template layout. In this case we define a distinct class `Layout` with a static field `view` corresponding to the layout function, as depicted in Listing 5.13. Then, it should include the partial view through the `addPartial` method (line 7).

**Listing 5.13:** vetList.html view inclusion in layout.html.

```
1  public class Layout {
2    static DynamicHtml view = view((v, model, partials) -> { v
3      .html()
4      ...
5        .div().attrClass("container")
6        ...
7          .of(__ -> v.addPartial(partials[0], model);)
8    }
9  }
```

In opposition to the inclusion approach followed by Thymeleaf templates, the HtmlFlow templates are agnostic with respect to the layout. On the other hand, the controller is responsible for composing the layout with the template view as presented in the following example that assembles the **VetList** view:

```
Layout.view.render(vets, VetList.view);
```

# 6  Performance Evaluation

To perform an unbiased comparison we used two of most popular benchmarks for template engines: 1) Comparing Template engines for Spring MVC, simply denoted as Spring templates benchmark [32] and 2) JMH benchmark for popular Java template engines [5]. We integrated the missing engines in our forks of these benchmarks available at Github repositories: xmlet/spring-comparing-template-engines and xmlet/template-benchmark. These tests were done on a local machine running Microsoft Windows 10, Education OS Version: 10.0.17134 with Java(TM) SE Runtime Environment 18.9 (build $11 + 28$) Java HotSpot(TM) 64-Bit Server VM 18.9 (build $11 + 28$, mixed mode) and with Intel(R) Core(TM) i7-7700 HQ CPU @ 2.80 GHz, 2808 MHz, 4 Cores.

## 6.1  Spring Templates Benchmark

This benchmark uses the Spring MVC framework to host a web application that provides a route for each template engine to benchmark. Each template engine uses the same template (i.e. **Presentations**) and receives the same information to fill the template, which makes it possible to flood all the routes with a high number of requests and asserts which route responds faster, consequently asserting which template engine is faster. Following the benchmark recommendation we used the Apache HTTP server benchmarking tool as a stress tester running it with 25 concurrent requests and 25000 requests in total, which corresponds to the following settings:

```
ab -n 25000 -c 25 -k http://localhost:8080/<template engine>
```

The performance of each template engine was measured according to the guidelines specified in the Spring benchmark repository, which states at least two dry runs with the exact same settings, to make sure that initialization of the engines, warm up of the JVM and additional caches have taken place.

After that, we calculate the average time taken by 5 iterations of the same benchmark for each template engine. The results are presented in Fig. 2 corresponding to the total time taken for processing 25000 requests with a concurrency level of 25 (lower is better).

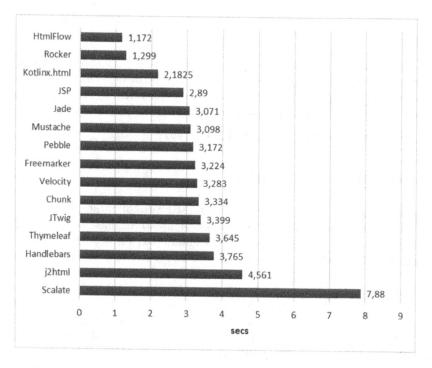

**Fig. 2.** Performance results in seconds for Spring templates benchmark.

This approach of measuring the template engines performance is misleading because the render time of the template engines is dismissible when compared to the overhead introduced by the Spring framework. Thus, the performance differences among some template engines are very tiny.

In this context, we mostly agree with the JMH templates benchmark proposal, which uses JMH to implement the benchmark. So we end up using the `Presentations` template from the Spring benchmark and integrated it in our fork of JMH templates benchmark to get more reliable measures.

## 6.2   JMH Benchmark for Java Template Engines

The advantage of this benchmark is that it focuses exclusively on evaluating the rendering process of each template engine. In this case, it does not use any web servers to handle a request, which is a more consistent approach. The general idea of this benchmark is the same, it includes many template engine solutions that define the same template and use the same data as a context object to generate the resulting HTML document. But, in this case, it uses Java Microbenchmark Harness, which is a Java tool to benchmark code. With JMH we indicate which methods to benchmark with annotations and configure different benchmark options such as the number of warm-up iterations, the number of measurement iterations, or the numbers of threads to run the benchmark method.

This benchmark contained eight different template engines: Freemarker, Handlebars, Mustache, Pebble, Thymeleaf, Trimou, Velocity, and Rocker. In addition, we integrated J2Html, KotlinX.html, and HtmlFlow.

The JMH templates benchmark used only one template, i.e. Stocks template. In addition we included the Presentations template from the Spring templates benchmark. By using two different templates the objective was to observe if the results were maintained throughout the different solutions. The main difference between both templates is that the Stocks template introduces much more binding operations: 1) it has more fields that will be accessed in the template, and 2) it has twenty objects in the default data set while Presentations only has ten objects in his data set. This means that the Stocks template will generate more string operations to the classic template engine solutions and more Java method calls for the solutions that have the template defined as a function in Java or Kotlin.

In Fig. 3 we present the results of the JMH templates benchmark corresponding to the mean value of five forked iterations, each one of the forks running eight different iterations, performed after five warm-up iterations. This approach intends to remove any outlier values from the benchmark. The benchmark values were obtained without any other programs running, nor background tasks, and only with the command line running the benchmark.

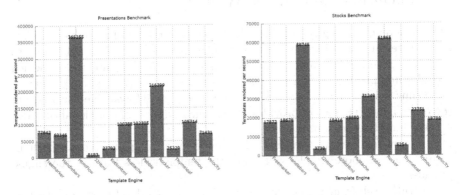

**Fig. 3.** Performance results in operations per second for JMH templates benchmark.

Regarding the classical template engines, i.e. Mustache, Pebble, Freemarker, Trimou, Velocity, Handlebars, and Thymeleaf, we can observe that most of them share the same level of performance, which should be expected since they all roughly have the same methodology. Regarding the remaining template engines, i.e. Rocker, J2Html, KotlinX.html, and HtmlFlow, the situation is diverse. On one hand, we have Rocker, which gives great performance when the number of placeholders increases, i.e. the `Stocks` benchmark, taking into consideration that it provides many compile-time verifications regarding the context objects, it presents a good improvement in comparison to the classical template engines. On the other hand, we have J2Html and KotlinX.html. Regarding J2Html we observe that the tradeoff of moving the template to a function of the environment language (i.e. Java) had a significant performance cost since it is consistently one of the two worst solutions performance-wise. Regarding KotlinX.html, its approach was definitely a step towards in the right direction since it validates the HTML rules and introduces compile-time validations, but, either due to the Kotlin language performance issues or poorly optimized code, it did not achieve the level of acceptable performance.

Lastly, HtmlFlow proved to have the best performance with the `Presentation` template. It achieved performance gains that surpass the second best solution by twice the operations per second. Regarding the `Stocks` template, the HtmlFlow held the top place even though the number of placeholders for dynamic information increased significantly. If we compare HtmlFlow to a similar solution, KotlinX.html, we observe a huge gain of performance on the HtmlFlow part.

In conclusion, HtmlFlow introduces domain language rule verification, removes the requirements of text files and additional syntaxes, adds many compile-time verifications, and, while doing all of that this, is still the best solution performance wise.

## 7 Conclusions and Future Work

Electing a template engine may be a choice between the set of available templating features and the simplicity of resulting templates. And, it is not viable to stretch both axis. For example, Mustache is a logic-less template syntax, which provides minimal templating through double-braces tags (i.e. $\{\{\ldots\}\}$ ), but at same time it is too much restrictive on the limited set of available features. On the other hand, Thymeleaf provides an enlarged number of functionalities, but it turns templates very intricated.

As more features we take from the engine more complex become the templates. And, as more simple we require the template, less features the engine provides.

In truth, web frameworks are build on top of a high-level programming language and enriching templating dialects will enforce developers to deal with two different programming languages. Moreover, these two languages are heterogeneous and have different building natures. While the host programming language spreads from the functional to imperative paradigms, the templating dialects are usually embedded in markups, which results in a mix of declarative and imperative idioms. This anti-paradigm inception of templating dialects turn templates difficult to manage as we have shown with 10 of the most used building blocks of Thymeleaf.

These problems arises from two unavoidable facts: 1. HTML is the main user interface programming language, and 2. HTML is a markup language with distinct characteristics from the host programming language. Thus we argue that empowering templating dialects is a counterproductive approach that leads to harmful templates.

In this work we propose a different methodology to answer developers needs on web templating. Rather than augmenting HTML markups with additional templating constructions we propose to keep HTML plain and let programmers interleave HTML with the use of the host programming language.

To that end we take advantage of an internal DSL to HTML to bring the power of the host programming language (such as Java) into web templates. We have shown the use of a DSL to HTML in three different hosting languages, namely Java, Kotlin and Javascript through the related DSL libraries HtmlFlow, KotlinX.Html and JSX. Furthermore, we have presented how the most used template patterns (e.g. using Thymeleaf) can be easily achieved with pure Java statements and the support of HtmlFlow Java library without any further dialect beyond the Java programming language.

To prove the effectiveness of our proposal we have used a well-known sample web application - PetClinic - and migrated the exiting Thymeleaf templates to Java with the support of HtmlFlow library. The last release of HtmlFlow (3.5) includes the translation tool `Flowifier` that allows the conversion of an HTML document in its equivalent definition in HtmlFlow idiom. This tool was essential to enhance the translation process of existing templates into the related HtmlFlow definition. The wide variety of templating idioms used in PetClinic and their successful translation to Java and Htmlflow, give us confidence about future applications of HtmlFlow to other real web applications.

# References

1. Alur, D., Malks, D., Crupi, J.: Core J2EE Patterns: Best Practices and Design Strategies. Prentice Hall PTR, Upper Saddle River (2001)
2. Ase, D.: Kotlin DSL for HTML. Technical report (2015). https://j2html.com/
3. Baker, H.G.: Iterators: signs of weakness in object-oriented languages. SIGPLAN OOPS Messenger 4(3), 18–25 (1993). https://doi.org/10.1145/165507.165514
4. Binder, W., Hulaas, J., Moret, P.: Advanced Java bytecode instrumentation. In: Proceedings of the 5th International Symposium on Principles and Practice of Programming in Java, PPPJ 2007, pp. 135–144. ACM, New York (2007). https://doi.org/10.1145/1294325.1294344, http://doi.acm.org/10.1145/1294325.1294344
5. Bösecke, M.: JMH benchmark of the most popular Java template engines. Technical report (2015). https://github.com/mbosecke/template-benchmark
6. Breslav, A.: Kotlin Language Documentation (2016). https://kotlinlang.org/docs/kotlin-docs.pdf

7. Brogden, B., D'Cruz, C., Gaither, M.: Cocoon 2 Programming: Web Publishing with XML and Java. Wiley, Hoboken (2006)
8. Carvalho, F.M.: HtmlFlow Java DSL to write typesafe HTML. Technical report (2017). https://htmlflow.org/
9. Carvalho., F.M., Duarte., L.: Modern type-safe template engines (2018). https://dzone.com/articles/modern-type-safe-template-engines
10. Carvalho., F.M., Duarte., L.: HoT: unleash web views with higher-order templates. In: Proceedings of the 15th International Conference on Web Information Systems and Technologies - Volume 1: WEBIST, WEBIST 2019, pp. 118–129. INSTICC, SciTePress (2019). https://doi.org/10.5220/0008167701180129
11. Donald, K., Isvy, M., Leau, C.: Spring petclinic sample application. Technical report (2013). https://projects.spring.io/spring-petclinic/
12. Duarte., L., Carvalho., F.M.: xmlet. Technical report (2018). https://github.com/xmlet
13. Krasner, G.E., Pope, S.: A description of the model-view-controller user interface paradigm in the smalltalk80 system. J. Object Oriented Program. JOOP 1, 26–49 (1988)
14. Evans, E., Fowler, M.: Domain-driven Design: Tackling Complexity in the Heart of Software. Addison-Wesley (2004). https://books.google.pt/books?id=7dlaMs0SECsC
15. Fernández, D.: Thymeleaf. Technical report (2011). https://www.thymeleaf.org/
16. Fowler, M.: Patterns of Enterprise Application Architecture. Addison-Wesley Longman Publishing Co., Inc., Boston (2002)
17. Fowler, M.: Domain Specific Languages, 1st edn. Addison-Wesley Professional, Boston (2010)
18. Freeman, S., Mackinnon, T., Pryce, N., Talevi, M., Walnes, J.: Jmock library for test-driven development with mock objects. Technical report (2008). http://jmock.org
19. Gamma, E., Helm, R., Johnson, R., Vlissides, J.: Design Patterns: Elements of Reusable Object-Oriented Software. Addison-Wesley Longman Publishing Co., Inc., Boston (1995)
20. Heijlsberg, A., Torgersen, M.: The.net standard query operators (2007)
21. Hors, A.L., et al.: Document object model (DOM) level 3 core specification. Technical report (2004). https://www.w3.org/TR/2004/REC-DOM-Level-3-Core-20040407/
22. Jin, X., Wah, B.W., Cheng, X., Wang, Y.: Significance and challenges of big data research. Big Data Res. 2(2), 59–64 (2015). https://doi.org/10.1016/j.bdr.2015.01.006
23. Johnson, R., et al.: The spring framework-reference documentation (2004). https://docs.spring.io/spring-framework/docs/3.2.x/spring-framework-reference/html/index.html
24. Landin, P.J.: Correspondence between ALGOL 60 and church's lambda-notation: Part I. Commun. ACM 8(2), 89–101 (1965)
25. Landin, P.J.: The next 700 programming languages. Commun. ACM 9(3), 157–166 (1966)
26. Marx, S., Odersky, M., Buckley, A.: Jsr 14: Add generic types to the Java. Technical report, Java Community Process (2004). https://jcp.org/en/jsr/detail?id=14
27. Mashkov, S.: Kotlin DSL for HTML. Technical report (2015). https://github.com/Kotlin/kotlinx.html
28. Meijer, E.: Your mouse is a database. Queue 10(3), 20:20–20:33 (2012). https://doi.org/10.1145/2168796.2169076, http://doi.acm.org/10.1145/2168796.2169076

29. Mutschler III, E.O., Stefaniak, J.P.: Method for extending the hypertext markup language (HTML) to support enterprise application data binding, 17 August 1999. US Patent 5,940,075
30. Parker, H.: Opinionated analysis development. PeerJ Prepr. **5**, e3210v1 (2017)
31. Parr, T.J.: Enforcing strict model-view separation in template engines. In: Proceedings of the 13th International Conference on World Wide Web, WWW 2004, pp. 224–233. ACM, New York (2004). https://doi.org/10.1145/988672.988703. http://doi.acm.org/10.1145/988672.988703
32. Reijn, J.: Comparing template engines for spring MVC. Technical report (2015). https://github.com/jreijn/spring-comparing-template-engines
33. Resig, J.: Pro JavaScript Techniques. Apress, New York (2007)
34. Singh, I., Johnson, M., Stearns, B.: Designing Enterprise Applications with the J2EE Platform. Addison-Wesley Professional, Boston (2002)
35. Ted, N.: Literary Machines. Mindful Press, Sausalito (1994)
36. Thompson, K.: Programming techniques: regular expression search algorithm. Commun. ACM **11**(6), 419–422 (1968). https://doi.org/10.1145/363347.363387
37. Walke, J.: React Javascript library for building user interfaces. Technical report (2013). https://reactjs.org/

# Resource Multiplexing and Prioritization in HTTP/2 over TCP Versus HTTP/3 over QUIC

Robin Marx[1,2]([✉]), Tom De Decker[1], Peter Quax[1,3], and Wim Lamotte[1]

[1] Hasselt University – tUL – EDM, Diepenbeek, Belgium
{robin.marx,tom.dedecker,peter.quax,wim.lamotte}@uhasselt.be
[2] Research Foundation Flanders, #1S02717N,
Brussels, Belgium
[3] Flanders Make, Lommel, Belgium

**Abstract.** Modern versions of the HTTP protocol, such as HTTP/2 over TCP and the upcoming HTTP/3 over QUIC, use just a single underlying connection to transfer multiple resources during a web page load. The resources are divided into chunks, optionally multiplexed on the connection, and reassembled at the receiver's side. This poses challenges, as there are many different ways simultaneously requested resources can share the available bandwidth, and not all approaches perform equally well with regards to achieving low loading times. Making matters worse, HTTP/2's prioritization system for directing this multiplexing behaviour is difficult to use and does not easily transfer to the new HTTP/3.

In this work, we discuss these challenges in detail and empirically evaluate the multiplexing behaviours of 10 different QUIC implementations, as well as 11 different prioritization schemes for HTTP/3. We find that there are large differences between strategies that can have a heavy impact on page load performance, of up to 5x load time speedup in specific conditions. However, these improvements are highly context-sensitive, depending on web page composition and network conditions, turning the best performers for one setup into the worst for others. As such, we also critically evaluate the ability of the newly proposed HTTP/3 prioritization mechanism to flexibly deal with changing conditions.

**Keywords:** Web performance · Resource prioritization · Bandwidth distribution · Network scheduling · Measurements

## 1 Introduction

The HTTP protocol has undergone some highly impactful changes in the past few years, starting with the standardization of HTTP/2 (H2) in 2015 and now the upcoming finalization of HTTP/3 (H3), barely five years later. This rapid evolution is driven mainly by the need for improvement in two key areas: performance and security, and this work focuses on the former. When loading web pages over

© Springer Nature Switzerland AG 2020
A. Bozzon et al. (Eds.): WEBIST 2019, LNBIP 399, pp. 96–126, 2020.
https://doi.org/10.1007/978-3-030-61750-9_5

HTTP, browsers typically request a large amount of different resources. These resources are spread over a range of different types, including HTML, CSS, JavaScript and image files. Over HTTP/1.1, only one of those resources can be in-flight on the underlying TCP connection at a time, holding up all further resources behind it until it is fully downloaded. This is called the Head-Of-Line (HOL) blocking problem. As a workaround to achieve better web page loading performance, browsers open up to six parallel HTTP/1.1 connections per domain, each carrying one resource at a time. By distributing resources over multiple domains this number of connections can grow to 30 or more. While this typically gives the intended benefit of faster page loads, it is also inefficient, as each TCP connection requires some memory and processing. Additionally, it introduces bandwidth contention problems, with each individual connection vying for their share. As TCP's congestion control mechanisms work on a per-connection basis and often use packet loss as their main backoff signal, this massive parallelism can lead to increased packet loss rates and fairness issues with other applications using less TCP connections.

As such, one of the main goals of H2 was to allow the multiplexing of a web page's resources on a single underlying TCP connection [11]. To this end, H2 subdivides resource payloads into smaller chunks which are prefixed with their unique resource identifier, allowing data from different resources to be interleaved on the wire. While this resolves HTTP/1.1's HOL blocking problem, it introduces new challenges. The question now becomes how exactly the individual resources should be multiplexed and scheduled on the single connection. It turns out that this depends on the specific resource: some file types (such as JavaScript or CSS) typically need to be downloaded in full by the browser before they can be used and executed. As such, it makes sense to send them sequentially, not multiplexed with data from other resources. On the opposite end, resource types such as HTML and various image formats can be processed and rendered incrementally, making them ideal targets for heavy interleaving with data from other resources. Getting these resource priorities right is key to achieving good web page loading performance [9,19]. To allow browsers maximum flexibility in this area, H2 includes a complex prioritization mechanism, using a so-called "dependency tree", to steer which resources should be sent first and how.

In practice, this dependency tree mechanism has turned out to be overly complex and difficult to use, for browsers and servers alike [8]. Few implementations use its full potential and several employ sub-optimal tree layouts, leading to higher page load times. Additionally, switching to a single underlying TCP connection surfaces the fact that TCP has a Head-Of-Line blocking problem of its own when faced with packet loss. As TCP is a reliable and strictly ordered protocol, even a single packet loss can block all other packets behind it, waiting for its retransmission. This is inefficient for H2, as at that layer the blocked packets can contain data for other H2 resources, and as such do not necessarily have to wait for the lost packet's retransmission to be useful to the browser.

Solving TCP's HOL blocking problem is one of the main reasons for the new QUIC transport protocol [4]. While TCP regards all its payload data as a single, contiguous and opaque byte stream, QUIC is instead aware of multiple, fully independent byte streams (and thus HTTP resources) being transported over a single connection. As such, QUIC can provide features such as reliability and in-order data delivery on a per-stream basis; it is no longer tied to the global connection level like TCP. While this ostensibly solves TCP's transport level HOL blocking problem, it is unclear how much of an advantage this delivers in practice and if its benefits hold in all conditions. Another consequence of QUIC's fundamental departure from TCP's single-stream model, is that it becomes difficult to impossible to port some application layer protocols that currently rely on TCP behaviour to the new transport protocol. A key example of this fact is H2, which does not have a straightforward mapping onto QUIC. The discrepancies are so large in fact, that a new version of the protocol, termed H3, is being developed in tandem with QUIC. While H3 retains most of the semantics and high level features of H2, the underlying systems for aspects such as HTTP header compression, server push and the aforementioned resource prioritization have been substantially reworked to deal with QUIC's specifics. As such, the introduction of these new protocols leads to many unanswered questions with regards to performance and best practices.

In this text we continue the groundwork from our previous publications on HTTP/2 and HTTP/3 prioritization [6,19] and contribute new evaluation results for the QUIC protocol. While QUIC and HTTP/3 are conceptually bound together, they are in essence still separate protocols. As such, we will first discuss them individually and then combine our findings in the discussion. Starting at the transport layer in Sect. 2, we look at how ten different QUIC implementations implement multiplexing and data retransmissions on the independent byte streams. We find that there are large differences in how various stacks employ the new protocol's options. In Sect. 3 we provide new data concerning QUIC's HOL blocking behaviour. We find that QUIC provides definite benefits over TCP in this area, but that they are highly dependent on the underlying resource multiplexing behaviour. We then explore our application layer results from previous work more deeply in Sects. 4 and 5, discussing the problems with H2's prioritization setup and why it had to change for H3. We present the results of evaluating 11 H3 prioritization schemes on 42 web pages, to again show the optimal approach to be highly context dependent. We end by combining insights from both QUIC and HTTP/3 and discuss how the results from our previous work helped initiate a radical change in H3's planned approach to prioritization. All our source code, results and visualizations are made publicly available at https://h3.edm.uhasselt.be.

## 2  QUIC Resource Multiplexing

### 2.1  Background: Resource Streams

QUIC supports the concept of multiple, independent byte streams being active on a connection at the same time. These streams are a rather abstract concept in QUIC itself, but map nicely to for example individual resource requests and responses at the HTTP layer. This is in stark contrast with TCP, which sees all the data it transports as part of a single opaque byte stream, even if it is in fact carrying data from multiple files for protocols such as H2.

This can be easily understood by looking at the protocols' mechanisms under the hood. TCP for instance, uses a *sequence number* in its packet header, indicating the starting byte offset of the data in the current packet within the larger stream. For example, a TCP packet 1400 bytes in size with a sequence number of 10, carries byte 10 up to and including byte 1409 of the payload. QUIC takes a different approach, not including the payload metadata in its packet header, but rather using an additional binary framing layer. QUIC's STREAM frames contain a stream identifier (ID), to indicate which byte stream this frame belongs to, and both offset and length fields. However, these offsets are separate per stream: if we have a STREAM frame for stream A with offset 10 and length 1400, we can also have a subsequent STREAM frame for stream B with offset 10 and length 1400 and they would carry completely independent data. In TCP, stream B's data would then rather have been given offset 1410, as it was being sent directly after A's data.

While it adds flexibility, QUIC's setup also provides new challenges. Where TCP just needs to transport its single byte stream as it receives it from the application layer, QUIC now has to decide which of the multiple in-progress streams gets to send data in each outgoing QUIC packet. Put differently: it has to decide on a multiplexing and scheduling approach. As we will see in Sect. 4, this decision can be driven by the application layer, for example by H2's and H3's prioritization system. However, since QUIC is a standalone transport protocol, intended for use besides HTTP as well, it is useful to consider these mechanics purely on the transport layer as well. It is important to note that while QUIC includes the abstract concept of streams, it knows not of the semantics tied to individual streams and thus also cannot derive relative stream priorities itself. Put differently, QUIC treats all streams as equally important.

Consider then some possible approaches for two streams, A and B. One possibility is a *sequential* scheme, in which we would keep sending stream A's (available) data in full, before starting to transport B. Another option is a *Round-Robin* (RR) scheduler, in which we send a limited amount of data for A before switching to B for some time, moving back to A afterwards and so on. There are many possible RR variants, depending on how much data each stream may send before switching. For example, the scheduler could switch after 40 packets, after just one packet, or could even aggregate a smaller STREAM frame from both A and B into a single QUIC packet. The question is then: which of these schemes and their variants performs best in which circumstances?

This question becomes even more complex when we consider reliability. Just like TCP, QUIC utilizes retransmissions based on acknowledgements and timeouts to ensure reliable data transfers. Unlike TCP, these retransmission are now also done on a per-stream basis. While QUIC still acknowledges full packets, endpoints are expected to keep track of which STREAM data was in which packet. As such, QUIC does not necessarily need to retransmit full packets, but only individual STREAM frames. In fact, not even that is needed: QUIC implementations only need to keep track of the ranges of a byte stream (offset + length) that have not been acknowledged. When packet loss is detected, the lost ranges can be re-packaged into new STREAM frames at will (e.g., two smaller ranges that were previously sent in two STREAM frames across two packets can just as well be combined into one large range in one packet for retransmission). As such, QUIC implementations also need to make decisions in how to schedule the retransmission of this lost data in comparison to the "normal" data. We will consider three main **Retransmission Approaches** (RAs), which are the ones observed in our experiments in Sect. 2.3. In the following example sequences, we assume a default RR scheduler over streams A, B, C and D, where streams A and B suffer some losses:

- **RA #1: Default scheduling:** to be retransmitted data is simply seen as "normal" data and is sent when the stream is next selected by the scheduler as part of normal operating procedure. It does not receive special treatment. An example sequence would be ABCDABCD.
- **RA #2: Priority retransmissions with default scheduling:** streams with lost data are given a higher priority, and between them the default scheduling applies. In the example with the default RR scheduler, it will first perform RR between streams with losses before going back to RR across all streams. An example sequence would be ABABCDCD.
- **RA #3: Priority retransmissions with special scheduling:** streams with lost data are given a higher priority, and between them a special scheduling applies. In the example with the default RR scheduler, this approach can first utilize a sequential (or other) scheduler between streams with losses, before going back to RR across all streams. An example sequence would be AABBCDCD. Conversely, in the case of a default sequential scheduler, RR could be used for lossy streams, resulting in for example ABABCCDD.

It should be evident that there is no immediate clear winner among these schedulers and RAs: each has their own tradeoffs and will perform better or worse depending on use case and on the specific types and frequencies of loss (e.g., bursty vs single packets). Given this large parameter space, we decided to evaluate the default choices made by current QUIC implementations. These will dictate the off-the-shelf behaviour and performance seen from QUIC stacks when not utilizing external prioritization signalling.

## 2.2 Experimental Setup

At the time of writing (January 2020), there are approximately 20 publicly announced IETF QUIC implementations[1], many of them tied to large internet companies. Note that we only look at the IETF QUIC proposed standard, not Google's original version of the QUIC protocol, which is implemented by much less different parties. Note too that, to our knowledge, we are the first to perform this type of evaluation on multiple IETF QUIC implementations, related work

---

[1] https://github.com/quicwg/base-drafts/wiki/Implementation.

being limited to either Google's original QUIC implementation or a single IETF QUIC stack.

Most of the IETF QUIC implementations provide a publicly hosted endpoint for testing, or are open source. After filtering out obviously broken, outdated, and closed source implementations without a public endpoint, we are left with 10 implementations: *aioquic*, *quiche* (Google), *lsquic* (LiteSpeed), *msquic* (Microsoft), *mvfst* (Facebook), *ngtcp2*, *picoquic*, *quiche* (Cloudflare), *ats* (Apache Foundation) and *quicly* (Fastly). Note that there are two implementations named *quiche*. Since Cloudflare named theirs first, we will henceforth refer to Google's quiche as simply *google*.

To execute our tests, we choose the *aioquic* client, as it implements all of QUIC's features, has excellent interoperability with the other implementations and is written in Python, which allows us to easily tweak its behaviour as needed. We run this client in a debian docker container and point it at the public endpoints to simultaneously request one to ten files, of various sizes between 1 KB and 10 MB. While we use H3 as a means to request these files out of convenience, no prioritization information is passed from H3 to the QUIC layer, allowing us to assess the transport layer's default behaviour.

We execute all our tests on two WAN networks. Firstly, on the Hasselt University network, providing 1 Gbps downlink and 10 Mbps uplink capacity. Secondly, on a residential Wi-Fi network, providing 35 Mbps downlink and 2 Mbps uplink. The first network allows us mainly to see multiplexing behaviour in optimal situations, while the second provides more insight in retransmission behaviour, as packet loss rates are somewhat higher on that network. All test permutations are run at least 10 times. For our analysis, we employ the logging output of the *aioquic* client in the *qlog* format [12]. *qlog* is a structured, JSON-based format which includes highly detailed endpoint event logs. We process the *qlog* events with custom scripts and visualize them using the qvis toolsuite at https://qvis. edm.uhasselt.be. For this, we contribute a new visualization to qvis, termed the "multiplexing graph", which helped produce the following images in this work.

### 2.3   Multiplexing Results and Discussion

Our main results are summarized in Fig. 1. We show the singular experiment configuration of ten simultaneously requested and downloaded 1 MB files across all tested endpoints. We visualize a single representative trace per endpoint. For *picoquic*, we include results before and after a major server-side code change (*picoquic_alt*). For *mvfst*, we include results after changing client-side parameters (*mvfst_alt*). Endpoints are loosely grouped by similar behaviour.

Figure 1 plots received QUIC STREAM frames (colored per individual stream) horizontally appended, thus hiding any inter-packet arrival time gaps. While this hides some contextual information, it helps to better view the overall multiplexing behaviour. Large contiguous blocks of the same color indicate a more sequential transfer for that stream, while rapid changes in color mean that an RR scheduler variant is being used. Black blocks are shown beneath

STREAM frames that contain retransmitted data. These are identified by continuously tracking gaps in each stream's byte ranges (assuming a sender always sends data in-order per stream). Whenever a new frame fills a gap that was created sufficiently long ago, it is considered a retransmit. If it fills a gap that was created shortly before, it is assumed to be a re-ordered frame caused by network jitter. As such, areas without black blocks beneath show the endpoint's default multiplexing behaviour, while the rest allows us to assess their retransmission approaches (RAs). Note that the traces shown in Fig. 1 are representative for each endpoint and that the trends discussed below were consistent across all traces unless otherwise mentioned.

We can observe some general trends in Fig. 1. Firstly, a majority of implementations use a RR scheduler, with only two stacks opting for a sequential approach. Within the RR group, most use the fine-grained option of switching streams on each individual packet. Only *msquic* and *google* choose larger contiguous blocks of a fixed size (respectively 4 and 14 packets). *lsquic*'s behaviour seems strange at first, but it was confirmed by its implementer that it is intentional: for ease of implementation and increased server performance, it chooses its block size based on the current congestion window size. Whenever data can be sent, the next stream is selected, which sends all its available data filling the congestion window. This explains why the trace starts with fine-grained RR and gets coarser as time progresses, only to condense again when loss is detected.

Secondly, the RAs are about evenly split between #1 and #2. The key visual difference between the two, is that for #1, the black areas are usually interleaved with small white gaps, where data from non-lossy streams is being sent, indicating that the retransmissions don't receive absolute priority. This is for example visible in the *quicly* trace. Conversely, for #2, the black areas are mostly contiguous, indicating the implementations give highest priority to retransmitted data. A good example is the first big black block in the *lsquic* trace. Similar behaviour can be seen on the right side for *ats* and *picoquic*: retransmittable purple data immediately interrupts the current yellow stream.. Finally, there is only a single implementation, *mvfst*, that opts to change its behaviour when retransmitting data as an example of RA #3. Where it normally employs per packet RR, it switches to a fully sequential approach when there was lost data. We will discuss the wider impact of these general findings in Sects. 3 and 6.

Next to the global findings, there are also several per-implementation quirks to be discovered. Firstly, both *ats* and *picoquic* employ a sequential scheme, but process the incoming requests in a Last-In First-Out (LIFO) order. Put differently, the tenth requested resource (pink) is sent first. While this might make sense in some use cases, it is generally not viewed as an optimal strategy. After conferring with the implementers, *ats* indicated they were aware of the behaviour, but are waiting for H3's new prioritization scheme to change their approach. On the other hand, *picoquic* was not expected to exhibit this behaviour. The maintainer implemented a fix[2], instead enforcing a First-In

---

[2] https://github.com/private-octopus/picoquic/commit/a66a5d0a0b02416f9fde46bb 0c447bcc0b7abd60.

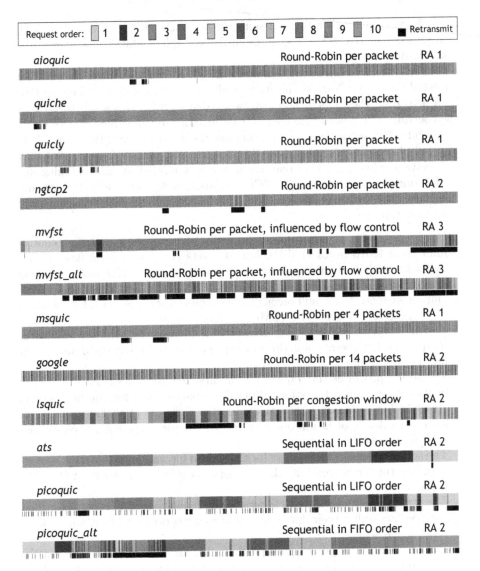

**Fig. 1.** QUIC endpoint multiplexing behaviour for ten simultaneously requested resources of 1 MB each. Per endpoint, the top line indicates the multiplexing of individual resource data (each small rectangle is one STREAM frame). Black areas in the bottom line indicate which frames in the top line contain retransmitted data. STREAM frames arrive at the client from left to right. (Color figure online)

First-Out (FIFO) approach, shown in *picoquic_alt*. Similarly, *ngtcp2* might at first glance look like it uses RA #3, as it seems to switch to a sequential mode for the later retransmits. After conferring with the author, this turned out to be due to a bug in their fair queuing implementation, which was subsequently fixed[3]. Now, all *ngtcp2*'s retransmissions use per-packet RR as intended, making it an example of RA #2 (trace of the updated implementation not shown due to size limits).

Secondly, *mvfst* consistently showed a large sequential transfer for the first requested stream (yellow) at the start of all its traces, before switching to RR. With help from the implementers, we were able to track this down to QUIC's flow control mechanisms. Like TCP, QUIC includes dynamic flow control limits to prevent a fast sender from overflowing buffers at the receiver. However, where TCP only has a single, connection-wide flow control window (sometimes called the receive window), QUIC instead has multiple separate flow control limits: one for the connection as a whole like TCP, but also one for each individual stream. This feature lead to a complex sequence of interlocking behaviours which we will now trace step by step:

1. In our test setup, the *aioquic* client sets the connection-level flow control limit to 1048576 bytes (1 MiB), but also sets the stream-level flow control limits for each individual stream to the same amount. This is done during the connection's handshake.
2. Our client sends ten simultaneous requests on ten streams, each for the same file of exactly 1000000 bytes (1 MB) in size.
3. The *mvfst* server processes each request individually as it comes in and works with a complex internal buffering system that fills the buffers up to the current flow control limits.
4. The server processes the request for the first file and puts it into the buffer in its entirety, since the stream-level flow control limit for the first stream (1048576 bytes) is larger than the requested file's size (1000000 bytes). This leaves just 48576 of headroom with regards to the over-arching connection-level flow control.
5. The server processes the request for the second file and puts 48576 bytes of its data into the buffer, reaching the connection-level flow control limit (1048576 bytes).
6. The server now incrementally processes the requests for the other eight files, but does not buffer their data, because the connection-level flow control limit is already reached.
7. The server starts sending, multiplexing with an RR scheduler between the data from just the first two streams, as can be seen at the very start of the *mvfst* trace. As the data from the second stream in the buffer soon runs out however, we end up just sending data from stream one.
8. After a while, the server receives an update to the connection-level flow control allowance from the client. At this point, it re-fills its internal buffers. As it now does have knowledge of all ten streams, it starts properly utilizing the RR scheduler across all of them.

We were able to easily confirm that this was the problem by changing the initial per-stream flow control limits to $\frac{1}{4}$th of the connection-level flow control.

---

[3] https://github.com/ngtcp2/ngtcp2/commit/4f705093d4c8f1ec5b231c2a1b557a6c96 6bc2f3.

The result can be seen in the *mvfst_alt* trace, which shows the server multiplexing data for the first four streams from the start of the connection. Note that, while the client's initial flow control setup was the same for all endpoints, only *mvfst* exhibited this behaviour. Its implementers indicated that, for a production deployment, it would make sense to limit the amount of data that can be buffered per stream (for example to 64 KB) if the intent is to use a RR scheduler. Further testing from our part on public *mvfst*-backed endpoints however, such as facebook.com and fbcdn.net, showed that they did not yet include this configuration change. It is interesting to note that flow control can be used by the client as a coarse prioritization/scheduling mechanism to dictate server behaviour, even overriding the server's normal intentions. For example, a RR server can be forced into sequential behaviour if the client only gives one stream flow control allowance at a time.

Thirdly, we looked at how implementations distribute STREAM frames over packets. While most stacks produce full-sized packets, all containing just a single STREAM frame for one stream, some implementations showed other behaviour. Notably *google* and *mvfst* had bugs that caused them to produce multiple, smaller STREAM frames for the same stream per packet. For example, one QUIC packet could contain 4 STREAM frames for stream one, sized 7, 500, 9, and 700 bytes respectively. The *mvfst* bug was since fixed[4], with Google indicating theirs was due to faulty re-use of HTTP/2 framing logic, which would be resolved in the future. Relatedly, *mvfst* was the only implementation we observed that occasionally multiplexed STREAM frames from **different** streams into a single QUIC packet. This only happened during retransmits, when for example stream one did not have enough retransmittable data to fill a full packet, which was completed with data from the next stream. Strangely, we also observed *mvfst* occasionally sending very small packets (e.g., 40 bytes). The reason was that *mvfst* adheres strictly to the current congestion window, which it measures in bytes instead of full packets. In some cases, the congestion window was not large enough to support another full packet, leading to a single smaller packet being sent instead. This sparked an interesting discussion with other implementers, who all indicated they instead rounded up to the next full packet in these situations. They felt that this (slight) overshooting of the congestion window was a good tradeoff between implementation complexity, correctness and performance. Note that, while it may seem that *mvfst* contained the most unexpected behaviours, this is mainly because it is a highly advanced implementation with complex logic. Additionally, its implementers were very receptive to our feedback and continued discussions with the authors of this work, leading to more in-depth scrutiny from our side over time. In practice, next to *quiche*, *mvfst* is the only QUIC implementation that has seen wide deployment and use in production with the facebook mobile app[5].

---

[4] https://github.com/facebookincubator/mvfst/commit/ec9d1ccd2088c64319f743541 b32789bb18ae2dc.

[5] https://www.youtube.com/watch?v=8lYHNzoPS2o.

Finally, we feel it is important to note that all tested implementations are active works in progress and that these results are not necessarily representative of the final products these companies may offer or deploy. The benefits however, of testing these implementations early, are manifold. Firstly, it helps to identify subtle bugs and quirks that can nevertheless have a noticeable impact. Secondly, it demonstrates differences between implementations, allowing implementers to re-assess their approaches. Thirdly, it highlights the inherent complexity of the QUIC protocol and the usefulness of specialized tooling and visualizations to perform debugging and analysis. Fourthly, and most importantly, it poses the question if the QUIC protocol should define a standardized interface to allow the application layer to manipulate QUIC's multiplexing behaviour. At the moment, the proposed QUIC specification [4] indicates that implementations **should** provide such an interface, but does not specify what such an interface should look like. As such, we end up not only with implementations choosing different default approaches, but also implementing different APIs (if they provide an API at all), making it more difficult for application layer protocol implementations to swap underlying QUIC stacks. Given that QUIC software is expected to be much more heterogeneous in behaviour than TCP deployments, this feels like an important point of action, allowing easier re-use of for example HTTP/3 implementations. For example, the recent "Pluginized QUIC" paper [3] can provide a possible starting point for a flexible API integration for this purpose. Further discussion on which multiplexing approach is optimal for performance follows in Sect. 5.3 and in the following exploration of Head-Of-Line Blocking.

## 3    QUIC Head-Of-Line Blocking

### 3.1    Background: Intra-Stream Blocking

Both QUIC and TCP are reliable protocols that deliver their received transported data to an application layer preserving the exact order in which that data was passed to the sender for transport. As seen in Sect. 2.1, TCP enforces this ordering across the entire connection as it collapses all data into a single byte stream, while QUIC instead only strictly orders data per individual byte

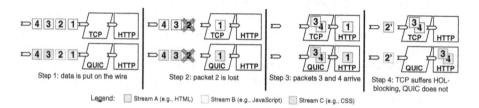

**Fig. 2.** Head-Of-Line blocking in TCP vs QUIC. Lacking knowledge of the three independent streams, TCP is forced to wait for the retransmit of packet 2 (2'). QUIC can instead pass packets 3 and 4 to HTTP immediately, where they are processed before packet 2' (source: [6]).

stream utilizing separate offsets in STREAM frames. Put differently, in TCP, a packet A sent before B, is always passed to the application layer before B, while in QUIC the order may well become B and then A, if the packets contain data for different streams and A becomes delayed. It follows that packet loss can thus create gaps in the byte streams, which can only be filled by retransmitting the lost data. In these instances, it is possible that data succeeding the gap is correctly received, for example if the gap is caused by an accidental loss of just one packet. However, the correctly received data cannot yet be passed on to the application layer, as this would break the ordering requirement. As such, even a single lost packet can conceivably block other packets behind it. This can be sub optimal for performance if the blocked packets contain data that could be processed independently from the lost data. This is called the Head-Of-Line blocking problem and it is illustrated in Fig. 2.

Because QUIC is no longer tied to a strict, connection-level ordering of its data, it is often said that it solves TCP's Head-Of-Line blocking problem. However, while it is true that QUIC removes TCP's inter-stream (connection-level) HOL blocking, it is still vulnerable to intra-stream HOL blocking. Put differently, if at the receiver QUIC stream A currently has a gap in its byte stream from offset 5000 to 6300, but has received and buffered stream A bytes 6301 to 40000 correctly, it still needs to wait for the gap to be filled. As soon as that happens, it can pass on bytes 5000 to 40000 in one large transfer to the application layer for processing, but not before. In this case, we could say 33699 bytes had been HOL blocked on this QUIC stream. The key advantage of QUIC over TCP is that if there were another QUIC stream B in progress, it would not be HOL blocked by loss on stream A. Note the exception to this: if QUIC implementations would multiplex STREAM frames of multiple streams into a single packet and that packet is lost, this does lead to (limited) inter-stream HOL blocking. As such, it is considered bad practice to multiplex data from multiple streams into a single QUIC packet. Absent this caveat however, on QUIC, the application layer should have to wait less time between receiving bursts of processable data from the transport layer than it would for TCP under the same network conditions. In the case of HTTP, this could then potentially translate into for example the browser being able to show a picture to the user sooner over QUIC.

## 3.2  Experimental Setup

Overall, it is difficult to assess whether QUIC's removal of inter-stream HOL blocking always has the intended effects and how much it actually reduces observed HOL-blocking in practice, due to the continued presence of intra-stream HOL blocking. Additionally, we can already intuitively predict that the chosen multiplexing behaviour will also influence the occurrence of this intra-stream HOL blocking. Consider that, with a purely sequential approach, there is always only a single stream in progress at a time and this stream will thus always HOL block itself upon packet loss. As there are no other streams active at the same time, there is no other data to provide to the application layer while waiting for the single stream to become unblocked. With an RR scheduler this is different, as simultaneously active streams that are not HOL blocked themselves can continue to make progress from the application layer's perspective. As such, we can predict that with an RR approach, the application layer should more frequently get smaller batches of data to process incrementally, versus rarer but larger bursts for a sequential scheduler.

To assess the actual impact of QUIC's inter-stream HOL blocking removal, we would ideally need to run the same experiments over both TCP and QUIC over identical network setups. However, this is difficult in practice, since network simulations are rarely deterministic and H3 does not support TCP (nor does H2 QUIC). Instead, we devise a different approach by employing the rich output logs from the previous experiment described in Sect. 2.2. The *qlog* format [12] utilizes the `data_moved` event to indicate when a given range of stream data was actually passed from the transport to the application layer. Additionally, the logs contain `packet_received` events which specify when STREAM frames were received. Correlating these two event types gives us a good indication of intra-stream HOL blocking at the QUIC layer (e.g., a `packet_received` not immediately followed by a `data_moved`, indicates data was blocked).

Subsequently, we can also use these events to simulate what would happen if QUIC would suffer from the same inter-stream HOL blocking as TCP. At the first encountered gap in one of the streams, we start pretending `data_moved` events from other streams have not proceeded and their data is blocked behind this stream's gap, as would be the case in TCP. We do this until this first gap was filled through retransmits, and then cascade the held-back `data_moved` events for other streams until the next tracked gap. As new gaps could have occurred while waiting behind the first gap, we track gaps in a contiguous manner, keeping a rolling log of missing stream data and which `data_moved` events they are blocking within TCP semantics. This approach allows us to derive a good estimate of TCP HOL blocking behaviour based on the QUIC traces, meaning we can now compare them on identical network setups and experiment parameters. It also allows us to confirm our intuition that the scheduling mechanism plays an important role, as some of the QUIC endpoints use RR schedulers while others employ sequential multiplexing.

## 3.3  HOL Blocking Results and Discussion

Tracking the `data_moved` events for QUIC and TCP produces two output lists, one for each protocol, their values indicating the amount of bytes blocked at each HOL blocking instance. Larger values indicate more data was held back and thus more HOL blocking was observed. To get a feel for this data, let's first consider the highest blocked byte amounts seen across all the traces. For TCP for example, the highest value seen was 3740019 bytes (in a *mvfst* trace), constituting over a third of the total amount of transmitted bytes on the connection (ten times 1 MB). Conversely, the highest value encountered for QUIC was 969151 bytes (unsurprisingly in a sequentially scheduled *picoquic* trace), a factor of three smaller than TCP.

The full set of results is shown in Fig. 3. Note that, as we use traces from experiments run over real networks, not every trace contains the same occurrences of packet loss or HOL blocking. As we are mainly interested in the worst-case differences that can occur between the protocols, we take the maximum blocked byte amount for each protocol. To be able to more easily compare TCP and QUIC measurements, we calculate the ratio between these two maximum values per trace:

$$ratio = \frac{max\_blocked\_bytes(QUIC)}{max\_blocked\_bytes(TCP)}$$

As such, ratios close to 1 indicate that the maximum values were very similar and QUIC suffered from HOL blocking more similarly to TCP. Conversely, ratios closer to 0 indicate that QUIC's maximum HOL blocked byte amount was (much) lower than TCP's, indicating it more frequently passes data to the application layer than the legacy transport protocol. Each trace's ratio is plotted as a point in Fig. 3. As traces without packet loss would give a ratio of exactly 1 (as both maxima would be the packet size), these are left out of the results, explaining the low amount of results for *google* and *ats*. Interpreting Fig. 3, we can see that for most endpoints and most traces, QUIC indeed achieves a much lower maximum amount of HOL blocked bytes than TCP, as most ratios are between 0.1 and 0.3. As predicted, the ratios shift upwards for the *picoquic* endpoint, as its sequential scheduler induces additional intra-stream HOL blocking compared to the other endpoints' RR schedulers. However, from these results alone it is difficult to assess the practical impact of QUIC's HOL blocking behaviour on application metrics such as page load times.

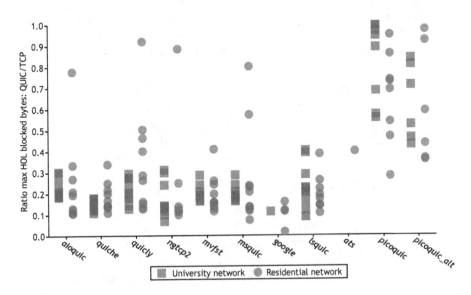

**Fig. 3.** Maximum HOL blocking ratios between TCP and QUIC. Each point is a single test run downloading ten 1 MB files. Higher values mean more HOL blocking in QUIC.

# 4   HTTP/2 Prioritization

Now that we understand how QUIC can approach general purpose multiplexing across different streams, it is time to look at how this behaviour can be influenced using semantics from the HTTP layer, which is necessary to achieve optimal page loading performance. While it may seem this is mainly important for H3, the concept of a prioritization system to dictate web page resource scheduling behaviour actually originates with the H2 protocol. This is because H2 includes its own stream abstraction and framing layer, also utilizing stream IDs in DATA frames for multiplexing [11]. This is incidentally one of the main reasons it is difficult to use H2 on QUIC directly, as this would lead to two separate and competing stream concepts, which can introduce much implementation complexity and inefficiencies. The choice was made instead to define a new mapping of H2 onto QUIC, which is now being called H3. In essence, the main change is that in H3, all of H2's stream-specific amenities have been removed in favor of utilizing QUIC's streams directly. This does mean that H3 still needs a prioritization system to steer QUIC and as such, it is interesting to first understand the details of H2's approach.

## 4.1   Background: The HTTP/2 Dependency Tree

In our discussion of the QUIC implementations' multiplexing behaviours in Sect. 2, it was clear they treated each resource and each stream in the same way. No individual requested file was considered more important than others; only retransmitted data was given a higher priority in some implementations. While this makes sense in the general purpose QUIC case, it does not when looking at HTTP semantics and the use case of loading a web page with multiple resources. Not all these resources are equally important and most have very distinct characteristics during the web page loading process. For example, HTML

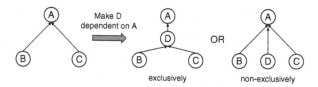

**Fig. 4.** HTTP/2 dependencies: exclusivity (source: [6]).

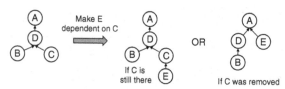

**Fig. 5.** HTTP/2 behaviour when referenced parent does not exist. E is added as a sibling of D on the root, (unintentionally) sharing its bandwidth (source: [6]).

and image files can conceptually be parsed, processed and rendered incrementally. This is different from JS and CSS files, which can be parsed as data comes in (at least in some browsers) but have to be fully downloaded to be actually executed and applied. Another issue is that the browser does not know about all the needed resources up-font, as they are discovered incrementally during the page load and resources can import other files dynamically. Finally, users typically only see a small part of the web page at a time due to screen sizes, which makes resources that are currently in the viewport extra important. These and other web page loading concepts make that web pages can have very complex resource interdependencies. Individual resource importance depends on its type, precise function (potentially) location within the HTML and how many children it will end up including. Relative resource priorities can also change over time, as new resources of a higher importance are discovered.

To be able to manage these volatile requirements, HTTP/2 includes an advanced prioritization system in the form of a 'dependency tree', in which each individual resource stream is represented as a node. Available bandwidth is then distributed across these nodes by means of two simple rules: parents are transferred in full before their children, and sibling nodes share bandwidth among each other based on assigned weights. For example, given a sibling A with weight 128 (out of a maximum of 256) and a sibling B with weight 64, A will receive 2/3 of the available bandwidth, leaving 1/3 for B. In an optimal implementation, this would result in the following scheduled frame sequence: AABAABAAB.... As HTTP/2 assumes that, between the two endpoints, the browsers have the best view of relative resource importance, it has the user agents build and maintain this dependency tree over time, which is then synchronized back to the server by means of PRIORITY frames. As such, the structure of the tree evolves over time on both endpoints, as new resources are discovered and added, and fully transferred nodes are pruned.

H2 provides two main ways to add nodes as children to a parent in the tree: exclusively and non-exclusively. As can be seen from Fig. 4, non-exclusive addition is the 'normal', less invasive way of adding nodes to the tree. Exclusive addition however, changes all of its potential siblings beneath its parent to instead become children of the newly added node itself. This allows aggressive (re-)prioritization, by displacing (large) groups of nodes in a single operation. One special case arises when the intended parent is no longer available at the server (i.e., because it was fully transmitted and was pruned from the tree). In this case, the child is added to the root node of the parent instead, leading to a possible desynchronization of the tree between client and server and a possible mis-prioritization of the new child, as it is now a sibling of other direct children of the root. An example of this can be seen in Fig. 5.

While this setup in general seems easy enough to comprehend, it can be difficult to implement correctly, especially if the tree updates frequently. Additionally, the possibility of desynchronization between the two endpoints can lead to unintended behaviours. Furthermore, the tree needs to be evaluated on the server for each packet that is to be sent, to determine which stream should received bandwidth, which can be computationally expensive for large trees. Given this complexity and these edge cases, one might wonder why it was decided that the browser should determine the resource priorities instead of the server. Could we not make a similar argument that the server (usually) already has all the resources for the web page and thus has a good overview from the start? While letting the server dictate priorities is certainly possible, it is quite complex in practice to know the resource priorities at the server at the start of the page load [7]. Still, H2 provides an option for this approach as well: servers are free to ignore the clients' PRIORITY messages and to concoct a more optimized bandwidth distribution from server-side info.

## 4.2   Prioritization: Theory vs. Practice

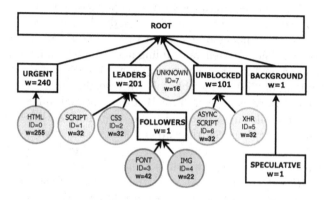

**Fig. 6.** Firefox's HTTP/2 dependency tree (source: [6]).

Given the high flexibility provided by H2's prioritization system and the choice between client and server-side prioritization, it is interesting to see how these amenities are actually being used in practice by real-world implementations. [19] looked at how modern browsers utilize H2's prioritization system in practice. They found that out of 10 investigated browsers, only Mozilla's Firefox constructs a non-trivial dependency tree (see Fig. 6). It uses "empty" nodes that are not tied to a real resource as placeholders to group other nodes and assigns heterogeneous weights. Other browsers like Chrome and Safari instead opt for much simpler schemes, the former creating a purely sequential model where all resources are added to a parent exclusively, the latter a RR variant where all resources are added non-exclusively to the root using different weights. The original Edge browser neglected to specify any priorities at all, relying on H2's default behaviour of adding all the resources to the root with identical weights, leading to pure RR.

Next, [2] looked at how various H2 servers actually adhere to client-side PRIORITY directives in practice. They find that out of 35 tested implementations, only 9 actually properly support (re-)prioritization. They posit this is due to faulty or inefficient implementations, servers ignoring client directives but failing to provide better server-side scheduling, and various forms of 'bufferbloat'. This last problem occurs when deployments use too large buffers: the risk exists that these buffers will be filled with low-priority data before the high-priority requests arrive [8]. This is similar to the problem encountered with *mvfst* in Sect. 2.3.

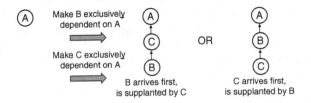

**Fig. 7.** Non-deterministic ordering over QUIC: intended structure of the dependency tree can become inverted (source: [6]).

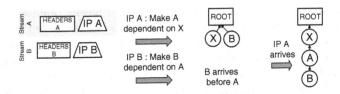

**Fig. 8.** Non-deterministic ordering over QUIC: B can end up 'stealing' bandwidth from X for a time. (IP: Initial PRIORITY message) (source: [6]).

Next to this H2 specific work, there are also contributions on resource prioritization in general. WProf [17] looks at resource dependencies and their impact on total page load performance. Polaris [7], Shandian [18] and Vroom [14] collect very detailed loading information and construct complex resource transmission and computation scheduling schemes, claiming 34%–50% faster page load times at the median. However, none of their implementations utilize H2's server-side prioritization, instead using JavaScript-based schedulers or H2 Server Push. At this time Cloudflare is the only commercial party experimenting with advanced server-side H2 prioritization at scale, for which they employ the *bucket* scheme from [9]. They claim improvements of up to 50% for the original Edge browser.

Overall, we can conclude that the flexibility of H2's prioritization system is barely used in practice, while its complexity leads to several bugs in real world deployments. Additionally, advanced server-side prioritization remains relatively unproven in practice and many servers that ignore the client's PRIORITY messages do not employ optimal custom scheduling logic.

## 4.3  Adaptation for HTTP/3

Given the complexities inherent in H2's prioritization system and its abysmal adoption in practice, there were already some who questioned whether the approach should be reworked for H3. This was then further compounded by the fact that directly using H2's setup to run in H3 over QUIC would be impossible due to QUIC's non-deterministic ordering, if PRIORITY messages are sent on different streams. This can be simply understood by looking at a few examples. Firstly, consider the two opposite outcomes if two H2 PRIORITY messages, each carrying an exclusive parenting operation, would become re-ordered over QUIC, see Fig. 7. Secondly, priority message re-ordering can lead to nodes being added to the default root node, if their intended parent had not yet been added to the tree, see Fig. 8. This is similar to the problem from Fig. 5. Several more similar edge-cases can occur within this setup.

Over time, the H3 designers debated multiple possible approaches and changes to H2's system to solve or at least alleviate these issues on H3. At one point, the proposed solution was to use a separate control stream to send priority updates. This would prevent them from becoming re-ordered, as messages within a single stream are of course delivered in-order. In tandem, a separate default parent node was used (termed the 'orphan' node) to prevent new nodes from being added to the root and stealing bandwidth from unintended siblings. This setup can be seen in Fig. 9. While this setup indeed made the worst edge cases manageable, it was still not ideal. For example, there was a form of HOL blocking where resources would be mis-prioritized for a full network round trip if there was loss on the control stream carrying the PRIORITY messages. A much more in-depth discussion of these issues and contemplated solutions can be found in our previous work [6]. Due to this added complexity to an already complex system, several people proposed alternative solutions to prioritization for H3. These are discussed and evaluated in Sect. 5.

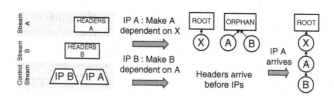

**Fig. 9.** Proposed H3 prioritization setup: control stream and separate default parent (orphan). (IP: Initial PRIORITY message) (source: [6]).

## 5  HTTP/3 Prioritization

### 5.1  Alternative Proposals

As many felt that the proposed integration of H2's dependency tree system in H3 was too complex, several alternative proposals were launched. Their first goal was trying to simplify the setup to make it easier to implement and reason about. A secondary goal was that it should be possible to back port the new approaches to H2 as well, to be able to fix the problems seen in current H2 deployments. A final goal was to make it easier to combine server-side information with client-side PRIORITY messages. As mentioned in Sect. 4.1, it is possible that a server has better information about a resource's relative importance than the client. However, in practice it is difficult for the server to integrate that knowledge into H2's dependency tree. As clients are free to build their tree in very different ways [19], it is almost impossible for a server implementation to automatically derive the semantics employed by various clients. This makes it difficult to determine the correct place in the tree for the (manually) prioritized resource. In practice for H2, servers either need to follow the client's setup, or ignore it completely and define a full new approach for all resources at the same time. As such, a new setup for H3 should ideally make it easier to combine client and server-side directives.

The first proposal, termed *bucket* by us, is one by Patrick Meenan from Cloudflare [10]. He proposes to drop the dependency tree setup and replace it with a simpler scheme of 'priority buckets', see Fig. 10. Buckets with a higher number are processed in full before buckets with a lower number. Within the buckets, there are three concurrency levels. Level three, called "Exclusive Sequential" preempts the other two and sends its contents sequentially by stream ID (streams that are opened earlier are sent first). Levels two ("Shared Sequential") and one ("Shared") are each given 50% of available bandwidth if level three is empty. Within level two, streams are again handled sequentially by lowest resource ID, while within level one, they follow a fair Round-Robin scheduler. As can be seen in Fig. 10, this allows a nice and fine-grained mapping to typical web page assets loading needs. This scheme was deployed for H2 as well on Cloudflare's edge servers and they claim impressive speedups [9]. Overall, this scheme is also easier to implement than the dependency tree: all that is needed is

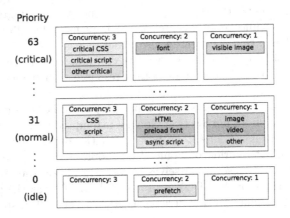

**Fig. 10.** Proposal for HTTP/3 prioritization based on priority buckets, from [10].

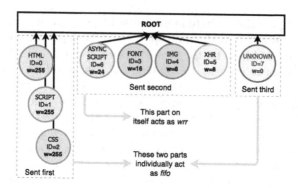

**Fig. 11.** Tree for our HTTP/3 zero weighting proposal (source: [6]).

a single byte per resource stream to carry the priority and concurrency numbers. Resources can easily be moved around by updating these numbers, though it is not possible to re-prioritize many resources at once. This scheme also makes it easier to incorporate server-side directives for particular resources, as there is a clear ordering of importance through the priority buckets.

Secondly, our own proposal[6] called 'zeroweight' has an aim to stay close to the idea of a dependency tree, but to significantly reduce ways in which new nodes can be added. The main change is that nodes can now have a weight between 0 and 255 (where before it was in the range 1–256). Nodes with weight 0 and 255 exhibit special behaviour, akin to Meenan's sequential concurrency levels: siblings with weight 255 are processed first, in full and sequentially in the lowest stream ID order. Then, all siblings with weight between 254 and 1 are processed in a weighted Round-Robin fashion (assigned bandwidth relative to their weights, see Sect. 4.1). Finally, if all other siblings are processed, do zero-weighted nodes get bandwidth, again sequentially in the lowest stream ID order. The resulting tree can be viewed in Fig. 11. This proposal requires just a few semantic changes to the H2 system, and is thus easy to integrate in existing implementations, while being much easier to implement for H3 than the more flexible dependency tree. This setup also makes it easy to integrate server-side directives, as changing per-resource weights can now have more impact and it is straightforward to promote or demote a resource to a higher 'tier' (change weight to 255 or 0).

Thirdly, we shortly discuss several other proposals. For example, the 'strict priorities' approach from Ian Swett at Google[7] attempted to integrate the semantics of Patrick Meenan's *bucket* proposal with the dependency tree setup to achieve a 'best of both worlds' outcome. As it should perform similarly to *bucket*, we did not evaluate this setup ourselves. Another proposal was to return to the prioritization scheme of the SPDY protocol [15]. SPDY was the predecessor of H2 and had just "eight levels of strict priorities". The SPDY specification did

---

[6] github.com/quicwg/base-drafts/pull/2723.

[7] github.com/quicwg/base-drafts/pull/2700.

not provide details on how resources should be allotted bandwidth, only that resources of higher priority levels should be sent first. In our evaluation in Sect. 5.3 we discuss a Round-Robin version of this setup, termed *spdyrr*, which processes the priority levels sequentially, but applies a fair RR scheduler between resources within a single level. More details on these and further proposals can be found in [16].

While at first glance these proposals seem to achieve the set goals, it is difficult to assess if they will indeed be able to provide similar or better web page loading performance when compared to the existing H2 setups seen in the different browser and server implementations. Without proof that these new setups would indeed be able to pull their own weight despite shedding considerable complexity, the H3 designers were reticent to drop the dependency tree. To aid their decision making, we implement and evaluate the different proposals.

## 5.2  Experimental Setup

In order to prove that the simpler H3 approaches can perform similarly or better than the existing H2 dependency tree configurations, we first need to determine a baseline for the performance of these different H2 schemes. While Wijnants et al. provide an extensive evaluation of these schemes [19], it is unclear if their findings also hold on H3 over QUIC. As such, next to the new H3 setups, we also implement and evaluate the main existing H2 schemes, resulting in a total of 11 different evaluated prioritization setups. Their main approaches are described in

**Table 1.** Prioritization schemes. The top seven are from actual browser H2 implementations and [19]. The bottom four are new proposals for H3 (source: [6]).

| Name | Description |
|---|---|
| *rr* (Edge) | Fully fair Round-Robin. Each resource gets equal bandwidth |
| *wrr* (Safari) | Weighted Round-Robin. Resources are interleaved, but non-equally, based on weights |
| *fifo* | First-In, First-Out. Fully sequential, lower stream IDs are sent in full first |
| *dfifo* (Chrome) | Dynamic FIFO. Sequential, but higher stream IDs of higher priority can interrupt lower stream IDs |
| *firefox* | Complex tree-based setup with multiple weighted placeholders and *wrr* for placeholder children. See Fig. 6 |
| *p+* | Parallel+. Combination of *dfifo* for high-priority with separate *wrr* for medium and low-priority resources [19] |
| *s+* | Serial+. Combination of *dfifo* for high and medium-priority with *firefox* for low-priority resources [19] |
| *spdyrr* | Five strict priority sequential buckets, each performing *wrr* on their children. The Round-Robin counterpart of *dfifo* |
| *bucket* | Patrick Meenan's proposal, Fig. 10 |
| *bucket HTML* | Our variation on Patrick Meenan's proposal, with HTML having a higher priority (bucket 63 instead of 31 in Fig. 10) |
| *zeroweight* | Our proposal, Fig. 11 |

Table 1 and Fig. 12 shows to what kind of data scheduling they lead in practice for an example page load. For example, as expected the fair Round-Robin *rr* clearly has a very spread out way of scheduling data for the various streams, as was also evident from similar approaches in our QUIC experiments. The *firefox, p+, s+* and *spdyrr* schemes are quite similar, but include subtle differences. Looking at the results for *bucket* we see that the HTML resource (and the font that is directly dependent on it) are delayed considerably, which seems non-ideal. As such, we propose our own variation, *bucket HTML*, which gives the HTML resource a higher priority. For this test page it dramatically shortens the HTML and font file's Time-To-Completion (TTC). Figures 6 and 11 show dependency tree layouts for two of the schemes; the rest can mostly be found in [19] and [16].

To make comparisons with earlier results easier, we test the 11 prioritization schemes on the test corpus of [19]. This corpus consists of 40 real web pages from the Alexa top 1000 and Moz top 500 lists. The corpus represents a good mix of simple and more complex pages (10–214 resources), as well as small and larger byte sizes (29 KB–7400 KB). We also add two synthetic test pages: one of our

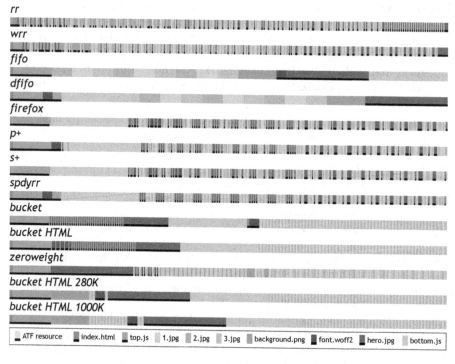

**Fig. 12.** Scheduling behaviour of various prioritization schemes for a single, synthetic test page from [2]. Each individual colored rectangle represents a single QUIC packet of 1400 bytes. Packets arrive at the client from left to right. The bottom two lines show results with non-zero send buffers. Resources in the legend are listed in request-order from left to right (source: [6]).

own design that tests all types of heuristics modern browses apply, and the one used by [2] (Sect. 4.2, Fig. 12). These two pages can be seen as "stress-tests" and are designed to highlight prioritization issues and behaviour. The full corpus is downloaded to disk and all files are served from a single H3+QUIC server.

For this QUIC server, we choose the open source TypeScript and NodeJS-based Quicker implementation [13] because the high level language makes it easy to implement the prioritization schemes. We have exhaustively tested the implementation to make sure any inefficiencies stemming from the underlying JavaScript engine did not lead to performance issues. As this part of our evaluation was run for of our previous work [6], it was performed several months before our tests of the various QUIC implementations in Sect. 2.2. At that time, the Quicker implementation was one of the few with a fully functional H3 implementation which allowed us to experiment with prioritization. During the intervening months, Quicker however became outdated with respects to the other implementations, which is the reason it was not evaluated in our tests for the QUIC implementations discussed earlier.

On the client side, there is currently sadly no browser available that (fully) supports H3. As such, we use the Quicker command line client instead. However, we do closely emulate the browser's expected behaviour by using the open source WProfX tool[8], an easy to use implementation of the concepts from the original WProf paper [17]. We host the test corpus on a local H2O optimized webserver and load the pages via the Google Chrome-integrated WProfX software. From this load, the tool can extract detailed resource inter-dependencies (e.g., was an image referenced in the HTML directly or from inside a CSS file) and request timing information. Our H3 Quicker client then performs a "smart play-back" of the WProfX recording, taking into account resource dependencies (e.g., if the current prioritization scheme causes a CSS file to be delayed, the images or fonts it references will also be delayed accordingly). The tool also indicates which resources are on the "critical path" and are thus most important to a fast page load.

At the time of our evaluation, none of the open source QUIC stacks (including Quicker) integrated a performant congestion control implementation that had been shown to perform on par with best in class TCP implementations. As we want to focus on the raw performance of the prioritization schemes and the order in which data is put on the wire, we do not want to run the risk of inefficient congestion controllers skewing our results. We instead manually tune the Quicker server to send out a single packet of 1400 bytes containing response data of exactly one resource stream every 10ms (i.e., simulating a steadily paced congestion controller). To see if we can replicate the results of [8], we also implement the option to use small and larger application-level send buffers, to assess the impact of "bufferbloat". Given these factors, our results represent an "ideal" upper bound of how well prioritization could perform in the absence of network congestion and retransmits. This approach also leads to exceptionally stable

---

[8] wprofx.cs.stonybrook.edu.

experimental conditions, with re-runs of individual experiments leading to near-identical results.

Due to our stable experimental setup we can not simply use, for example, the total web page download time as our metric, as these values are all identical per tested page across the different schemes. This can easily be seen by understanding that each scheme still needs to send the exact same amount of data; it just does so in a different order. Instead, we will mainly look at so-called "Above The Fold" (ATF) resources. These are the resources that are either on the browser's critical render path (meaning they would delay the load and usage of other resources) or that contribute substantially to what the user sees first (e.g., large hero images). We combine WProfX's critical path calculations with a few manual additions to arrive at an appropriate ATF resource set for each test page. This ATF set typically contains the HTML, important JS and CSS, all fonts and prominent 'hero images'. Non-hero (e.g., background) images that are rendered above the fold are consciously not included in this set (e.g., see "background.png" in Fig. 12), as they should have less of an impact on user experience. Furthermore, to highlight the power that comes from combining client and server-side directives, our implementations of both *bucket* and *zeroweight* use small parts of these ATF resource lists to simulate explicit manual web developer prioritization interventions. Concretely, the hero images are given a higher server-side priority than what they would normally receive from the client. For example, Fig. 10 mentions a 'visible image' for the *bucket* scheme, while in practice, browsers have no way of definitively knowing which images will eventually be visible or not. Since the other discussed schemes do not utilize this additional metadata, this will in part explain the seemingly best-in-class performance of *bucket* and *zeroweight* in our results.

However, to report these results, we also cannot directly use, for example, the mean TTC for these ATF resources as our metric. For example, receiving most of the ATF files very early and then receiving just a single one late is generally considered better for user experience than receiving all together at an intermediate point, though both situations would give a similar mean TTC. To get a better idea of the progress over time, we use the ByteIndex (BI) web performance metric [1]. This metric estimates (visual) loading progress over time by looking at the TTCs of (visually impactful, e.g., ATF) resources. At a fixed time interval of 100 ms we look at which of the resources under consideration have been **fully** downloaded. The BI is then defined as taking the integral of the area above the curve we get by plotting this download progress, see Fig. 13. Consequently as with normal web page load times, lower BI values are better. Practically, we instrument Quicker to log the full H3 page loads in the *qlog* format [12]. We then write custom tools to extract the needed BI values from these logs, as well as new visualizations to display and verify our results (Figs. 12 and 14).

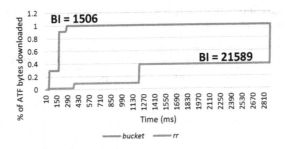

**Fig. 13.** ByteIndex (BI) for *bucket* and *rr* schemes. *Bucket* is clearly faster for ATF resources. Looking at these schemes in Fig. 12, it is immediately clear why (source: [6]).

## 5.3 Prioritization Results

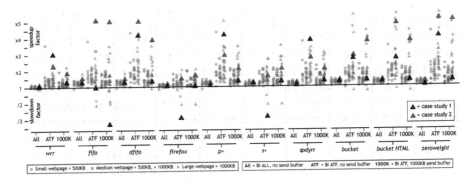

**Fig. 14.** ByteIndex (BI) speedup and slowdown ratios for 10 prioritization schemes compared to the baseline *rr* scheme. Each datapoint represents a single web page, split out by total page byte size. Higher y values are better (source: [6]).

Our main results are presented in Fig. 14 and Table 2. Like [19], when processing the results we quickly saw that the *rr* scheme is by far the worst performing of all tested setups, with almost no data points performing worse. This is mainly because for many high-priority ATF resources (e.g., JS, CSS, fonts) it is imperative that they are downloaded **in full** as soon as possible. As can be seen at the top of Fig. 12, RR bandwidth interleaving leads to resource downloads being completed very late. As such, a more sequential scheduler, which sends a single resource at a time, is a better approach for many types of critical resources, while a RR scheme is more apt for lower-priority resources that can be incrementally used (e.g., progressive images).

**Table 2.** Mean speedup ratios compared to *rr* per other prioritization scheme from Fig. 14. Higher mean values are better (source: [6]).

| Name | Mean All | Mean ATF | Mean 1000K |
|---:|:---:|:---:|:---:|
| *wrr* | **1.05** | 1.49 | **1.28** |
| *fifo* | **1.27** | 1.93 | 1.57 |
| *dfifo* | **1.27** | 2.30 | 1.72 |
| *firefox* | 1.07 | **1.22** | 1.25 |
| *p+* | 1.17 | 2.20 | 1.64 |
| *s+* | 1.14 | 1.45 | 1.56 |
| *spdyrr* | 1.14 | 1.96 | 1.57 |
| *bucket* | 1.20 | 2.13 | **1.82** |
| *bucket HTML* | 1.20 | **2.49** | **1.83** |
| *zeroweight* | 1.15 | **2.8** | **1.9** |

Consequently, we take *rr* as the baseline and present the other measurements in terms of a relative speedup to that baseline result. As such, a speedup of x2 for scheme Y means that, for a baseline *rr* BI of 1500, Y achieves a BI of 750. Symmetrically, a slowdown of /3 indicates that Y had a BI of 4500. We have tested the schemes with application-level send buffers of 14 KB (about 10 packets and similar to the default minimum H2 frame size of 16 KB [11]), 280 KB and 1000 KB, but found that these had relatively small effects until the buffer grows substantially large. As such, we focus on results for send buffers of 1000 KB here. As seen from the *mvfst* example in Sect. 2.3, this is a realistic value.

A few things are immediately clear from Fig. 14: a) Almost all data points are indeed faster than *rr*. b) With the exception of a few bad performers (i.e., *firefox*, *wrr*, *s+*), all schemes are able to provide impressive gains of x3.5 to x5+ speedup factors for individual web pages. c) Medium sized pages seem to profit less from prioritization overall, with smaller and larger pages showing higher relative advancements. d) Of the well-performing schemes, there is not a clear, single winner or a scheme that consistently improves heavily upon *rr* for -all- tested pages. e) The impact of the 1000KB send buffer is visible, but less impressively so than perhaps indicated by previous work [8], which quoted slowdowns of /2 compared to small/non-existent send buffers.

When looking at the mean ratios in Table 2, we see similar trends. We have highlighted some of the highest and lowest values for each column. Taking into account all page assets, even though the speedups are all modest, it is clear that *fifo* is a far better default choice than *rr*. Looking at ATF resources only, it is remarkable how badly some schemes implemented by browsers perform (i.e., *firefox* and Safari's *wrr*), while Chrome's *dfifo* is almost optimal, after *bucket HTML* and *zeroweight*. Though all schemes suffer from larger send buffers, *bucket HTML* and *zeroweight* again come out on top. As mentioned before, this good performance of these latter two schemes can be partially attributed to giving hero images a higher server-side priority, highlighting that indeed, there might be merit in combining client and server-side directives.

While the reduced observed impact of larger send buffers might seem unexpected and contrary to the findings of [2], it has a simple explanation in two parts. Firstly, larger send buffers mainly impact the ability of the scheme to re-prioritize its scheduler in response to late discovered but important resources. In our data set however, we seem to have few web pages that contain such highly important late discoveries. Indeed, the test page showing the most remarkable slowdown from the larger send buffers was that introduced in [2] itself (dropping from x9 speedup without send buffer to x3 with 1000K). Secondly, as the size of the send buffer grows, the resulting behaviour more and more becomes that of *fifo*, as requested resources can be put into the buffer in their entirety immediately (similar to *mvfst*'s flow control behaviour in Sect. 2.3). This is clearly visible in Fig. 12. As we have seen, *fifo* performs well overall, so even larger send buffers will also keep performing relatively well. It is our opinion that the results seen in [2] for faulty prioritizations in the wild might be less due to 'bufferbloat' and more due to misconfigured or badly implemented H2 servers, or to their choice of a highly tuned test page.

To dig a bit deeper into some of the outliers, we discuss two case studies. The first is outlined in black on Fig. 14. This web page suffers a slowdown of about /3 for three separate schemes, yet sees major improvements of x4 in others. This specific page has relatively few resources with highly specific roles. Most importantly, it features a single, page-spanning hero image that is relatively small in byte size. Next, it includes several very large JS files which, even though included in the HTML <head>, are marked as "defer". This means they will only execute once the full page has finished downloading. As such, the hero image is marked as an ATF resource, but the JS files are not. As the image is discovered after the JS files, it is stuck behind them in *fifo*. For *firefox* (and similarly *s+*), the image is in the "FOLLOWERS" category (see Fig. 6), while the JS files are in "UNBLOCKED". While the group of the image receives about twice the bandwidth as the JS (via the parent "LEADERS" placeholder), the image is competing with a critical CSS in the leaders, thus being delayed. For the speedups, the schemes either know there is a hero image (*bucket (HTML)* and *zeroweight*), allow the smaller hero image to make fast progress via a (semi) Round-Robin scheme or, in the case of *dfifo*, accurately assign low priority to the JS files.

The second case study is outlined in blue on Fig. 14. This web page interestingly has a few instances where the 1000k send buffer outperforms the normal ATF case. This is because this page's HTML file is comparatively very large (167 KB). As explained before, a large send buffer exhibits *fifo*-alike behaviour. Thus, for schemes where normally the large HTML would be competing with other resources (e.g., *bucket* and *firefox*), it now gets to fill the send buffers in its entirety, completing much faster. Where in the previous case study Round-Robin-alike schemes led to smaller resources completing faster, here the large HTML file is instead smeared out over a longer period of time due to interleaving with the other (ATF) resources.

# 6  Conclusion

## 6.1  HTTP/3's New Priority System

Based on our evaluation of the different prioritization schemes in Sect. 5.3, we can draw two general conclusions to help guide the choice for an appropriate H3 prioritization approach. Firstly, that it is perfectly possible to switch to a simplified prioritization framework while still fully supporting the web browsing use case and without losing performance. Schemes such as *bucket HTML* and *zeroweight* are easy to implement performantly without a dependency tree structure and seem to provide a good baseline performance for most web pages.

Secondly, that such a simpler scheme should nevertheless still allow enough flexibility. As our results and case studies have clearly shown, no single scheme performs well for all types of web pages. This is a conclusion we and related work keep repeating: it is almost impossible to come up with a perfect general purpose scheme. This is emphasized by the good results achieved by combining client-side priority indicators with server-side priority information in our *bucket HTML* and *zeroweight* schemes. This is also why efforts such as 'Priority Hints'[9] give developers options to manually indicate per-resource priorities. As such, any new chosen system should allow the integration of similar client and server-side overrides and behaviour tuning on a per-page basis.

These prioritization results and conclusions were first presented in our previous work [6] in June 2019, and were brought to the attention of the IETF QUIC and HTTP working groups. Based partly on our input and other insights, it was finally decided to remove the dependency tree setup from H3 completely and to instead develop a new system. As the alternative proposals tested in our evaluation were still deemed to be too complex, an even simpler proposal named "Extensible Prioritization Scheme for HTTP" [5] was adopted. This new proposal is simple in that it defines resource priorities based on just two parameters, termed 'Urgency' and 'Incremental'. The Urgency parameter is defined as an integer of value between 0 and 7. Intuitively, these values can be seen as individual priority buckets or levels, similar to the *spdyrr* scheme. These buckets are intended to be given bandwidth from low to high. The Incremental boolean parameter then defines whether resources sharing the same Urgency level should best be sent using a sequential (Incremental = 0) or an RR (Incremental = 1) scheduler. As such, unlike in the dependency tree setup, a resource's priority is no longer directly dependent on its relationship to other resources (parent or child), but is rather defined in a standalone, declarative fashion.

While simple in nature, this setup nevertheless provides all the benefits we had envisioned. Firstly, it can emulate (simplified versions of) both the *zeroweight* and *Bucket HTML* schemes. Secondly, it makes it easy to incorporate server-side overrides, as this only requires changing the Urgency and/or Incremental parameter values. Similarly, this makes it easy to re-prioritize resources. Thirdly, it can easily be emulated by a dependency tree in existing H2 deployments. Fourthly, it is easy to extend with more semantic parameters later (e.g.,

---

[9] github.com/WICG/priority-hints.

to indicate the resource is RenderBlocking or OnScreen) to provide more fine-grained scheduling options.

At the time of writing, implementation of this new scheme is expected to start soon in several HTTP/3 implementations and thus an evaluation of this setup is left for future work.

## 6.2 Transport Layer Multiplexing

Evaluating both QUIC transport layer (Sect. 2.3) and HTTP/3 application layer (Sect. 5.3) behaviours allows us to draw conclusions about their possible interplays.

The problems that might arise are most evident in our discussions of Round-Robin schedulers. As we have shown for H3, these can lead to worst case web page loading performance, as they can delay the full download of key resources compared to a sequential scheduler. Consequently, it is somewhat counter-intuitive to find that RR was the default for H2 and that a majority of QUIC implementations in fact implements RR as their default scheduler. The latter could be explained by the fact that QUIC can be used as a general purpose transport protocol, and is probably implemented that way in most stacks. As such, it should indeed not just be tuned for HTTP/3, as other use cases might in fact prefer Round-Robin schedulers. Still, this again highlights the need for clear and flexible QUIC-level prioritization APIs to allow H3 implementations running on top to specify more sequential behaviours as needed. As discussed in Sect. 2.3, these APIs are currently not well defined, which might lead to problems down the line.

Somewhat contradictory to the previous paragraph is that, while we have found RR to perform badly for loading web pages on lossless networks, we have also seen it is the optimal approach for reducing transport layer HOL blocking. This is in opposition to more sequential schemes, which seem better for web page loading, but are more at risk of becoming HOL blocked. However, it is unclear how much of an impact HOL blocking actually has on web page loading, as we only explored its behaviour on the transport layer. Future work is needed to explore the impact of the complex combination of congestion control, packet loss and application layer multiplexing behaviour.

## References

1. Bocchi, E., De Cicco, L., Rossi, D.: Measuring the quality of experience of web users. In: Proceedings of the 2016 Workshop on QoE-based Analysis of Data Communication Networks, Internet-QoE 2016, pp. 37–42. ACM (2016)
2. Davies, A., Meenan, P.: HTTP/2 priorities test page. https://github.com/andydavies/http2-prioritization-issues. Accessed Dec 2018
3. De Coninck, Q., et al.: Pluginizing QUIC. In: Proceedings of the ACM Special Interest Group on Data Communication, pp. 59–74. ACM (2019)
4. Iyengar, J., Thomson, M.: QUIC: A UDP-based multiplexed and secure transport. Internet-Draft 24, IETF Secretariat, November 2019. http://www.ietf.org/internet-drafts/draft-ietf-quic-transport-24

5. Oku, K., Pardue, L.: Extensible Prioritization Scheme for HTTP. https:// github.com/httpwg/http-extensions/blob/master/draft-ietf-httpbis-priority.md. Accessed Dec 2019

6. Marx, R., De Decker, T., Quax, P., Lamotte, W.: Of the utmost importance: resource prioritization in HTTP/3 over QUIC. In: Proceedings of the 15th International Conference on Web Information Systems and Technologies: WEBIST, pp. 130–143. INSTICC, SciTePress (2019)

7. Netravali, R., Goyal, A., Mickens, J., Balakrishnan, H.: Polaris: faster page loads using fine-grained dependency tracking. In: Proceedings of the 13th USENIX Conference on Networked Systems Design and Implementation, NSDI 2016, pp. 123–136, March 2016

8. Meenan, P.: Optimizing HTTP/2 prioritization with BBR and tcp_notsent_lowat. https://blog.cloudflare.com/http-2-prioritization-with-nginx. Accessed Oct 2018

9. Meenan, P.: HTTP/2 priorities test page. https://blog.cloudflare.com/better-http-2-prioritization-for-a-faster-web. Accessed Mar 2019

10. Meenan, P.: HTTP/3 prioritization proposal. https://github.com/pmeenan/http3-prioritization-proposal. Accessed Feb 2019

11. RFC7540: HTTP/2. https://tools.ietf.org/html/rfc7540. Accessed May 2015

12. Marx, R.: qlog logging format. https://github.com/quiclog/internet-drafts. Accessed Oct 2019

13. Marx, R., De Decker, T.: Quicker: TypeScript QUIC and HTTP/3 implementation. https://github.com/rmarx/quicker. Accessed June 2019

14. Ruamviboonsuk, V., Netravali, R., Uluyol, M., Madhyastha, H.V.: Vroom: accelerating the mobile web with server-aided dependency resolution. In: Proceedings of the ACM SIG on Data Communication, pp. 390–403. ACM (2017)

15. SPDY: SPDY Protocol (2014). https://www.chromium.org/spdy/spdy-protocol

16. Swett, I., Marx, R.: IETF QUIC interim: HTTP/3 priorities status update. https://github.com/quicwg/wg-materials/blob/master/interim-19-05/priorities. pdf. Accessed May 2019

17. Wang, X.S., Balasubramanian, A., Krishnamurthy, A., Wetherall, D.: Demystifying page load performance with WProf. In: Proceedings of the USENIX Conference on Networked Systems Design and Implementation, NSDI 2013, pp. 473–486, April 2013

18. Wang, X.S., Krishnamurthy, A., Wetherall, D.: Speeding up web page loads with Shandian. In: Proceedings of the 13th USENIX Conference on Networked Systems Design and Implementation, NSDI 2016, pp. 109–122, March 2016

19. Wijnants, M., Marx, R., Quax, P., Lamotte, W.: HTTP/2 prioritization and its impact on web performance. In: Proceedings of the 2018 World Wide Web Conference, WWW 2018, pp. 1755–1764. ACM (2018). https://doi.org/10.1145/3178876. 3186181

# CATI: An Extensible Platform Supporting Assisted Classification of Large Datasets

Gabriela Bosetti⬭ and Előd Egyed-Zsigmond(✉)⬭

Université de Lyon, LIRIS UMR 5205 CNRS, Bâtiment Blaise Pascal,
20 Avenue Albert Einstein, 69621 Villeurbanne, France
{gabriela.bosetti,elod.egyed-zsigmond}@insa-lyon.fr

**Abstract.** More and more, researchers in humanities and companies need large classified document data-sets. These users are not familiar with information retrieval or data science notions. For data scientists, there is also often a need for those classified document data-sets as ground truth. There are multiple tools that allow users to carry out this classification task on large data-sets, involving always a quite expert level in computer and data science. More over, these tools are not usually oriented to the domain of micro-blogs or do not always take into account meta data and attached images as additional dimensions to improve the classification. In this work, we present a platform to enable end users to classify large document collections of several hundred thousands documents in an assisted way, within a humanly acceptable number of clicks, with no coding and without having data science and information retrieval expert knowledge. The system includes a graphical user interface with several classification assistants doing text- and image-based event detection, geographical filtering, image clustering, search services with rich visual metaphors to visualize their results and finally Active Learning (AL) with different sampling strategies. We also present a comparative study on the impact of using different and interchangeable AL components on the number of clicks needed to reach a stable level of accuracy.

**Keywords:** Document classification · Active learning · Human-computer interaction · User-centric systems · Web information filtering and retrieval

## 1 Introduction

Today, there are plenty of tools and techniques to classify large datasets, assigning one or multiple categories to documents according to their content (which may be of diverse nature, e.g. textual, visual). There are very flexible and

Supported by LABEX IMU under the project IDENUM: Identitées numériques urbaines. http://imu.universite-lyon.fr/projet/idenum-identites-numeriques-urbaines.

A. Bozzon et al. (Eds.): WEBIST 2019, LNBIP 399, pp. 127–147, 2020.
https://doi.org/10.1007/978-3-030-61750-9_6

low-level frameworks and libraries like Mallet [15], Apache openNLP[1], GEN-SIM [17], spaCy [10] or NLTK [9], that allow creating classification solutions in conjunction with well-known languages like R, Python or Java. These solutions are nevertheless only for those who have some background in software development and data science or who are willing to go first through a learning stage, which may turn out time-consuming and difficult.

Moreover, there are hardly any solution to classify large document collections at a higher level of abstraction and user friendly interface for those users without knowledge in Natural Language Processing (NLP) or a technological background but a deep understanding of the domain problem to solve. On the other hand, NLP experts usually need help from domain specialists when building ground truth training corpora, for instance, when annotating clinical documents [7]. This work has been developed around the need of generating tools for analyzing the use of social networks and urban digital data to "get the pulse" of the city of Lyon, France. The name of the general project is IDENUM[2], which integrates the interests of partners from the local government, industry and the academia, the Social and the Computer Sciences. As computer scientists, our challenge, then, is to provide the means to overcome the gap between domain experts and data scientists and provide tools usable by all the partners of the project enabling the collection and analysis of large data-sets. End users are people who do not necessarily know about the software development process and technologies, but who are capable of understanding the meaning of the collected information an know how to combine high-level constructs to handle their data in different ways by applying diverse functionalities to it or configuring some of their parameters with the more convenient values. This is what Lieberman [13] calls Parameterization, and in the context of document classification these users can be very useful at the moment of carrying out a classification process to generate ground truth datasets.

Today, there are multiple Parametrization tools facilitating data scientists the classification and annotation of large collections of documents (see Sect. 4). However, very few empower users to build their own classified corpora in the domain of microblogs and targetting event detection on textual and visual content, and their results may not always match the whole amount of documents in the dataset. For instance, MABED [8] is a tool allowing users to detect events based on textual features, but before running the algorythm they must specify how many events it should try to detect, and this number may not cover the full amount of events and documents in the dataset. The situation may be worst if the user has little or no information at all about a large dataset. In contexts like this, annotating the remaining documents (those not included in the detected events) can be expensive.

In general terms, the task of annotating large datasets might be expensive and time-consuming to perform for a human in a non-assisted way. Sometimes there are training sets that can be used with an existing model to automatically classify the data, but sometimes not. Or soemtimes, there is a training set but the

---

[1] https://opennlp.apache.org.

[2] http://imu.universite-lyon.fr/projet/idenum-identites-numeriques-urbaines.

available labels are scarce. Fortunately, Active Learning (AL) [18] helps to overcome these problems by the construction and refinement of classifiers through incremental enhancements and requiring only minimal supervision. The idea behind AL in a machine learning classification process is to improve the quality of the training set in an iterative way by selecting carefully additional elements to submit to a manual classification. AL is useful specially in situations where we have a large dataset to classify with a very small initial training dataset. It can start from scratch by selecting the "N" most informative instances (usually called sample queries) from a fully unclassified dataset and asking an oracle (an entity, usually a human) to label them with a category, moving these labeled instances into the training set, after the first set of labeling, a first classification model is trained. The full process is repeated until a stopping criterion is met (e.g. max number of iterations or labeled data, exhausted labeling budget, etc.). This way, assisting users to carry out a classification can be beneficial. And it is, even if the initial classified data is imbalanced. In this sense, Miller et al. [16] demonstrated that Active Learning with an Uncertainty Sampling strategy performs better in such conditions.

In a previous work [2], we presented a platform assisting end users to quickly and easily classify documents in any domain. We presented a preliminary study based on just two Active Learning sampling strategies and a single dataset. Now, we extend this work by using a wider spectrum of components, fields, vectorizers, models, and datasets. In this work, we present:

- CATI: a user friendly web platform assisting and minimizing user efforts in classifying large document collections. Its target users may have no or little knowledge in data science and programming.
- A visual interface to conduct the AL based assisted classification.
- A study comparing the Active Learning results of diverse datasets, using different attributes, vectorizers, classification models and sampling strategies. The goal is to detect which combination minimizes the required number of clicks to classify the datasets.

We tested our system with collections containing Tweets and journal articles.

This article is organized as follows: Sect. 2 introduces our approach and our supporting tool; Sect. 4 presents the state-of-the-art; Sect. 3 reports a study on the use of the diverse components of our tool over different datasets; finally, Sect. 4.1 presents the conclusions and perspectives of our work.

## 2   An Assisted System for Large Document Collection Classification

In this work, we propose a new means for end users to produce a classified dataset from a corpus of time-stamped documents (tweets, journal articles,...), eventually accompanied with images and other metadata (geographical coordinates, author identifier,...). To do so, we propose an approach supported by a pipeline of assistants that allow end users to classify the documents in 3 stages (see Fig. 1), and a platform supporting such pipeline, called CATI. The methods for each stage may be combined in different ways, and the platform we provide is extensible, so new methods can be added by developers if needed.

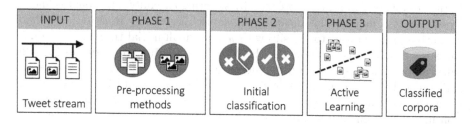

**Fig. 1.** Overall flow of the proposed pipeline [2].

Our system, CATI is helping users classify a document collection in a binary way: into a positive and a negative class. In CATI we can have several collections and for each collection we can create as many binary classification *sessions* as we want. Each *session* corresponds to a binary classification criteria. For example, a tweet dataset collected with the keyword "Lyon" (our city) in December, month when a big light festival takes place in the town can be classified in a first *session* according to the relatedness of the tweets to the light festival event, and in a second *session* according to their relatedness to football. The classification criteria are freely definable and the objective of CATI is to provide the right assistants to help the user carry out the classification quickly and with a good accuracy even for datasets containing several hundred thousands documents.

Figure 1 shows an overview of CATI's workflow. It is composed of 3 phases.

The first phase of the workflow consists in importing a new collection, pre-processing it and creating at least one session. New sessions can be created on an already imported collection later. The pre-processing phase includes event detection [5], image content based document clustering [6], word bi and tri-gram extraction and indexing an can be extended later with other feature extractors. This first phase may be time consuming, but can be executed off-line without needing the presence of the user.

The second phase is a highly interactive one. Its goal is to classify the largest subset of the collection with the fewer clicks possible in order to train a classifier model. We implemented a set of *helpers* to do this. A *helper* is a functionality, that enables a user to classify a (possibly large) subset of documents quickly, typically with less then 5 mouse clicks, based on the preprocessed features extracted in phase 1. For example: a helper detects automatically events [2] in the collection, assigns documents to the events, presents the detected events in a synthetic manner and enables users to classify with one click all the documents assigned to a given event. Another helper clusters documents according to the similarity of the accompanying images, and enables users to classify all the documents in a same image cluster with one click. A third helper groups together very similar documents according to their textual content and lets user classify each group with one click. We implemented a helper that projects geolocated documents on a map and enables users to select documents by their location drawing a polygon on the map. Another helper shows the most frequent word bi or tri-grams of the collection and enables the classification of all documents containing a selected n-gram with one click. We added filters that enable working on the collection's fragments according to their classification for the current session: only the unclassified ones, only the positive or the negative ones. We also implemented a key-phrase based search engine using elasticsearch. The search results can be filtered using all the helpers and filters mentioned above. For example, a simple way to do the initial classification would be to carry out two searches: one with a word closely related to the criteria corresponding to the current session, and another one not at all related to it. When searching, our platform provides different representations of the results; we present them in different visual modules that we call "helpers". For instance, you can observe in Fig. 2 that the results of the query with the keyword "fête" (festival) associated with geo-location are presented on a map, then the top bi-grams of all the documents matching the keyword are presented in a second frame and so on, until the final helper that simply presents a list of the individual documents.

Another way of conducting the first phase could be using the automatic event-detection helper and use textual, time and image content based features if available [5] to get a list of event-related clusters, or event-related image clusters. All the documents in such clusters can be quickly and massively annotated with the "positive" and "negative" classes with a single click.

As the classified documents usually represent a small part of the dataset, the third phase assists the user through Active Learning in the classification of the remaining documents. As you can see in Fig. 4, the process starts with the selection of the sampling algorithm (tabs) and some basic parameters. Successive forms let them choose more details on which components to use, and then the model is trained once with the initial set of annotated documents (phase 2). The non-annotated documents (in the target set) are then sorted according to the sampler's strategy. For instance, sorting them in descending order according to their distance to the classifier's hyperplane. Finally, the top documents (10 by default) are presented to the user along with the predictions of their annotations. If the predictions are wrong, the user can change them. If the user wants to continue training the model, these top documents with their labels (predicted or corrected) are moved to the training set and then model is re-trained.

Our supporting platform is called "CATI" (Classification Assistée de Textes et Images) and it is available online, as well as its documentation and demonstration videos[3]. It uses methods described in [2,8] and [5] for event detection, but we also provide alternative methods for the first two phases. The system was evaluated on short-text documents but it can be used on any time-stamped text documents that eventually have associated meta-data, like news articles.

---

[3] CATI's documentation, videos and source code: https://bitbucket.org/idenum/cati/wiki/Home.

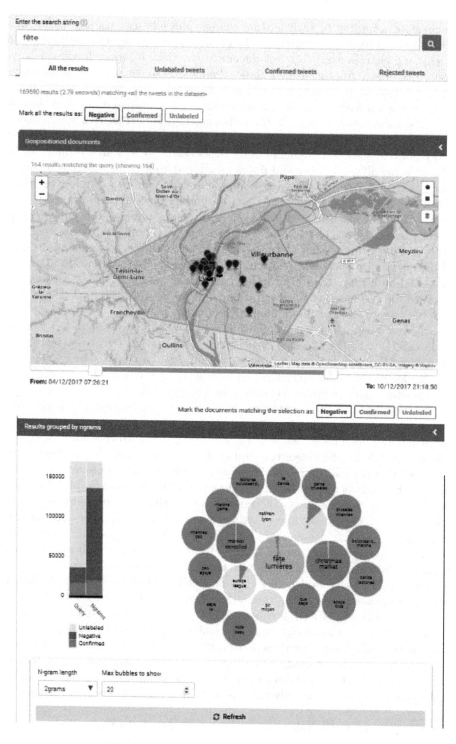

Fig. 2. Search and selection helpers in CATI.

## 2.1  Phase 1: Preprocessing Methods

At the beginning of the pipeline, the goal is to obtain subsets of documents that will be later classified as positive or negative. The objective is to have an initial classification, so there must be both positive and negative documents annotated.

One strategy to identify those subsets is through event detection, and we used two methods that were already evaluated with tweets: MABED [8] and MABED++ [5]. The first one focuses on a classification based on textual features and uses anomaly detection on word frequency to extract events. The latter improves the first and also relies on image similarity among the ones associated with different tweets. MABED++ improves MABED in two aspects: it considers the images (when present) associated to the tweets during the event detection process and it allows to retrieve documents related to a detected event. In order to include associated images to the text based event detection process, we cluster the images using a very fast almost identical image search method [6], assign a unique identifier to each image cluster and append the class identifier to the text of the documents containing the images. This way the text of the documents carrying similar images gets common tokens. The detected events are a possible target for our initial classification. An example of one of these events is presented in Fig. 3-a. You can note, that one of the characteristic keywords of the event (cluster286)is an image cluster identifier. MABED++ also clusters the tweets with images based on the image content. This is to say that for each event cluster, there are sub-clusters of images that the users may also use in the initial classification. Figure 3-b presents one of these image clusters in our platform. It is possible to classify the whole cluster with one click.

Other ways to identify subsets is by using the helpers associated to our search form: each time the user searches for some keywords, the platform presents the individual documents that match the search criteria but also some extra sections that try to provide more insights on the results. Such a query can contain several words or none. In the latter case, the search applies to the full dataset and so do the helpers. The current helpers allow users to get:

- **N-grams.** We provide a visualization of a pie-cloud with the top n-grams extracted from the documents matching the query. Each cake presents an n-gram and is divided according to the percentage of documents labeled as positive, negative or unclassified (as in Fig. 3-d). By clicking on each bi-gram, the user can access and classify all its related documents. It is also possible to filter the n-grams under a certain classification category. For example, the end user could make use of such feature to request just those that are extracted from the documents that are not yet classified.
- **Image clusters.** This helper presents the image clusters processed by MABED++. When using it together with the search functionality, we are not presenting them in relation to an event but to a specific search criteria.
- **Duplicated content.** A ranking on top duplicated-content documents is presented by this helper. In the domain of this work, most of its content may be re-tweets or re-posts 3-c. In this case, users can classify a whole group of duplicated content with one click.

It is worth to highlight that users can trigger a full-match query, that is, a query with no keywords, in order to get the top n-grams, image clusters, geo-locations and re-tweets of the whole dataset. This lets them explore the dataset and have some insight about which are the most representative terms that can be used to query and identify the target clusters for the initial classification.

## 2.2    Phase 2: Initial Classification

At this point the user should just annotate the clusters obtained in the previous phase to have an initial amount of documents for both categories: positive and negative. Therefore this phase is quite easy, since our system provides mechanisms to fully classify the clusters with just one click each. In addition the pre calculated clusters and search results can be further filtered. Fragments of the visual interface to carry out the initial classification using the events is presented in Fig. 3. These documents will be used later for the training of the AL process.

As shown in Fig. 3, the events are presented on a timeline with a list of associated words (a) and image clusters (b). A full event or an image cluster can be classified by clicking on the "Confirmed" or the "Negative" button. Therefore, not more than a single click for each cluster is required. However, in some cases the descriptive image of a cluster may not be very meaningful and it may be necessary to retrieve and check (with an extra click) the related tweets to make a decision based on their textual content. Each item on the top duplicated content (c) can be classified with a single click, while each set of tweets containing a given n-gram (d) can be classified with two clicks.

We also reused the helpers from our search form (the n-grams visualization, the duplicated content presentation) on the presentation of the event-detection results. The main motivation of these frames is to be able to understand in general terms the predominant content of the event in order to make a decision regarding its full classification.

## 2.3    Phase 3: The Active Learning (AL) Process

The most important aspect of AL is how to select the most informative instances to be presented to the oracle for manual classification. There are many methods to do so, usually referred to as "Query Learning Strategies" [18] or sampling methods. The well knwon Uncertainty Sampling method takes the instances that are closer to the hyperplane (for which it is least certain how to label), ignoring the instances it is already confident about. Then, it makes the decision based on the confidence of a measure of uncertainty, like the lower predicted label's distance to the hyperplane, to sort all the documents and to get the top queries. CATI supports different sampling methods and it is also possible to extend them. In this work, we choose to present the implementation of two sampling methods for the purpose of our evaluation: the uncertainty method and a random method. We also introduce and evaluate other extensible components, concretely the use of three classifier models and three document vectorizer methods, listed below.

- Sampling methods. The following components return a collection of documents and their predicted annotations so these can be checked by a user. A sampling method should be configured with regard to a classifier model.
  - Uncertainty Sampling [18]. It returns a list of N documents composed by the those documents with smaller values of confidence (closer to the hyperplane).
  - Random Sampling. It returns a list of N documents randomly retrieved from the unlabeled set. For the evaluation we set to run multiple times this method and calculate average values.
- Classifier approaches. Different models are used to obtain a classification based on the annotated documents provided in the training set.
  - Linear Support Vector Classification. This is a supervised learning model that takes a collection of annotated documents (represented by features) and assigns new examples to the available categories (in our case, positive and negative). The training documents are represented as points in a space, separated by a hyper-plane into different categories, and then the unlabeled documents are mapped according to their predictions into the existing categories.
  - Decision Tree Based Model. The tree is build through an iterative splitting the data into partitions to generate the rules from the analysed features, until the a decision tree covers the features in the full training set. Then, it predicts the values by learning decision rules inferred from the vector features.
  - K Nearest Neighbors Based Model. It assumes that similar things are usually clustered together, so the classification is performed through the vote of the majority of the nearest neighbors of each document.

In our architecture, a model must be configured with a vectorizer. The vectorizer precises how to get the input vectors for the classifier from the original documents.

- Vectorizers. Given a collection of documents and a target field to be considered (e.g. the text field of a tweet), these components are in charge of converting the documents into a feature vector. This vector will be used by the models to classify the documents and predict their classes.
  - Tf-Idf (Term Frequency-Inverse Document Frequency) Vectorizer. It converts a collection of documents into a matrix of features. Each row corresponds to a document and each column corresponds to a term. It is intended to appreciate the relevance of a term contained in a document at its turn being part of a collection of documents.
  - Count-Based Vectorizer (bag of words). It converts a collection of documents into a matrix of token counts. First it tokenizes a documents by using white-spaces and punctuation as token separators, and then it counts the ocurrences of each token on each document. It threats each token occurrence frequency as a feature.
  - Neural network based word embedding. Doc2Vec Based Vectorizer. It is an unsupervised algorithm to generate vector representations for documents, derivated from the word2vec algorithm.

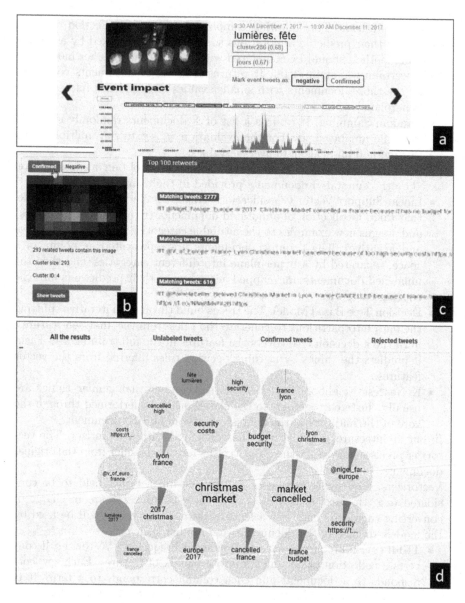

**Fig. 3.** Classification visual interface [2].

Regarding the user interface, the process is presented to the users in a separate section where they can choose the query strategy through tabs. The process is supported with a carousel (Fig. 4), and users should loop through the steps (a) and (b) until they achieve a classification they consider satisfactory. In the first step, they are presented with the predictions for the selected documents as queries (Fig. 4(a)). If any prediction is wrong, the user can toggle its value.

Then, the model is re-trained and the new classification is presented in step (b), so the user can analyze the results and decide to continue for a further loop or not.

## 3  An Evaluation on the Active Learning Strategy

In this section we present an analysis on the supported Active Learning artifacts in CATI. The goal is to check which is the most convenient configuration in terms of attribute, vectorizer, classification model and sampler to conduct Active Learning assisted binary classification on documents. We call such a combination of components a configuration. In this section we present the experiments we conducted in order to find the best configuration.

### 3.1  Groundtruth

In order to evaluate our assisted classification system, we used 4 different data-sets associated to one different classification criteria each. Each data-set has two sessions: one for the groundtruth and another one for the target experiment based on the same classification criteria. We call our sessions: FDL17, FOOT16, AFR and GEO_LYO.

Below, we mention how we harvested and annotated the documents for the groundtruth sessions:

- FDL17: for this collection, the documents were collected from December 2 to 13, 2017, using the Twitter streaming API and querying the word "Lyon". They were analysed with regards to their link with the "Fête des Lumiéres" (a light festival) event. It has 21912 documents, of which 5727 documents were annotated with the "positive" label and the remaining ones with the "negative" label. A filtering criteria was that all the documents have –at least– one image associated. The positive documents are those whose content is related to the Fête des Lumiéres 2017, and the negative documents are those that are not linked to such event. The annotation was carried out manually by 4 persons.
- FOOT16: The documents were collected from November 24 to December 12, 2016, using the Twitter API and querying the word "Lyon". The positive documents are those whose content is linked to football, and the negative documents are those that are not linked to such events. This collection has 47109 documents, of which 32252 were annotated as "positive" and the remaining ones as "negative". All the documents have –at least– one image associated.
- AFR: The documents are journal articles and were collected from December 7 to 11, 2015 in the frame of an international classification challenge and provided with their annotations[4]. The documents on this dataset have no images associated. The positive documents are those whose content is linked

---

[4] https://dataverse.harvard.edu/dataset.xhtml?persistentId=doi:10.7910/DVN/28075.

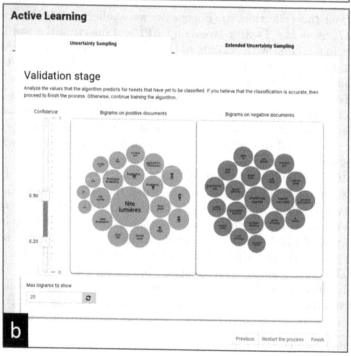

**Fig. 4.** Active learning interface [2]

to any kind of protest, and the negative documents are those that are not linked to such topic. It has 48451 documents, of which 12341 were annotated as "positive" and the remaining ones as "negative".

- GEO_LYO: This is again a Tweet dataset. The documents were collected from September 13, 2017, to February 22, 2019. The documents on this dataset have no images associated but are all precisely geo-located. The positive documents are those geo-located within the boundaries of the city of Lyon (France) and the negative documents are those with a different location. This dataset has 55496 documents, of which 20851 were annotated as "positive" and the remaining ones as "negative".

In the first two cases and the last one, the datasets come from Twitter and were collected using the same method and keywords. In all cases, the content of the documents is of short length. In all cases, there are repeated documents (e.g. retweets or republished articles).

In the following subsections, we present the a general overview of how we conducted our experiments, each individual scenario and the results for each case.

## 3.2  Experiment Setup

In all the cases, we started by annotating some documents in each experimental session. The way we choose those documents were the following: we analyzed the top bi-grams in the full dataset to have an idea of the most representative words. Then we picked two words : one representing the target criteria (e.g. Football for the FOOT16 session to get potentially positive documents), and another word representing another non related event (Christmas for the FOOT16 session to retrieve potentially negative documents). Then, we used CATI's search engine to search for documents containing those words, and we annotated some documents as positive or negative. For the FOOT16, FDL17 and AFR sessions, we annotated the Top-5 repeated content (the documents having the most frequently repeated content: re-tweets or identical journal articles) presented in the search results. For the GEO_LYO session, we annotated 10 documents as positive and 10 documents as negative, since the retweets we analized were not completely localized in Lyon and we adopted a different strategy to avoid introducing wrongly annotated documents in the training set. In all cases, the annotated documents represented the initial classification, and were used as the first training set for the Active Learning process.

- FDL17: we choose to annotate the Top-5 retweets presented in the search results, when searching for "foot" (1324 documents were marked as negative) and for "fête" (1231 documents marked as positive). These documents represented the initial classification, and were used as the training set for the Active Learning process.
- FOOT16: we annotated the Top-5 retweets matching "8décembre" marked as negative (217) and the Top-5 retweets matching "league" marked as positive (918).

- AFR: we annotated the Top-5 retweets matching "exchange + fighters" marked as negative (21), and the Top-5 retweets matching "demonstrations" marked as positive (37).
- GEO_LYO: as the tweets in the groundtruth were marked by localization, marking full retweets was not a possibility since that introduced wrong elements in the training set. Therefore, we annotated 10 tweets matching "Bellecour" as positive, and 10 tweets matching "gare paris" as negative. We checked that those tweets were geolocalized in Lyon and in Paris for the latter.

Then, we run 10 loops of the the Active Learning process with each possible combination of attribute, vectorizer, clasification model and sampler available in our platform. These components are listed below:

- Attributes: text and bi-grams.
- Vectorizers: TFIDF, token count and Doc2Vec.
- Clasification models: Linear SVC, Decision Tree, KNeighbors.
- Samplers: a Random Sampler and an Uncertainty Sampler.

For each possible combination of these components, we logged the results of the 10 loops in separate numbered files that we call "configuration files". Such a configuration file is identified by a number, but it contains the information regarding which attribute, vectorizer, learner and sampler were used in order to get the accuracy at each loop.

Here are some configuration examples (configuration number and components:

- #001 is calculated on the text as attribute, composed of the TFIDF vectorizer, the Uncertainty sampler and the Linear SVC classification model
- #018 is calculated on frequent bi-grams as attributes, composed of the TFIDF vectorizer, the Random sampler and the Linear SVC classification model
- #024 is calculated on frequent bi-grams as attributes, composed of the count based vectorizer, the Random sampler and the Linear SVC classification model

Finally, we took the results of the experiments for each configuration file and for each dataset and reported the ones that performed best taking into account the results in all scenarios. To get the best combinations, we calculated a score for each configuration file in the 4 datasets as shown in Eqs. (1), (2) and (3). This score combines components concerning accuracy and gives a sorted list of the best configurations.

For each (configuration, dataset) pair we get 10 values of accuracy across the 10 loops of active learning. The goal of this experiment is to get the configurations that give best accuracy over all the datasets and show a homogeneous increasing tendency in accuracy. In order to evaluate this we created a score (1) that is given by a linear combination of accuracy values and the *shape* of the histogram given by the accuracy values across the active learning loops.

Equation (1) sums two parts : accuracy and shape. The first part of the sum : $\frac{Acc_{c,d}}{loops_{c,d}}$ represents the average of the accuracy ($Acc_{c,d}$) in the 10 loops of a configuration (c) for a given dataset (d), where $Acc_{c,d}$ is the sum of accuracy values of the classification results of different active learning loops and $loops_{c,d}$ is the number of active learning loops (here = 10). We get an accuracy score for a given configuration on a given dataset across 10 active learning loops.

$$Q_{c,d} = \alpha \frac{Acc_{c,d}}{loops_{c,d}} + (1-\alpha)(1 - \frac{\sum(abs(negGrad_{c,d}))}{\sum(abs(grad_{c,d}))}) \tag{1}$$

The second part of the sum in Eq. (1) concerns the shape of the histograms. It allows avoiding big decreases in the individual curves of accuracy. This is to say, we expect to favour those configurations which curves are growing and not decreasing a lot. To do so, we traversed all the accuracy values across the 10 loops from each configuration with a same number, and we summed the values of the negative gradients ($negGrad$) across values corresponding to consecutive loop pairs. Then, we divided the result by the sum of all the gradients ($grad$). This way we get a number between 0 and 1, that will be subtracted from 1, so the curves with a low amount of negative values will have a higher scores and will be better positioned than the ones with big amount of negative gradients. A constantly increasing histogram denotes a better configuration, since the active learning loops are supposed to improve the global accuracy of the classification.

The two parts of the equation are combined using a weight coefficient $\alpha \in [0,1]$, that allows us control which part of the global score has more weight. We tested all the multiple values of 0.1 between 0 and 1, and we finally choose $\alpha = 0.2$ as the best value. This is to say that the second part of the formula was more important to get better results.

Equation (2) gives a score $C_{c,D}$ to a configuration c over all the datasets $D$ that avoids having configurations with high divergence for all the datasets. The results of a configuration (c) with a same number is taken from each dataset (d) –e.g. #001 drom AFR, #001 from FDL17, etc–, and then their accuracy values measured across 10 loops. The accuracy values give a histogram for each dataset. We calculate the Kullback-Leibler divergence between each pair of histograms. $KL_{c,i,j}$ denotes the Kullback-Leibnitz divergence of histograms over datasets $i$ and $j$ calculated with configuration c. We get a sum of divergence values that are then used to get an average divergence value. In the Eq. (2) we denote $Subs_D = \{(i,j)|i \neq j, i \in D, j \in D\}$ the set of all distinct dataset pairs in the set $D$ of the datasets. This value is divided by the maximum divergence value ($max_{((i,j) \in Subs_D)}(KL_{c,i,j})$) so the result is normalized, as in the previous equation, to a number between 0 and 1. The higher such value, the higher is the divergence and we want to avoid this, so we subtract this value from 1 in the final score.

$$C_{c,D} = 1 - \frac{\frac{\sum_{(i,j) \in Subs_D}(KL_{c,i,j})}{count(Subs_D)}}{max_{((i,j) \in Subs_D)}(KL_{c,i,j})} \tag{2}$$

Finally, a general score is calculated for each configuration contemplating its values on each datatset. Equation 3 shows the weignhted sum of the formulas

1 and 2, being pondered by a $\beta$ value. In our case, we fond out that $\beta = 0.9$ generats the best results, presented in Sect. 3.3, which tells us that the quality of the dataset is, in this context, more important than the coherence across the datasets.

$$Score_{c,D} = \beta * Q_{c,d} + (1 - \beta) * C_{c,D} \tag{3}$$

## 3.3  Results

In this section we present the results of the experiments concerning accuracy. First, we observed which are the top-10 best configurations for each dataset, and try to identify if there is any configuration repeated in the 4 rankings. We could observe that configurations 6, 7, 8 and 18 were present on 3 of the rankings, as you can check in Table 1.

Table 1. Top-10 best configurations for each dataset.

| Ranking | FOOT16 | LYO | FDL17 | AFR |
|---------|--------|-----|-------|-----|
| 1 | **018** | 015 | **006** | **007** |
| 2 | 024 | **018** | 024 | 025 |
| 3 | 022 | 030 | 027 | 026 |
| 4 | **006** | 031 | **018** | 001 |
| 5 | 027 | 019 | 021 | **006** |
| 6 | 013 | 020 | 003 | 000 |
| 7 | 026 | **007** | **008** | **008** |
| 8 | **008** | 005 | **007** | 009 |
| 9 | 002 | 032 | 009 | 013 |
| 10 | 020 | 000 | 023 | 031 |

But those combinations are not present in all the datasets, so we got the best combination of components across all the datasets by aplying the Eq. (3). Using this score, we sorted all the configurations. Figure 5 presents a fragment of the sorted configurations represented by histograms with curves for all the 4 datasets. The vertical scale shows the accuracy of the classification obtained at the active learning loop corrsponding to the x axis. As you can observe, the values at the top-left of the figure (configuration #018) are better than the ones at the right-bottom area (configuration #028); graphs at the top present more coherent and high values than the ones in the bottom.

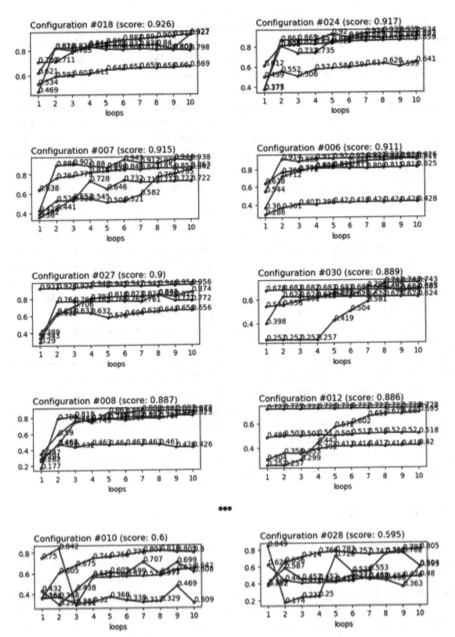

**Fig. 5.** General results on accuracy covering all the datasets.

All the possible combinations of components resulted in 36 configuration files. Figure 5 presents the first 6 best configurations, and the lasttwo worst configurations. There you can observe that 3 of the 4 configurations highlighted in Table 1 are also among the top-4 best configurations obtained with the Eq. 3.

The best configuration is #018, which was also one of the best ones in Table 1. Such configuration combines the processing of the "bigrams" field of the documents, which was vectorized with our TfidfBasedVectorizer component. The model used was a Linear SVC, and the sampler was random. The number of negative gradients in the curve "accuracy & loop number" was 3 over 10 loops. The average accuracy across all the datasets is 0.7651. The general score obtained with Formula 3 was 0.926. This combination of components has also one of the best averages on corrective clicks, which is 3.2 clicks by loop. This is to say that the predictions on the samples presented to the user were mostly right, and that few clicks were needed to correct the few wrong predictions. Therefore, it is good from a user interaction point of view, since it requires less clicks to get a good accuracy.

Configuration #024 achieved the best second place with an average accuracy of 0.7589 across all the datasets, and a general score of 0.917. This combination included vectorizing the "2grams" arrtibute with our CountBasedVectorizer, classifying the documents with a Linear SVC and sampling with a random sampler. The configuration #006, at the fourth place, has the same combination of components, but vectorizing a different attribute: "text" instead of "2grams". It achieved an average accuracy of 0.7167 and a score of 0.911.

The third place belongs to the configuration #007, and it is the first configuration with a different sampler: the UncertaintySampler. It vectorized the "text" field with a CountBasedVectorizer and the model used was a Linear SVC. The average accuracy across all the datasets is 0.7253, and the general score is 0.915. The average number of clicks across the 10 loops was 5.

As you go down in Fig. 5 to the lower graphs, you can see how the curves of the 4 datasets in each of them are less homogeneous: either because they differ in shape or in value. In contrast, the curves shown in the upper part of the Figure have a more similar shape, they start at much higher values at the first loop and reach much higher values at the end of the process.

## 4    Related Work

GATE (General Architecture for Text Engineering) [4] is a big family of tools for developing software components for Natural Language Processing (NLP). It allows achieving document annotation and classification, but it is not intended for non-technical users. They depend, at some point, on NLP experts to develop or combine some components data structures and algorithms. GATE can be extended to deal with micro-blogs content classification, like TwitIE [1]; it is a NLP pipeline to deal with micro-blog text. However, carrying out the classification still requires a higher level of knowledge for users to operate with GATE.

NLPReViz [20] is another annotation tool but specialized in the medical field that reduces the time to create an annotated corpus by interactively and continuously improving the accuracy of its predictive model by involving the user in the process. As in this example, there are other tools specialized in a concrete domain and targetting microblog content but CATI has the advantage to not be tied to a single domain; it enables the user to massively label a whole class of documents associated with a certain image, event, n-gram or simply with all the results retrieved from a search.

MonkeyLearn[5] is an online Machine Learning platform for Text Analysis allowing users to process different kinds of documents (e.g. tweets, chats) and create and test their models through a graphical interface. This tool, compared to the previous ones, is conceived from a user-centered and general-purpose point of view. Nevertheless, we have not found documentation on the design of the models to contrast our work, but we can differentiate since CATI also uses the images associated with the documents to cluster them and into related documents, and that the user can easily apply different classification methods to the same dataset. Our method implements in addition, a non supervised event detection method in the preprocessing phase.

Concerning context of event detection, Guille & Favre [8] consider this kind of event as something that happens at a specific time and may be discussed by traditional media. Events can be of different nature; planned social events, such as celebrations, shows, plays, conferences, marathons, social demonstrations but also unplanned events, like natural or practical events as natural disasters, traffic crashes, something taking place in quarters, buildings, in a unique or multiple locations. In this context, Katragadda et al. [12] propose a topic evolution model to quickly detect events from Twitter streaming in real-time. They conducted an experiment where tweets were collected in micro-batches of a same time period. Then, it detects the start of an event by comparing the terms frequency over the most recent time periods to the historical frequencies of the same term. As a result, they generate a co-occurrences graph, that later is pruned to reduce the number of nodes, and clustered with a voltage based clustering algorithm. Finally, some clusters are eliminated and the resulting ones represent the collection of detected events.

Cai et al. [3] present STM-TwitterLDA (Spatio-Temporal Multimodal TwitterLDA), which differentiates from TwitterLDA in the distribution they use to model the topic (location- vs user-specific), and the number of features they consider. One of their main contributions is the consideration of images as a feature; this is, the visual properties of the images associated to a tweet. They filter some images, as the ones representing "stop words" (cartoons, landscapes, diagrams or text-based screenshots) and "general words" (noisy images) so they just keep "specific images", which are the ones meant to visually describe the event. Then, they apply convolutional neural network to represent images as text.

Concerning Active Learning, Spina et al. [19] analyze its effectiveness for entity filtering in social media; extracting topics, conversations, and trends around a concrete entity. They used a linear Support Vector Machine and different sampling methods (random, uncertainty and density sampling) to compare their results. They retrain the model after every single query labeled by the user. The authors find out that using uncertainty sampling is effective and the strategy that works best for this task (among the ones they used).

---

[5] https://monkeylearn.com/.

Regarding AL and microblogging, Hu et al. [11] model textual content to incorporate social network information to later analyze whether the social relations can improve the active learning results. They propose two query sampling methods: a global one, aimed at labeling highly representative documents in a network to propagate the information through a big number of nodes in a whole network; or a local one, aimed at finding the most representative local documents from within-group connections rather than between-group (global) connections. In the evaluation, the authors use a Support Vector Machine classifier and compare different query strategies, as Random Sampling, Uncertainty Sampling or Query by Committee against two of their methods with a global or local selection strategy. In contrast, we do not directly consider the relationships between users in the AL process.

Makki et al. [14] proposes a user-driven approach for the retrieval of Twitter content through AL strategies. The aim is to improve the searching in social media by supporting the exploration of potentially relevant tweets. They propose starting with an initial unsupervised retrieval (extracting discriminative features using tf-idf) with no user intervention and then a second component applies 4 AL query sampling strategies comprising the highest similarity to a debate, similar content (not exactly the same), frequent hashtags and post replies. In contrast, our starting clusters represent events or images, not used in this approach, and our sampling strategies consider exactly duplicated documents and bigrams as well.

### 4.1 Conclusions

In this work, we presented an extensible platform to assist and try to minimize the user efforts in the construction of an annotated corpus from large datasets. The platform does not require users to have knowledge in data science and classification; it is intended for anyone. The platform have different extension points to add new components at the different stages of a proposed pipeline: preprocessing, initial classification and Active Learning.

All the combinations of the available components of the Active Learning stage were used in an evaluation. In this way we were able to obtain the combination of components that best suits 4 datasets. The challenge was also to find a way to classify all possible combinations and their results to know which is the best combination; we proposed a formula to do that.

The evaluation was carried out on a total of 10 loops in the Active Learning process, with a sampling of only 10 documents in each loop. In general terms we can say that CATI allows to reach a high level of accuracy with a reasonable number of clicks (less than 100 clicks).

## References

1. Bontcheva, K., Derczynski, L., Funk, A., Greenwood, M.A., Maynard, D., Aswani, N.: TwitIE: an open-source information extraction pipeline for microblog text. In: Proceedings of the International Conference Recent Advances in Natural Language Processing, pp. 83–90 (2013)

2. Bosetti, G., Egyed-Zsigmond, E., Ono, L.: CATI: an active learning system for event detection on mibroblogs' large datasets. In: Proceedings of the 15th International Conference on Web Information Systems and Technologies. Scitepress (2019). https://doi.org/10.5220/0008355301510160, https://www.scitepress.org/ProceedingsDetails.aspx?ID=tv9WTo7buso=&t=1

3. Cai, H., Yang, Y., Li, X., Huang, Z.: What are popular : exploring twitter features for event detection, tracking and visualization. In: Proceedings of the 23rd ACM International Conference on Multimedia, pp. 89–98 (2015)

4. Cunningham, H., Maynard, D., Bontcheva, K.: Text Processing with Gate. Gateway Press, Sheffield (2011)

5. Odeh, F.: Event detection in heterogeneous data streams. Technical report Lyon (2018)

6. Gaillard, M., Egyed-Zsigmond, E.: Large scale reverse image search-a method comparison for almost identical image retrieval. In: INFORSID, pp. 127–142 (2017)

7. Gobbel Dr, G.T., et al.: Assisted annotation of medical free text using RapTAT. J. Am. Med. Inf. Assoc. 21(5), 833–841 (2014)

8. Guille, A., Favre, C.: Mention-anomaly-based event detection and tracking in twitter. In: ASONAM 2014 - Proceedings of the 2014 IEEE/ACM International Conference on Advances in Social Networks Analysis and Mining, pp. 375–382 (2014)

9. Hardeniya, N., Perkins, J., Chopra, D., Joshi, N., Mathur, I.: Natural Language Processing: Python and NLTK. Packt Publishing Ltd., Sebastopol (2016)

10. Honnibal, M., Montani, I.: spacy 2: natural language understanding with bloom embeddings, convolutional neural networks and incremental parsing (2017)

11. Hu, X., Tang, J., Gao, H., Liu, H.: ActNeT: Active Learning for Networked Texts in Microblogging (2013)

12. Katragadda, S., Virani, S., Benton, R., Raghavan, V.: Detection of event onset using Twitter. In: Proceedings of the International Joint Conference on Neural Networks, pp. 1539–1546 (2016).https://doi.org/10.1109/IJCNN.2016.7727381

13. Lieberman, H., Paternò, F., Klann, M., Wulf, V.: End-user development: an emerging paradigm. In: Lieberman, H., Paternò, F., Wulf, V. (eds.) End User Development, Chapter 1, pp. 1–8. Springer, Netherlands, Dordrecht (2006). https://doi.org/10.1007/1-4020-5386-X_1

14. Makki, R.: ATR-Vis: visual and interactive information retrieval for parliamentary discussions in twitter. ACM Trans. Knowl. Disc. Data 12(1), 33 (2018)

15. McCallum, A.: MALLET: A Machine Learning for Language Toolkit. http://mallet.cs.umass.edu (2002)

16. Miller, B., Linder, F., Mebane Jr., W.R.: Active Learning Approaches for Labeling Text. Technical report, University of Michigan, Ann Arbor, MI (2018). http://www-personal.umich.edu/~wmebane/active-learning-approaches-4-18-2018.pdf

17. Řehůřek, R., Sojka, P.: Gensim - statistical semantics in python. In: EuroScipy (2011)

18. Settles, B.: Active learning literature survey. University of Wisconsin-Madison Department of Computer Sciences, Technical report (2009)

19. Spina, D., Peetz, M.H., de Rijke, M.: Active Learning for Entity Filtering in Microblog Streams, pp. 975–978. ACM, New York (2015). https://doi.org/10.1145/2766462.2767839

20. Trivedi, G., Pham, P., Chapman, W.W., Hwa, R., Wiebe, J., Hochheiser, H.: NLPReViz: an interactive tool for natural language processing on clinical text. J. Am. Med. Inf. Assoc. 25(1), 81–87 (2018)

# Progress in Adaptive Web Surveys: Comparing Three Standard Strategies and Selecting the Best

Thomas M. Prinz$^{(\boxtimes)}$, Jan Plötner, Maximilian Croissant, and Anja Vetterlein

Course Evaluation Service, Friedrich Schiller University Jena, Jena, Germany
{Thomas.Prinz,Jan.Ploetner,Maximilian.Croissant,
Anja.Vetterlein}@uni-jena.de

**Abstract.** Progress indicators inform the participants of web surveys about their state of completion and play a role in motivating participants with a special impact on dropout and answer behaviour. Researchers and practitioners should be aware of this impact and, therefore, should select the right indicator for their surveys with care. In some cases, the calculation of the progress becomes, however, more difficult than expected, especially, in adaptive surveys (with branches). Previous work explains how to compute the progress in such cases based on different prediction strategies, although the quality of prediction of these strategies still varies for different surveys. In this revised paper of a conference paper, we demonstrate the challenges of finding the best strategy for progress computation by presenting a way to select the best strategy via the RMSE measure. We show the application of this method in experimental designs with data from two large real-world surveys and in a simulation study with over $10k$ surveys. The experiments compare three prediction strategies taking into account the minimum, average, and maximum number of items that participants have to answer by the end of the survey. Selecting the mean as strategy is usually a good choice. However, we found that there is no single best strategy for every case, indicating a high dependence on the structure of the survey to produce good predictions.

**Keywords:** Progress indicator · Web survey · Prediction strategy · Simulation study

## 1 Introduction

As web information systems, web surveys are an important tool in evaluation research to provide a fast and straight-forward way to collect information from a user. They usually include a variety of questions or statements to be rated by the participants. In order to not overwhelm the user, these questions are often separated into different pages. To show the participant how much of the survey is left, many surveys include progress indicators (PIs).

© Springer Nature Switzerland AG 2020
A. Bozzon et al. (Eds.): WEBIST 2019, LNBIP 399, pp. 148–167, 2020.
https://doi.org/10.1007/978-3-030-61750-9_7

PIs serve not only informative purposes, but are linked to user's motivation to continue the survey thoroughly and answer every question diligently [6]. Typically, the PI displays the progress in percentage between 0 and 100%. There are three main differences between PIs of web surveys and PIs of other usual tasks in software, e.g., for machine learning [14] and database queries [12]. Participants of web surveys 1) have to focus on the task, 2) can influence the PI, and 3) do not necessarily have an interest on the result of the survey [21]. This means that web survey PIs take on a special role of motivating participants to continue and finish the survey. In keeping with this, it has been shown that web survey participants prefer to have a PI to be aware of their real progress [16, 21], which also functions as an indication of how much more effort is needed to finish. However, the computation of the progress can be difficult in case of surveys with *adaptivity* (branches). In previous work [19], we propose an equation to compute the progress in adaptive surveys, based on the *number of remaining items* (questions) at each point of time. This number of remaining items depends on a chosen *prediction strategy*. Such a strategy tries to predict the number of remaining items for each page since the participants may take different paths in the survey with different numbers of remaining items. For example, three known prediction strategies are: 1) take the minimum, 2) average, or 3) maximum number of remaining items [10]. However, we suspect that it depends on the structure of the survey which prediction strategy is the best. Furthermore, the comparison of the quality of the strategies seems to be not trivial.

This paper is a revised version of a conference paper [20]. It is extended with additional related work and examples. Furthermore, it provides more evidence showing that none of the three known mentioned prediction strategies is always the best, based on a simulation study with over $10k$ surveys. One main goal of this research is to find a measure in order to select the strategy that provides a prediction of the remaining items closest to the *true* number of remaining items and, therefore, the *true* progress. The *true* progress is the actual degree of completion of the survey. We support the idea of displaying the *true* progress since research in Human-Computer Interaction (HCI) reveals probable side-effects of PIs on the answer and dropout behaviour of participants [21]. Especially the progress speed (the rate in which the PI increases) seems to influence the decision whether a participant finishes a long survey [17, 21]. For example, a PI that is slow at the beginning and gets faster towards the end seems to discourage participants and causes higher dropout rates [1, 2, 15]. A meta-analysis of PI speeds by Villar et al. [21] supports these observations.

A different pattern can be observed for fast-to-slow PIs, which actually have been found to encourage the participants to finish the survey. While this might seem like a desirable outcome, there is no research regarding the perception of the whole process, i.e., how frustrating the survey was, especially towards the end. The perception of being misguided could therefore decrease any willingness to participate in future surveys and even result in a changing motivation to properly answer the survey throughout.

On the contrary, PIs which try to display the true progress and can therefore be viewed as honest representations should reduce any side-effects, could strengthen long-term motivation, and hold a greater informational value.

The recognition of imprecise PIs by the participants seems to lead to higher dropout rates as a study of Crawford et al. implies [3]. If the growth of the PI is unexpected, e.g., it does not match the amount of time mentioned in the introduction of a survey, the dropout rate increases significantly [6,22].

There are lot of discussions regarding PIs' impact on the dropout behaviour of participants. Some studies suggest that surveys without any PI have lower dropouts than surveys with a PI [3,13]. However, conversely, Heerwegh and Loosveldt state that PIs can have a positive effect on the dropout rate, as they are a highly requested tool to constantly reassess the cost of a given survey [6]. As an indication of when a survey ends could increase the motivation to finish and may therefore reduce the dropout rate [5,6]. When used as a psychological frame of reference, the effects of PIs may differ individually, as the demographic background of the participants seems to decide whether a PI has a positive or negative effect on the completion rate [3]. Other studies on the other hand claim that the effect of the PI on the dropout rate might be negligible altogether [13,22].

Besides the effect on the completion rate, survey design principles and the participant's volition have to be taken into account. As mentioned, most participants prefer to have a PI [6,16,21]. In addition, design principles, e.g., of Dillman et al. [4], claim that PIs should be typical parts of web surveys. In other words, sometimes PIs are necessary to accommodate the participants wishes and there is no room for discussions if a PI should be used or not. In those cases, the effect of the PI on the dropout rate might be small, but could be seen as a mere addition to the positive effects from a perspective of design and preference. As discussed before, this should be the case if the PI tries to show the *true* progress.

If the *true* progress should be displayed, different prediction strategies should be comparable to select the one whose predictions are nearest to the true progress. To reach the aim of a more precise progress computation, we argue in this paper that the *Root Mean Square Error (RMSE)* is the most fitting measure to describe the quality of prediction strategies for progress computation. Researchers conducting surveys can use the RMSE to determine the best known strategy for each survey and can give the participant a PI, which represents the true progress as well as possible. Furthermore, this paper shows as a second goal that the trivial prediction strategies, mentioned earlier, can lead to bad predictions in specific cases and that there is no single best strategy for all surveys. Further research should find solutions for these cases.

The paper has the following structure: First of all, we will explain in Sect. 2 how the computation of progress in adaptive surveys work and how the prediction strategies can be applied. Following this, four different measures as indicators for quality of the prediction strategy will be compared in Sect. 3. Findings will then be applied in experimental designs in Sect. 4. Section 4 argues further which measure is most suitable and explains some disadvantages with current prediction strategies. It also contains a simulation study with over 10$k$ surveys. Section 5 provides some concluding thoughts and prospects for further research.

## 2   Related Work and Preliminaries

Many studies in research take into account the differences in PI speeds. However, it is not the focus of research *how* to calculate an exact progress in web surveys (especially in surveys with high adaptivity). The first work (to the best of the authors' knowledge) is the thesis of Kaczmirek [10] that presents an equation of progress calculation in adaptive surveys. Based on this equation, our previous work [19] describes a general algorithm to predict the number of remaining items, which is part of that equation. The number of remaining items is typically unknown because of the unknown *"path"* in a survey taken by a participant. Our general algorithm allows to apply different prediction strategies to tune the progress as closely as possible to the *true* progress.

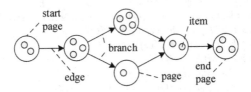

**Fig. 1.** A simple questionnaire graph (taken from the conference paper [20]).

Surveys can be considered as acyclic, connected and directed graphs (digraphs) where vertices describe pages and edges describe the control flow between these pages. Our above mentioned algorithm is based on such an abstract survey model that is called the *questionnaire graph* or in short *Q-graph*. It is an acyclic, connected digraph $Q = (\mathbb{P}, \mathbb{E})$ with a set of pages $\mathbb{P} = \mathbb{P}(Q)$ and a set of *edges* $\mathbb{E} = \mathbb{E}(Q)$, which connect the pages. Q-graphs have exactly one page without any incoming edge (the *starting page*) and exactly one page without any outgoing edge (the *ending page*). Each page of the Q-graph contains *items* (questions, etc. at the page). Therefore, each page is a finite set $\{i_1, i_2, \ldots\}$ of items $i_1, i_2, \ldots$ which are not specified in detail and are assumed to be unique in this context. Since a page $P$ is a set, $|P|$ is the number of items at $P$. Figure 1 illustrates a simple Q-graph.

A participant can reach a certain page in the Q-graph if there is a *path* from the current page to that page. A path is a sequence $W = (P_0, \ldots, P_m)$, $m \geq 0$, of pages, $P_0, \ldots, P_m \in \mathbb{P}(Q)$, where an edge exists for each two pages appearing consecutively: $\forall\, 0 \leq i < m \colon (P_i, P_{i+1}) \in \mathbb{E}(Q)$.

In our previous work [19], we generalized Kaczmireks equation to compute the progress in item precision for arbitrary Q-graphs. This equation is recursive and returns values between 0 and 1 (i.e., 0 and 100%):

$$\rho(P) = \rho(P_{prev}) + |P|\frac{1 - \rho(P_{prev})}{rem(P)} \tag{1}$$

It describes how to calculate the progress $\rho(P)$ at the current page $P$. The calculation of the current progress sums the progress $\rho(P_{prev})$ of the previous page $P_{prev}$ and the impact on the progress of the current page, $|P|\frac{1-\rho(P_{prev})}{rem(P)}$. If the current page $P$ is the starting page, then the progress $\rho(P_{prev})$ of the previous page is 0. The impact on progress of the current page depends on the number of items $|P|$ at $P$ and the impact of a single item $\frac{1-\rho(P_{prev})}{rem(P)}$. The impact of a single item contains the *remaining progress* $(1-\rho(P_{prev}))$ and the *number of remaining items* $(rem(P))$. The usage of the remaining progress in the equation allows the progress to adopt to the number of remaining items. For example, if a participant follows a branch, which reduces the number of remaining items, then the impact of each item increases, accelerating the growth of the PI. Otherwise, if the number of remaining items increases, the impact with each item decreases, decelerating the growth of the PI.

**Input:** A Q-graph $Q$ and a selection operator $\sqcup$.
**Output:** For each $P \in \mathbb{P}(Q)$ the remaining items $rem(P)$.
  Set $rem(P) = 0$ for each $P \in \mathbb{P}(Q)$
  $worklist \leftarrow queue\big(\mathbb{P}(Q)\big), visited \leftarrow \emptyset$
  **while** $worklist \neq \emptyset$ **do**
    $P \leftarrow dequeue(worklist)$
    $directSucc \leftarrow \{succ: (P, Succ) \in \mathbb{E}(Q)\}$
    **if** $directSucc \subseteq visited$ **then**
      **if** $directSucc = \emptyset$ **then**
        $rem(P) \leftarrow |P|$
      **else if** $|directSucc| = |\{Succ\}| = 1$ **then**
        $rem(P) \leftarrow |P| + rem(Succ)$
      **else**
        $rem(P) \leftarrow |P| + \bigsqcup\limits_{Succ \in directSucc} rem(Succ)$
      $visited \leftarrow visited \cup \{P\}$
    **else**
      $enqueue(worklist, P)$

**Fig. 2.** The general algorithm for computing the number of remaining items for arbitrary prediction strategies (taken from previous work [19]).

The number of remaining items $rem(P)$ is the only unknown part of (1). This number highly depends on the path a participant takes throughout the survey—which is usually unknown too. Therefore, it is necessary to predict the number of remaining items.

Different prediction strategies are possible making the computation of the progress a challenge. Our general algorithm for calculating the number of remaining items [19] allows such different strategies. An input of the algorithm is a *selection operator* $\sqcup$ representing these strategies. This operator combines different numbers of remaining items to a single prediction if the survey forks. Figure 2 shows the algorithm.

Our algorithm considers exactly three situations during the prediction of the remaining items for a page $P$ in the inner if-then-else-structure: either $P$ has 1) no successor, 2) exactly one direct successor, or 3) more than one direct successor. The number of remaining items for the first situation 1) is simply the number of items on $P$, $|P|$, since $P$ has no successor and, therefore, is the ending page. In situation 2), the number of remaining items is the sum of the number of items on $P$, $|P|$, and the number of remaining items $rem(Succ)$ of its direct successor $Succ$. Different numbers of remaining items may be possible after $P$ in situation 3) since $P$ has multiple direct successors $Succ_1, \ldots, Succ_n, n \geq 2$. This situation solves the selection operator that combines all those numbers to a single prediction. So the operator receives all those numbers as input, $\sqcup(rem(Succ_1), \ldots, rem(Succ_n))$, and gives a prediction $rem(P)$.

Typical examples of prediction strategies (i.e., selection operators) are the *minimum*, *mean*, and *maximum* functions. Taking the minimum, the number of remaining items is the *smallest* number of items. As a result, the progress is fast at the beginning and becomes slower if the participant takes a path containing more items than the operator has detected. For the maximum, it is vice versa. It represents the *largest* number of items. In the case of the *mean*, the number of remaining items of a page is always the average of numbers of remaining items of the direct successor pages.

Take a look at Fig. 3. It shows a Q-graph with 13 pages where the names of the pages are assigned to the circles. The best solution to traverse the path

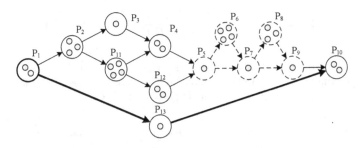

**Fig. 3.** A more complex questionnaire graph (Q-graph).

**Table 1.** The number of remaining items $rem_{min}$, $rem_{mean}$, and $rem_{max}$ for each page of the Q-graph in Fig. 3. The estimations are based on the *maximum*, *mean*, and *minimum* prediction strategies. The table shows the pages in a reverse topological order.

| Page | $rem_{min}$ | $rem_{mean}$ | $rem_{max}$ | Page | $rem_{min}$ | $rem_{mean}$ | $rem_{max}$ |
|------|------|------|------|------|------|------|------|
| $P_{10}$ | 2 | 2 | 2 | $P_3$ | 8 | 11.5 | 15 |
| $P_9$ | 3 | 3 | 3 | $P_{12}$ | 7 | 10.5 | 14 |
| $P_8$ | 6 | 6 | 6 | $P_{11}$ | 11 | 14.5 | 18 |
| $P_7$ | 4 | 5.5 | 7 | $P_2$ | 11 | 16 | 21 |
| $P_6$ | 8 | 9.5 | 11 | $P_{13}$ | 3 | 3 | 3 |
| $P_5$ | 5 | 8.5 | 12 | $P_1$ | 5 | 11.5 | 23 |
| $P_4$ | 7 | 10.5 | 14 | | | | |

is by visiting the pages in reverse topological order beginning from the ending page $P_{10}$ [19]. In a reverse topological order, each page is processed if all of its direct successor pages are processed.

For the ending page, the number of remaining items $rem(P_{10})$ is 2. This belongs to situation 1) mentioned earlier. The number of remaining items of $P_9$ is 3. It is computed by the number of remaining items of its direct successor page ($P_{10}$, 2) added with the number of its own items, 1. This belongs to situation 2). Similar holds for the number of remaining items at $P_8$ with $rem(P_8) = 6$. For page $P_7$, however, there are two direct successor pages and, therefore, two possible numbers of remaining items 6 and 3 after it. This belongs to situation 3) and the selection operator (i.e., prediction strategy) combines both values. For example, if the selection operator is the minimum function, then $rem(P_7) = min(3,6)+1 = 4$. Taking the maximum function, the number of remaining items $rem(P_7)$ is $max(3,6)+1 = 7$. Table 1 shows the number of remaining items for the Q-graph for three strategies *min*imum, *mean*, and *max*imum.

Table 1 shows obvious differences especially for the pages at the begin of the Q-graph (e.g., the remaining items on $P_1$ and $P_2$). Assume a participant takes the path $(P_1, P_2, P_{11}, P_4, P_5, P_7, P_8, P_9, P_{10})$ through the survey. Depending on the differences in the numbers of remaining items, the displayed progress differs between different strategies. For example, for the minimum strategy the progress after finishing the starting page is:

$$\rho(P_1) = \rho(P_{prev}) + |P_1|\frac{1 - \rho(P_{prev})}{rem_{min}(P_1)} = 0 + 2 * 1/5 = 40\%$$

**Table 2.** The predicted (displayed) progress $\rho_{min}$, $\rho_{mean}$, and $\rho_{max}$ for the different strategies *min*imum, *mean*, and *max*imum and the true progress $\rho_{true}$ for the path $(P_1, P_2, P_{11}, P_4, P_5, P_7, P_8, P_9, P_{10})$ of the Q-graph in Fig. 3.

| Page | $\rho_{min}$ [%] | $\rho_{mean}$ [%] | $\rho_{max}$ [%] | $\rho_{true}$ [%] |
|---|---|---|---|---|
| $P_1$ | 40.0 | 17.4 | 8.7 | 10.5 |
| $P_2$ | $40.0+3\cdot60.0/11 = 56.4$ | $17.4+3\cdot82.6/16 = 32.9$ | $8.7+3\cdot91.3/21 = 21.7$ | 26.3 |
| $P_{11}$ | 72.2 | 51.4 | 39.1 | 47.4 |
| $P_4$ | 80.2 | 60.7 | 47.8 | 57.9 |
| $P_5$ | 84.1 | 65.3 | 52.2 | 63.2 |
| $P_7$ | 88.1 | 71.6 | 59.0 | 68.4 |
| $P_8$ | 94.0 | 85.8 | 79.5 | 84.2 |
| $P_9$ | 96.0 | 90.5 | 86.3 | 89.5 |
| $P_{10}$ | 100.0 | 100.0 | 100.0 | 100.0 |

For the *mean* strategy, the displayed progress after the starting page is $2 * 1/11.5 \approx 17.4\%$, and for the maximum strategy it is $2 * 1/23 \approx 8.7\%$. Table 2 contains the progresses for all strategies for all pages on the mentioned path. It further contains the *true* progress that can be easily computed since the exact number of remaining items on this path is known. The reader may identify the (sometimes large) discrepancies between the progresses, especially at the begin of the survey. Where the progress of the minimum strategy is really fast at 50%, the progresses of the other strategies and of the true progress grow more slowly.

## 3 Selecting the Best Prediction Strategy

As shown in the example of the last section, different prediction strategies usually result in different predicted progresses. To allow the selection of a strategy for a given survey, we need a measure to compare the precision of them.

In the introduction of this paper, we argued that a PI should represent the *true* progress as well as possible. However, calculating the true progress needs the exact number of remaining items—that is only known *after* the participant has finished the survey. In other words, only after a participant completes the survey on a path $W = (P_1, \ldots, P_n)$, $n \geq 1$, the calculation knows the exact number of remaining items on each page $P_1, \ldots, P_n$ and can compute the true progress $\rho^*$.

The predicted and true progress usually have discrepancies. Given a set $\{\sqcup_1, \sqcup_2, \ldots, \sqcup_n\}$, $n \geq 1$, of prediction strategies, the *best* strategy should minimize these discrepancies. Literature proposes many measures regarding prediction accuracy and many recommendations explain in which situations a specific measure should be applied. Hyndman and Koehler [7] consider different measures of prediction accuracy in detail and provide a good overview about them. These measures have in common that they are based on the discrepancy between the predicted and the actual measured value (in our specific case, the true progress).

Imagine some people have participated in a survey. Then, the predicted/displayed and true progress are known. We can now can bring them in relation. That means, we have a value pair $(\rho^*(P), \rho(P))$ of the true and displayed progress for each page $P$ on all paths participants have visited. The pair $(\rho^*(P), \rho(P))$ can be read as "on page $P$ the true progress was $\rho^*(P)$ but the progress $\rho(P)$ was displayed". That means, all those pairs are given as a set $\mathcal{M}$. For the comparison of different strategies $\sqcup_1, \ldots, \sqcup_n$, $n \geq 2$, there is such a set for each strategy: $\mathcal{M}_1, \ldots, \mathcal{M}_n$.

If the predicted progress differs from the true progress, it results in an error $e(P) = \rho(P) - \rho^*(P)$. Notice that $\rho^*$ and $\rho$ have percentage scales. As a result, the error also has a percentage scale and measures based on percentage errors are applicable. Hyndman and Koehler [7] mention four typical measures of percentage errors:

1. *Mean Absolute Error (MAE)*, $\overline{|e|}$
2. *Median Absolute Error (MdAE)*, $median(|e|)$
3. *Root Mean Square Error (RMSE)*, $\sqrt{\overline{e^2}}$
4. *Root Median Square Error (RMdSE)*, $\sqrt{median(e^2)}$.

The MAE and the RMSE are common measures to evaluate prediction accuracies. The MAE uses the absolute differences between the predicted and true progresses and as a consequence treats these errors proportionally, whereas the

RMSE squares these errors. As a result, larger are weighted more strongly. The MdAE and RMdSE are similar measures, which use the median instead of the mean and as a result are more robust against outliers. Applying these measures to the errors produces fit measures for each strategy. Since all fit measures are on the same scale, they can be compared with each other. The strategy with the lowest value is the best one of the considered strategies.

If a strategy predicts the true progress exactly, each measure produces a value 0, i.e., the error between the true and predicted progress is zero. One disadvantage of the RMSE and RMdSE is that they are infinite, undefined, or skewed when all *observed* values (i.e., the true progress) are 0 or near to 0 [7]. Since the true progress has values in the range from 0 to 100%, this disadvantage does not affect them.

In fact, the MdAE and RMdSE result in almost the same values (see the appendix). It has no benefit to consider both measures in an empirical study. Our opinion is that the RMdSE should not be used since it is more difficult to compute and to interpret.

The explained approach relies on the knowledge of the true progress and, therefore, on empirical data. Unfortunately, as with any empirical study, these data is usually not available before the survey starts. It is *not* possible to select the best strategy for a survey without additional effort on collecting empirical data. To overcome this problem, data can be generated by *pilot studies*, *simulations*, or *path-explorations* of the survey for example. *Pilot studies* refer to conducting the survey with a subset of the population to obtain data for strategy selection. In *simulations* virtual participants answer the questionnaire and result in simulated data for strategy selection. In a *path-exploration*, an algorithm computes all (or most) paths of the survey and computes sample progresses for each path. But the number of such paths in adaptive surveys may be large (or exponential). All three possibilities have in common that they should represent a "realistic" usage of the different paths. Different weights exist for the paths influencing the measure and makes the generation of data more difficult. The researcher should be aware of this.

The last section considered the example Q-graph of Fig. 3 and divergences in progresses after applying three prediction strategies *minimum*, *mean*, and *maximum* (cf. Table 2). Table 3 contains the errors $e$ between the displayed and true progress for each page of the path $(P_1, P_2, P_{11}, P_4, P_5, P_7, P_8, P_9, P_{10})$. The minimum strategy has the highest errors followed by the maximum strategy. The four measures MAE, MdAE, RMSE, and RMdSE support this observation. The RMSE has the highest value except for the minimum strategy where the median measures are a little higher. As mentioned, the MdAE and RMdSE are equal. The reason is the odd length of the path (see the appendix).

**Table 3.** Errors $e_{min}$, $e_{mean}$, and $e_{max}$ between the predicted (displayed) and the true progress for the different strategies *minimum*, *mean*, and *maximum* at the path $(P_1, P_2, P_{11}, P_4, P_5, P_7, P_8, P_9, P_{10})$ of the Q-graph in Fig. 3 and the progress values of Table 2. The table further contains the *MAE*, *MdAE*, *RMSE*, and *RMdSE* values for each strategy. The mean strategy has the best values for four measures.

| Page | $e_{min}$ [%] | $e_{mean}$ [%] | $e_{max}$ [%] |
|------|------|------|------|
| $P_1$ | 29.5 | 6.9 | −1.8 |
| $P_2$ | 30.0 | 6.6 | −4.6 |
| $P_{11}$ | 24.9 | 4.0 | −8.2 |
| $P_4$ | 22.3 | 2.8 | −10.1 |
| $P_5$ | 21.0 | 2.1 | −11.0 |
| $P_7$ | 19.7 | 3.2 | −9.4 |
| $P_8$ | 9.8 | 1.6 | −4.7 |
| $P_9$ | 6.6 | 1.1 | −3.1 |
| $P_{10}$ | 0.0 | 0.0 | 0.0 |
| *MAE* | 18.2 | 3.1 | 5.9 |
| *MdAE* | 21.0 | 2.8 | 4.7 |
| *RMSE* | 20.7 | 3.8 | 7.0 |
| *RMdSE* | 21.0 | 2.8 | 4.7 |

## 4     Experiments

The last section described four measures that can be applied to compare different prediction strategies. A first experiment with two real and large surveys examines which measure is most suitable for comparison. In a second experiment, a simulation study with over $10k$ surveys examines if there is a single best strategy for all surveys and, if not, which trivial strategy performs best in most cases.

### 4.1     Experiment with Real Surveys

Our department conducts large surveys with many variables, items, and adaptivity that result in a high number of possible paths participants can "walk". We store the paths on which the participants walked through the surveys with the survey engine *Coast* [18]. With these paths, it is possible to compute the true number of remaining items for each visited page for each participant. Furthermore, for each prediction strategy, the predicted number of remaining items can be calculated in retrospect with Eq. (1) and the algorithm of Fig. 2. As a result, data sets with true and displayed progresses for each strategy and for each survey are available. This data can be used to determine the most suitable measure and the best strategy.

In general, we want to answer the following research questions with our first experiment:

**Table 4.** Structure and important empirical properties of *survey A* and *survey B*. $N_{Participants}$ is the number of participants, $N_{Branches}$ describes the number of branching pages in Q-graph, $|Path|$ is the empirical length of paths, $N_{Items}$ is the empirical number of items seen, *rem(start)* describes the number of remaining items on the starting page (values in parentheses are adjustments explained in the text). (Table taken from the conference paper [20])

| | Survey A | Survey B | | | Survey A | Survey B |
|---|---|---|---|---|---|---|
| $N_{Participants}$ | 1041 | 193 | $N_{Items}$ | | | |
| $N_{Branches}$ | 11 | 38 | *min* | | 4 | 6 |
| $|Path|$ | | | *mean* | | 246.70 | 290.97 |
| *min* | 2 | 2 | *max* | | 339 | 377 |
| *mean* | 16.34 | 18.49 | *rem(start)* | | | |
| *max* | 25 | 23 | $\sqcup = min$ | | 46 (167) | 7 (258) |
| *Var* | 48.56 | 24.63 | $\sqcup = mean$ | | 115 (241) | 254 (495) |
| | | | $\sqcup = max$ | | 345 (288) | 706 (700) |

**R1** Which measure is most suitable for comparing different prediction strategies?

**R2** Is there a single best prediction strategy?

**Experimental Settings.** For the first experiment, we considered two of our surveys that we call *survey A* and *survey B* since their content is irrelevant. Table 4 shows characteristics of the surveys where some of the characteristics are based on empirical data. In the table, $N_{Branches}$ describes the number of pages with branches, $|Path|$ refers to the number of pages within a path, and $N_{Items}$ is the number of items a participant has seen. Both surveys have similar structures except for $N_{Participants}$ and $N_{Branches}$. Survey $A$ has more available data sets, whereas survey $B$ has much more branches.

The experiment examines the previously mentioned three prediction strategies: minimum (*min*), *mean*, and maximum (*max*). The *mean* strategy does *not* represent the empirical average of items on the paths, but the selection operator used in the general algorithm.

For all three strategies and both surveys, Eq. (1) and the algorithm of Fig. 2 produced data sets. The expected remaining items on the starting page vary for both surveys (cf. Table 4, *rem(start)*) and are higher for survey $B$ except for the *min* approach, which is very small with a value of 7. The values in parentheses represent adjustments on the surveys explained in the following.

**Lessons Learned.** During the performance of the experiments, we observed two critical characteristics of surveys resulting in bad predictions. We called them *screening paths* and *adaptive page chains*.

*Screening paths* are paths at the beginning of surveys in which participants receive a few key questions to determine if they are part of the survey-specific target population. Depending on their answers, the survey either continues or ends quickly. As a result, screening paths end with shortcuts (exit paths) to the ending page without many items. For example, Fig. 3 has a screening path containing only page $P_1$ and resulting in the exit path $(P_{13}, P_{10})$.

The inclusion of screening paths in progress calculation usually produces bad predictions, this was the first lesson we learned. Especially by taking the *min* strategy, the exit path has the fewest remaining items and, therefore, decreases the number of remaining items on all paths at the beginning of the survey (cf. $rem(start)$ in Table 4 or the remaining items of $P_1$ in Table 1 of our example survey of Fig. 3). This leads to progresses near 100% for survey $B$ after passing the last page of the screening path. We observed no great impact of screening paths for strategies *mean* and *max*.

*Adaptive page chains* are subgraphs with many adaptive pages, however, each participant only sees a small number of them. The survey of Fig. 3 has a little page chain between pages $P_5$ and $P_9$ for example. Survey $B$ consists of a lot of such pages that describe special topics. In general, each participant has only seen one or two of these approx. 30 pages. Adaptive page chains disappear for the *min* strategy in progress calculation skewing the results as most participants nevertheless see at least one page. The *max* strategy includes each adaptive page in the chain resulting in high numbers of remaining items. The *mean* strategy smooths high numbers of remaining items, however, usually only by half. In Table 4, $N_{Branches}$ indicates adaptive page chains in survey $B$ with a value of 38 instead of 11 in survey $A$. It was the second lesson we learned that such chains of adaptive pages also produce bad predictions.

As a consequence, we revised our experiments with surveys $A$ and $B$ by eliminating screening paths from progress calculation. It is useless, otherwise, to compare the results of the different strategies. Our revisions result in new numbers of remaining items for each strategy (see $rem(start)$ in parentheses in Table 4). We left adaptive page chains as they contain important items.

**Experimental Results and Discussion.** Figure 4 shows the results of the first experiment. The $x$ axis describes the true and the $y$ axis the displayed (predicted) progress. In other words, the figure visualizes the measurement points $\mathcal{M}$ (cf. Sect. 3). The black line illustrates the true progress and a perfect prediction strategy, respectively. The *min* approach obviously results in overestimations of the progress, whereas the *max* approach results in underestimations. For survey $A$, *mean* has values above and below the true progress line. For survey $B$, the values of *mean* are all below the line. This is caused by the adaptive page chains described earlier.

Besides the measurements of true and predicted progresses, Fig. 4 contains values for measures MAE, MdAE, RMSE, and RMdSE. Actually, the MdAE and RMdSE result in equivalent values as mentioned.

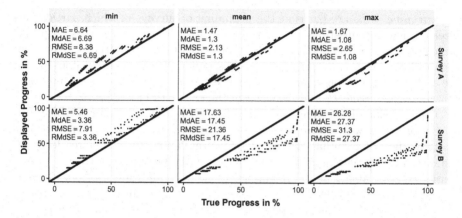

**Fig. 4.** Charts with displayed progresses and the computed measures MAE, MdAE, RMSE, and RMSE for the three prediction strategies *min*, *mean*, and *max* for two surveys *A* and *B*. For survey *A*, the *mean* strategy has the lowest MAE and RMSE and the *max* strategy has the lowest MdAE and RMdSE. For survey *B*, the *min* approach is the best and the *max* strategy is the worst one for all four measures. But all strategies perform worse in survey *B*  (taken from the conference paper [20]).

For survey *A*, the *mean* strategy has the lowest MAE of 1.47 and RMSE of 2.13, but the *max* strategy has the lowest MdAE and RMdSE with both 1.08. The *mean* and *max* strategies seem to estimate the true progress best. The *min* strategy is the worst approach. The distribution of the points supports the result.

For survey *B*, the strategies perform contrary: the *min* approach is the best and the *max* strategy is the worst one for all four measures. All strategies perform worse for survey *B*. No strategy predicts the true progress well. Even though *min* has the lowest measures, a visual inspection of the predicted values in Fig. 4 shows that for many participants the displayed progress is near 100% even though they still have around 25% of the survey to go. This is a result of adaptive page chains, because the *min* strategy predicts that all adaptive pages will be skipped, where in most cases a participant visited at least one adaptive page. In comparison to survey *A*, all fit measures are higher, showing that progress predictions are generally worse in survey *B*. As a whole, the results show that there is no single best strategy for both surveys. We take these first results to tendentially answer research question *R2* "Is there a single best prediction strategy?" with "*No*", rather it is important to look at the characteristics of a given survey, as was seen with the adaptive page chains in survey *B*. It could also be possible that in the future a more elaborate selection strategy could be offer the best prediction for different kinds of surveys.

In our application context, high errors should be penalized more than smaller errors since higher errors have a stronger impact on the overall progress calculation and can lead to noticeable deviations from the true progress. Small errors on the contrary should be almost invisible to the participant. The RMSE is, therefore, a good choice, because it gives large errors more weight by squaring the error. Like Fig. 4 shows, the RMSE is always the highest. The squaring of the error in RMdSE has no great effect on the resulting value. Actually, it is always close to the MdAE as mentioned before.

For survey $A$, the *mean* (MAE and RMSE) and the *max* strategies (MdAE and RMdSE) have low values. We can see in Fig. 4 that the *max* strategy has more outliers for survey $A$ than the *mean* strategy. Following the above argumentation, the *mean* strategy should be used since the outliers may lead to noticeable deviations. This is supported by a higher RMSE.

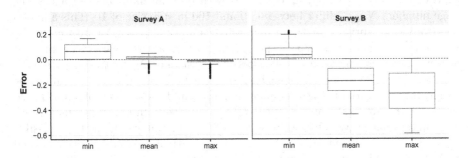

**Fig. 5.** Error distribution of the strategies *min*, *mean*, and *max* for surveys $A$ and $B$. For survey $A$, the *mean* and *max* strategies result in errors near zero with less variance. The *min* strategy has a higher variance. In contrast, for survey $B$, the *max* and *mean* strategies have a very high variance and the *min* approach has a small variance (taken from the conference paper [20]).

Figure 5 illustrates the error distribution for all strategies in both surveys and, therefore, also the number of outliers. For survey $A$, the *mean* and *max* strategies have a median error near zero with less variance and only a minor number of outliers. Instead, the *min* strategy results in a higher variance of the error. The *max* and *mean* strategies have a very high variance with many outliers for survey $B$. The *min* approach has better results with a smaller variance. Altogether, Fig. 5 supports the previous observations and the usage of the RMSE.

Altogether, we recommend to use the RMSE for comparing different prediction strategies for PIs. It is most sensitive to high deviations. This answers research question *R1* "Which measure is most suitable for comparing different prediction strategies?".

## 4.2 Experiment with Simulated Surveys

The second experiment examines simulated surveys. Since our department has indeed large surveys, but does not conduct many different variants, we generated over $10k$ random surveys. It is important to note that only Q-graphs and branch conditions with their variables were randomized and *not* complete surveys with all of their items.

The second experiment should answer research question *R2* "Is there a single best strategy?" in more detail. Including this research question, there are two questions to examine in this experiment:

**R2** Is there a single best strategy?
**R3** Which of the three strategies *min*, *mean*, and *max* is the best?

**Experimental Settings.** The experiment contains exactly 11 200 randomized surveys that are separated in 10 groups with differing numbers of pages. The page numbers $N_{Pages}$ differ between 10 and 100 in step-size of 10. This allows a wide variety of surveys. With an increasing number of pages, we also increased the number of generated survey per group to increase the variety of different surveys. Further, the number of pages with branches $N_{Branching\,pages}$ and the number of items $N_{Items}$ vary for each survey. The variables, the values that can be assigned to the variables, the number of clauses, and the number of axioms used in conditions are based on empirical values of surveys on our department. Our real surveys have 6 variables in conditions $N_{Variables}$ on average with 3 possible values that are assigned $M_{Possible\,values}$. The conditions are in disjunctive normal form (DNF). The average number of clauses $M_{Clauses}$ is 1.84 and the average number of axioms $M_{Axioms}$ per clause is 1.4. Table 5 gives an overview about the surveys and their empirical properties.

**Table 5.** Properties of the computer-generated surveys. $N_{Pages}$ describes the number of pages, $N$ the number of surveys, $N_{Branching\,pages}$ is the number of pages with at least two succeeding pages, $N_{Items}$ is the total number of items, $N_{Paths}$ is the number of paths available, $N_{Variables}$ is the number of variables used in the conditions, $M_{Possible\,values}$ is the average of possible characteristics per variable, $M_{Clauses}$ is the average number of clauses per condition, and $M_{Axioms}$ is the average number of axioms per clause.

| $N_{Pages}$ | $N$ | $N_{Branching}$ pages | | | $N_{Items}$ | $N_{Paths}$ | | | $N_{Variables}$ | | | $M_{Possible}$ values | $M_{Clauses}$ | $M_{Axioms}$ |
|---|---|---|---|---|---|---|---|---|---|---|---|---|---|---|
| | | min | M | max | | min | M | max | min | M | max | | | |
| 10 | 400 | 1 | 2 | 4 | 200 – 1000 | 1 | 3 | 7 | 1 | 4 | 10 | 2.97 | 1.83 | 1.42 |
| 20 | 800 | 1 | 3 | 7 | 200 – 1000 | 1 | 5 | 24 | 1 | 6 | 12 | 2.98 | 1.86 | 1.4 |
| 30 | 1000 | 1 | 4 | 8 | 200 – 1000 | 1 | 5 | 30 | 1 | 6 | 12 | 3.01 | 1.85 | 1.44 |
| 40 | 1000 | 1 | 5 | 11 | 200 – 1000 | 1 | 10 | 176 | 1 | 6 | 15 | 3 | 1.86 | 1.42 |
| 50 | 1000 | 2 | 7 | 14 | 200 – 1000 | 1 | 17 | 234 | 1 | 7 | 16 | 3 | 1.85 | 1.42 |
| 60 | 1000 | 4 | 9 | 15 | 200 – 1000 | 1 | 30 | 339 | 1 | 8 | 16 | 3 | 1.84 | 1.42 |
| 70 | 1200 | 4 | 10 | 17 | 200 – 1000 | 1 | 41 | 452 | 1 | 8 | 16 | 3 | 1.85 | 1.42 |
| 80 | 1400 | 4 | 11 | 19 | 200 – 1000 | 1 | 57 | 571 | 1 | 8 | 17 | 3 | 1.85 | 1.41 |
| 90 | 1600 | 4 | 12 | 21 | 200 – 1000 | 1 | 68 | 712 | 1 | 8 | 16 | 2.99 | 1.84 | 1.42 |
| 100 | 1800 | 4 | 13 | 24 | 200 – 1000 | 1 | 82 | 799 | 1 | 8 | 18 | 3 | 1.84 | 1.42 |

It is not trivial to randomly generate realistic-looking surveys (Q-graphs). Their construction is based on the generation of so-called *Program Structure*

*Trees* (PST) [8,9]. A PST represents a computer program as a tree with *sequences* of *instructions* and *bonds* (branches and loops). For its generation, the algorithm divides the given number of pages at first into a given number of branching pages (bonds) and normal pages (instructions). The second step assigns a random number of pages (instructions and bonds) to the bonds. The constructed PST is then transformed into a Q-graph by adding additional edges and joining pages. Such PSTs always result in well-structured Q-graphs. To get also some *irreducible* Q-graphs, a random number of additional edges were inserted into the Q-graph. The number of items for each page were assigned on that Q-graph randomly. Each page gets at maximum two times the average number of items per page to avoid imbalanced surveys.

Conditions on branches cause individual paths for participants. Without conditions, either all participants would take the same path or each branch is visited equal-distributed. Our random Q-graphs get conditions for each branch where each branching page has at least one default edge that is followed if none of the other branching conditions hold. The conditions are based on DNF, i.e., they consists of axioms and clauses. Each axiom consists of a variable, a comparison operator, and one possible value of the variable. The variables with their possible values are also randomly generated for each Q-graph. Sometimes, conditions are generated which never evaluate to true. But their prevention corresponds with the *SAT* problem[1] that is NP complete. We accepted this inaccuracy as improperly designed surveys.

**Table 6.** Descriptive statistics of the results of the second experiment. It compares the *Strategies* regarding the *RMSE*. The *mean* strategy has the lowest *RMSE* in minimum, mean, and maximum.

| Strategy | $RMSE$ | | |
|---|---|---|---|
| | min | M | max |
| min | 0 | 10.35 | 53.87 |
| mean | 0 | 5.83 | 46.89 |
| max | 0 | 8.81 | 51.86 |

We simulated 1 000 participants for each survey. The participants were simulated by pre-assigning their answers to all variables used in the conditions in an uniform distribution. Differences in assigned answers may result in differences in paths in the surveys. All simulated participants answer the survey and use their own paths. Based on these paths, the predicted and actual progress as well as the RMSE for the three strategies *min*imum, *mean*, and *max*imum were computed.

**Experimental Results and Discussion.** Table 6 summarizes the results of the second experiment. For each strategy exists at least one survey for which the

---

[1] The *Boolean satisfiability problem* is a decision problem whether variables of Boolean formula can be replaced by *true* or *false* so that the formula evaluates to *true*.

strategy produces a perfect estimation of the true progress (the *minimum* of the *RMSE* is 0). But for each strategy exists also at least one survey where the estimation is bad (the *maximum* of the *RMSE* is greater than 20). The *mean* strategy seems to perform best with an average RMSE of 5.83. This is followed by the *max* (8.81) and *min* (10.35) strategies.

The averages of the three strategies show a tendency that the *mean* strategy estimates the true progress best. But sometimes outliers are hidden by the average. For this reason, we ranked each strategy for each survey from best (1) to worst (3). Figure 6 shows the three strategies and their placements, totally and relatively. The relative numbers belong to the total number of surveys.

The *mean* strategy has most placements on the first rank. It leads to the best progress estimations for about 71.9% of the surveys. If it does not perform best, it always ranked second and never third. For 28.1% of the surveys, either the *min* or *max* strategies have better RMSE. Although the *max* strategy has a better average than the *min* strategy, the *min* strategy has more rank one places than *max*. But the *min* strategy has the worst predictions in approx. 60% of the surveys. Altogether, Fig. 6 supports the conclusion drawn from comparing the average RMSE values.

The descriptive statistics show that the *mean* strategy is usually the best one of the three strategies. This answers research question *R3* "Which of the three strategies *min*, *mean*, and *max* is the best?". But the results also accentuate that non of the three strategies is best for every survey (research question *R2*). Research in future should examine strategies performing better than the strategies examined here. However, to find a strategy that performs well for each

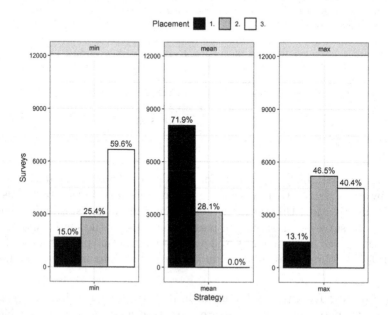

**Fig. 6.** Comparison of the three prediction strategies *min*, *mean*, and *max* related to their placement for a single survey. The relative values belong to the number of surveys.

survey, it becomes necessary to further investigate the factors, that influence the prediction of the progress for a given survey. We examined the describing factors of the surveys in Table 5. However, we find no significant correlations between those factors and the RMSE. These factors do not seem to describe the structure of surveys accurately in terms of progress prediction. Therefore, we need further factors that describe the structure better. One possibility is to use measures describing graph similarity. But there are a lot of such measures with individual benefits and disadvantages [11]. These measures, however, are out of the scope of this paper.

## 5   Conclusion

In this paper, we argued for a measure to compare prediction strategies for calculating the progress in adaptive surveys. Measures from statistics as well as experiments recommend the RMSE measure as good choice of comparing different strategies for the same survey. That strategy with the lowest RMSE is the best one. Experiments in this paper compared three standard prediction strategies: taking the minimum, average, and maximum number of items by the end of the survey. The comparison showed that the mean strategy is usually a good choice when little is known about the characteristics of the survey. In over 70% of over 10$k$ simulated surveys, this strategy performs best. In all other cases, it comes in second place. However, there are surveys where even the mean strategy has poor predictions and therefore scores poorly. Our experiments with real-world and a large number of simulated surveys accentuates that *no single strategy is the best for all surveys*. The strategy is survey-dependent. Further research is necessary to provide a guide or tool for selecting the best strategy.

This study showed that using the RMSE for comparison is promising. But there is still need for empirical data. Additional research has to find ways to generate this data precisely, e.g., by further simulation or path-weighting. Furthermore, future research has to find survey characteristics that influence the accuracy of different prediction strategies. This characteristics may help to select a well-fitting strategy without having empirical data.

Sometimes it may be possible that a prediction strategy has the best RMSE within a set of strategies, but another strategy may be better in practice; for example, if simulated data does not reflect the actual population of the survey, the survey population varies over time, or there is simply an yet unknown, better strategy. We examined three basic strategies, future research should focus on finding better strategies, especially ones that can handle adaptive page chains.

## Appendix

Section 3 mentioned that the MdAE and RMdSE mostly result in almost the same values. In this appendix, we are going to investigate this fact.

Assume a vector of (real) values $v = \{v_1, \ldots, v_n\}$, $n \geq 1$. The first step of computing the median $\tilde{v}$ is to order the values of $v$ by size. By taking the

MdAE, the ordering is performed on $|v|$. For RMdSE, the ordering is performed on $v^2$. Since for each two arbitrary (real) values $v_1$ and $v_2$ it holds true that $|v_1| \leq |v_2| \iff v_1^2 \leq v_2^2$, it is easy to confirm that the ordering of $|v|$ is equal to the ordering of $v^2$. Let $(a_1, \ldots, a_n)$ be the resulting order of the absolute and $(s_1, \ldots, s_n)$ be the ordering for the squared values. The following is valid:

$$\forall 1 \leq i \leq n \colon a_i = \sqrt{s_i} \tag{2}$$

The second step of computing the median depends on the number of dimensions $n$ of $v$. There are two cases:

1. $n$ is odd. The median is the value on position $n/2$ of the ordering. It is $a_{n/2}$ for MdAE and $s_{n/2}$ for RMdSE. For RMdSE, we have to take the root median, i.e., RMdSE is $\sqrt{s_{n/2}}$. With Eq. 2 in mind, the MdAE and RMdSE are equal.
2. $n$ is even. The median is half the sum of the values on positions $n/2$ and $n/2 + 1$. It is $1/2(a_{n/2} + a_{n/2+1})$ for MdAE and $1/2(s_{n/2} + s_{n/2+1})$ for RMdSE. For RMdSE, we take again the rooted median, $\sqrt{1/2(s_{n/2} + s_{n/2+1})}$. Actually, the MdAE and RMdSE are *unequal*. But on closer inspection, the value of $1/2(s_{n/2} + s_{n/2+1})$ is always between $s_{n/2}$ and $s_{n/2+1}$, and therefore, the RMdSE is always between $a_{n/2}$ and $a_{n/2+1}$ with regard on Eq. 2.

Both cases result in the following facts:

1. MdAE and RMdSE are equal if $n$ is odd.
2. MdAE and RMdSE are almost equal if $n$ is even and the values on positions $n/2$ and $n/2 + 1$ are close to each other.

# References

1. Conrad, F.G., Couper, M.P., Tourangeau, R.: Effectiveness of progress indicators in web surveys: it's what's up front that counts. In: Banks, R. (ed.) Survey and statistical computing IV. The impact of technology on the survey process, vol. V, pp. 1–10. Association for Survey Computing, London (2003)
2. Conrad, F.G., Couper, M.P., Tourangeau, R., Peytchev, A.: The impact of progress indicators on task completion. Interact. Comput. **5**, 417–427 (2010)
3. Crawford, S.D., Couper, M.P., Lamias, M.J.: Web surveys: perceptions of burden. Soc. Sci. Comput. Rev. **19**(2), 146–162 (2001). https://doi.org/10.1177/089443930101900202
4. Dillman, D.A., Tortora, R.D., Bowker, D.: Principles for constructing web surveys. Technical report 98–50, Social and Economic Sciences Research Center (SESRC), Washington State University, Pullman, Washington, USA (1998)
5. Healey, B., Macpherson, T., Kuijten, B.: An empirical evaluation of three web survey design principles. Market. Bull. **16**, 1–9 (2005)
6. Heerwegh, D., Loosveldt, G.: An experimental study on the effects of personalization, survey length statements, progress indicators, and survey sponsor logos in web surveys. J. Official Stat. **22**(2), 191–210 (2006)
7. Hyndman, R.J., Koehler, A.B.: Another look at measures of forecast accuracy. Int. J. Forecasting **22**(4), 679–688 (2006). https://doi.org/10.1016/j.ijforecast.2006.03.001

8. Johnson, R., Pearson, D., Pingali, K.: Finding regions fast: single entry single exit and control regions in linear time. Technical report TR 93–1365, Cornell University, Ithaca, NY, USA, July 1993

9. Johnson, R., Pearson, D., Pingali, K.: The program structure tree: computing control regions in linear time. In: Sarkar, V., Ryder, B.G., Soffa, M.L. (eds.) Proceedings of the ACM SIGPLAN 1994 Conference on Programming Language Design and Implementation (PLDI), Orlando, Florida, USA, 20–24 June 1994, pp. 171–185. ACM (1994). http://dl.acm.org/citation.cfm?id=178243

10. Kaczmirek, L.: Human Survey-Interaction. Usability and Nonresponse in Online Surveys. No. 6 in Neue Schriften zur Online-Forschung, Herbert von Halem Verlag, Cologne, Germany, 1st edn. (2009)

11. Koutra, D., Parikh, A., Ramdas, A., Xiang, J.: Algorithms for graph similarity and subgraph matching. Technical report, Carnegie Mellon University, December 2011

12. Li, J., Nehme, R.V., Naughton, J.: GSLPI: a cost-based query progress indicator. In: 2012 IEEE 28th International Conference on Data Engineering, pp. 678–689, April 2012. https://doi.org/10.1109/ICDE.2012.74

13. Liu, M., Wronski, L.: Examining completion rates in web surveys via over 25,000 real-world surveys. Soc. Sci. Comput. Rev. **36**(1), 116–124 (2018)

14. Luo, G.: Toward a progress indicator for machine learning model building and data mining algorithm execution: a position paper. SIGKDD Explor. Newsl. **19**(2), 13–24 (2017). https://doi.org/10.1145/3166054.3166057

15. Matzat, U., Snijders, C., van der Horst, W.: Effects of different types of progress indicators on drop-out rates in web surveys. Soc. Psychol. **40**, 43–52 (2009)

16. Myers, B.A.: INCENSE: a system for displaying data structures. SIGGRAPH Comput. Graph. **17**(3), 115–125 (1983). https://doi.org/10.1145/964967.801140

17. Myers, B.A.: The importance of percent-done progress indicators for computer-human interfaces. SIGCHI Bull. **16**(4), 11–17 (1985). https://doi.org/10.1145/1165385.317459

18. Prinz, T.M., Apel, S., Bernhardt, R., Plötner, J., Vetterlein, A.: Model-centric and phase-spanning software architecture for surveys - report on the tool Coast and lessons learned. Int. J. Adv. Softw. **12**(1&2), 152–165 (2019). iSSN 1942–2628

19. Prinz, T.M., Bernhardt, R., Plötner, J., Vetterlein, A.: Progress indicators in web surveys reconsidered – a general progress algorithm. In: Kokil, U., Ota, T. (eds.) ACHI 2019: The Twelfth International Conference on Advances in Computer-Human Interactions, Proceedings, IARIA Conference, ThinkMind Digital Library Athens, Greece, 24–28 February 2019, vol. 9, pp. 101–107 (2019)

20. Prinz, T.M., Plötner, J., Vetterlein, A.: The problem of finding the best strategy for progress computation in adaptive web surveys. In: Bozzon, A., Mayo, F.D., Filipe, J. (eds.) Proceedings of the 15th International Conference on Web Information Systems and Technologies (WEBIST 2019), Vienna, Austria, pp. 307–313, September 2019

21. Villar, A., Callegaro, M., Yang, Y.: Where am I? A meta-analysis of experiments on the effects of progress indicators for web surveys. Soc. Sci. Comput. Rev. **31**(6), 744–762 (2013). https://doi.org/10.1177/0894439313497468

22. Yan, T., Conrad, F., Tourangeau, R., Couper, M.: Should I stay or should I go: the effects of progress feedback, promised task duration, and length of questionnaire on completing web surveys. Int. J. Public Opin. Res. **23**, 131–147 (2011). https://doi.org/10.1093/ijpor/edq046

# A New Approach for Processing Natural-Language Queries to Semantic Web Triplestores

Shane Peelar$^{(\boxtimes)}$ and Richard A. Frost

School of Computer Science, University of Windsor, Windsor, ON, Canada
{peelar,richard}@uwindsor.ca

**Abstract.** Natural Language Query Interfaces (NLQIs) have once again captured the public imagination, but developing them for the Semantic Web has proven to be non-trivial. This is unfortunate, because the Semantic Web offers many opportunities for interacting with smart devices, including those connected to the Internet of Things. In this paper, we present an NLQI to the Semantic Web based on a Compositional Semantics (CS) that can accommodate many particularly tricky aspects of the English language, including nested $n$-ary transitive verbs, superlatives, and chained prepositional phrases, and even ambiguity. Key to our approach is a new data structure which has proven to be useful in answering NL queries. As a consequence of this, our system is able to handle NL features that are often considered to be non-compositional. We also present a novel method to memoize sub-expressions of a query formed from CS, drastically improving query execution times with respect to large triplestores. Our approach is agnostic to any particular database query language. A live demonstration of our NLQI is available online.

**Keywords:** Natural language processing · Natural Language Query Interfaces · Compositional Semantics · Event Semantics · Quantification

## 1 Introduction

This is an extended version of the paper by Frost and Peelar [14] that was presented at WEBIST 2019 in Vienna, Austria. That paper was selected as one of the best papers at WEBIST 2019 and the authors were invited to submit an extended version for publication. In this paper we expand upon the compositionality of our NLQI, including the parsing framework and semantic implementations, we introduce a novel method to accommodate superlatives using compositional semantics, and we discuss a novel approach to memoization and triplestore retrieval. We also significantly expand upon how our NLQI is implemented.

Supported by NSERC of Canada.

A. Bozzon et al. (Eds.): WEBIST 2019, LNBIP 399, pp. 168–194, 2020.
https://doi.org/10.1007/978-3-030-61750-9_8

We begin by describing a Natural Language Query Interface (NLQI) that we have built. We hope that the interface will motivate readers to look into our modifications to MS. In Sect. 2, we explain how our NL Query interface (NLQI) can be accessed through the Web. In Sect. 3, we describe the compositional aspects of our NLQI. In Sect. 4, we describe the Semantic Web triplestore. In Sect. 5 we discuss example queries and their results, including examples of what are often referred to as "non-compositional" features of NL that our NLQI can handle. With each of the examples we provide an informal explanation of how the answer is, or could be, computed. In Sect. 6, we describe the new FDBR data structure which is central to our approach. In Sect. 7 and Sect. 8, we describe how our system accommodates chained prepositional phrases with superlatives. In Sect. 9, we describe how to use our approach with relational databases. In Sect. 10, we provide a system overview and implementation details on how our semantics are realized. Section 11 discusses how our work fits into the framework of existing work in this area. We close with Sect. 12 and Sect. 13 where we discuss future research directions and our conclusions.

Much of our semantics is based on MS. We differ in these ways:

1. We add events to the basic ontological concepts of entities and truth values.
2. Each event has a number of roles associated with it. Each role has an entity as a value.
3. For efficiency, we use sets of entities rather than characteristic functions of those sets as is the case in MS.
4. We define transitive $n$-ary verbs in terms of sets of events, each with $n$ roles.
5. We compute FDBRs, the novel data structure presented in this paper, from sets of events and use them in the denotations of transitive verbs and in computing results of queries containing prepositional phrases. Although not referred to as an FDBR, the use of relational images in denotations of verbs was first proposed by Frost and Launchbury in 1989 [12].

We hope that this paper reawakens an interest in Compositional Semantics, in particular for NL query processing.

## 2  How to Access Our NLQI

Our NL interface is accessible via the following URL, and is speech enabled for both voice-in and voice-out in browsers that support the Web Speech API:

http://speechweb2.cs.uwindsor.ca/solarman4/demo_sparql.html

## 3  Compositionality

Compositionality is a useful property of any system as it facilitates understanding, construction, modification, extension, proof of properties, and reuse in different situations. When building our system, we tried to make it as compositional as possible: a compositional syntax processor is systematically combined with a compositional semantics.

## 3.1   The Compositionality of Our Syntactic Processor

Our parser is designed and built using the Haskell programming language, using parser combinators [13]. The approach enables parsers to be constructed as executable specifications of context-free grammars with explicit and implicit left-recursive productions, which is useful for defining grammars for NL. The result of applying our parser is the set of all parse trees for ambiguous grammars. The trees are represented efficiently using a Tomita-style [20] compact graph in which trees share common components.

In 2008, Frost and Hafiz [13] demonstrated that it is possible to efficiently implement context-free parsing using combinators, with their approach having $O(n^4)$ complexity in the worst case and $O(n^3)$ complexity in the average case.

The following example was featured in Frost and Hafiz [13]. To demonstrate use of our combinators, consider the following ambiguous grammar from Tomita [20]:

```
s    ::= np vp  |  s pp       np    ::= noun  |  det noun  |  np pp
pp   ::= prep np              vp    ::= verb np
det  ::= "a"    |  "the"      noun ::= "i"    |  "man"  |  "park"  |  "bat"
verb ::= "saw"                prep ::= "in"   |  "with"
```

In this grammar, the non-terminal s stands for sentence, np for nounphrase, vp for verbphrase, det for determiner, pp for prepositional phrase, and prep for preposition. It is left recursive in the rules for s and np. The Haskell code below defines a parser for the above grammar using our combinators term (terminal), <+> (alternative), and *> (sequence) [13]:

```
data Label = S | ... | PREP
s    = memoize S    $ np *> vp <+> s *> pp
np   = memoize NP   $ noun <+> det *> noun <+> np *> pp
pp   = memoize PP   $ prep *> np
vp   = memoize VP   $ verb *> np
det  = memoize DET  $ term "a" <+> term "the"
noun = memoize NOUN
         $ term "i" <+> term "man" <+> term "park" <+> term "bat"
verb = memoize VERB $ term "saw"
prep = memoize PREP $ term "in" <+> term "with"
```

Parsers written in this fashion are highly compositional, and can be easily extended with new rules if needed. Parsers constructed with our combinators have $O(n^3)$ worst case time complexity for non-left-recursive ambiguous grammars (where $n$ is the length of the input), and $O(n^4)$ for left recursive ambiguous grammars. This compares well with $O(n^3)$ limits on standard algorithms for CFGs such as Earley-style parsers [8]. The increase to $n^4$ is due to expansion of the left recursive non-terminals in the grammar. The potentially exponential number of parse trees for highly-ambiguous input are represented in polynomial space as in Tomita's algorithm.

## 3.2    The Compositionality of Our Semantics

The semantics on which our system is based is similar to Montague Semantics. All phrases of the same syntactic category have meanings of the same semantic type. The meaning of all words and phrases are functions defined over sets of base terms which are entities, events and Boolean values. The meaning of a complex phrase is obtained by applying the functions which are the meanings of its parts, to each other in an order determined by the syntactic structure of the whole. Our system was easy to construct, and is easy to extend. Additional language features are accommodated by adding their syntactic structure and then defining their semantics by viewing the semantics of words and phrases of the same syntactic category.

## 3.3    The Compositionality of the Whole NL Processor

Our processor is built as an executable specification of a fully general attribute grammar. Compositional semantic rules are added to each syntactic production using the technique of Frost, Hafiz and Callaghan [13]. The attribute grammar is fully general as it can accommodate left recursive context-free grammars and fully-general dependencies between inherited and synthesized attributes. Haskell allows any computational dependency between attributes to be defined. Also, Haskell's lazy evaluation strategy enables our language processor to be efficient. For example, no attribute computation is carried out until a successful parse has been obtained. We have also developed a variation of memoization using monads [13] in order to reduce the complexity of syntactic and semantic evaluation. In the paper by Frost and Peelar [14] we discuss how we accommodate, using our compositional approach, various English phrases that are often given as examples of non-compositional constructs.

# 4    The Triplestore that Is Queried

Our NLQI computes answers with respect to an *event-based* Semantic Web triplestore containing data about the planets, the moons that orbit them, and the people who discovered those moons, and when, where and with what implement they were discovered. Briefly, a triplestore is a database of 3-tuples, called triples, that have the form *(subject, predicate, object)*, where *subject, predicate* and *object* are Uniform Resource Identifiers (URIs).

An *event-based triple* has a *subject* that identifies an event rather than an entity [19]. In these triples, the *predicate* identifies a *role* through which the *object* participates in the event. That is, an event-based triple $(e, r, o)$ expresses that $o$ participates in $e$ through role $r$. We call $o$ the event $e$'s "$r$ property". For example, in Table 1, "hall" is event "event1045"'s *subject* property. Triplestores consisting of event-based triples are called *event-based triplestores*.

The advantage of event-based triplestores is that additional information about the events and entities participating in those events is immediately available. This is not the case in an entity-based triplestore, where some form of *reification* is necessary to obtain additional information about a fact expressed in a triple. For example, obtaining the location where "hall discovered phobos" in an entity-based triplestore, described by (*hall*, *discovered*, *phobos*), is not possible without reification.

We assume that each event will at minimum contain a role *ev_type* that identifies the type of the event, with the general expectation that events of the same type will contain similar roles. This implies the existence of a schema that describes the types of roles that an event may contain. As a consequence of this, each event could be equally well be represented by a row in a relational database. We discuss this further in Sect. 9.

Going forward, when we refer to the type of an event or set of events, we are referring to their *ev_type* property. Likewise, when we refer to events of a particular type, we are referring to events whose *ev_type* property corresponds to that type. As a shorthand, we use *t*-type events to refer to events with type *t*. For example, "discover" events refers to events that have *ev_type* property "discover".

The triplestore contains triples such as those in Table 1 which represent the event in which `hall` (in the role of *subject*) discovered `phobos` (in the role of *object*) in 1877 (in the role of *year*) with the `refractor_telescope_1` (in the role of *implement*) at the `us_naval_observatory` (in the role of *location*). Events representing set membership are represented as shown in Table 2.

**Table 1.** Triples describing an event of type "discover" [14]. The full URIs of the events, roles, and entities have been omitted here.

| Event | Role | Entity |
|-------|------|--------|
| event1045 | subject | hall |
| event1045 | object | phobos |
| event1045 | ev_type | discover_ev |
| event1045 | year | 1877 |
| event1045 | location | us_naval_observatory |
| event1045 | implement | refractor_telescope_1 |

**Table 2.** Triples describing an event of type "membership" [14].

| Event | Role | Entity |
|-------|------|--------|
| event1128 | subject | galileo |
| event1128 | object | person |
| event1128 | ev_type | membership |

The complete triplestore, which contains tens of thousands of triples, is hosted on a remote server using the Virtuoso software [9] and can be accessed by following the link at the beginning of Sect. 2.

# 5    Example Queries

Our NLQI can answer millions of queries with respect to the triplestore discussed above. The NLQI can accommodate queries containing common and proper nouns, adjectives, conjunction and disjunction, intransitive and transitive verbs, nested quantification, superlatives, chained prepositional phrases containing quantifiers, comparatives and polysemantic words. In the following sections, we provide an informal explanation of how the answer is computed. If a query is syntactically ambiguous, the results from each possible interpretation of the query are denoted with a semicolon.

## 5.1    Queries Demonstrating the Range of NL Features that Our NLQI Can Accommodate

phobos spins $\Rightarrow$ *True*
phobos is a moon $\Rightarrow$ *True*

The function denoted by phobos checks to see if $e_{phobos}$ is a member of the *spin* set, and secondly if $e_{phobos}$ is a member of the *moon* set.

a moon spins $\Rightarrow$ *True*
every moon spins $\Rightarrow$ *True*
an atmospheric moon exists $\Rightarrow$ *True*

The function denoted by "a" checks to see if the intersection of the set of *moons* and the set of *spins* is non-empty. The function denoted by "every" checks to see if the set of moons is a subset of the *spins* set. The denotations of a and every that we use are set-theoretic event-based versions of the denotations from MS which uses characteristic functions. The answer to the third query is obtained by checking if the intersection of the *atmospheric* set and the *moon* set is non-empty.

hall discovered $\Rightarrow$ *True*

All of the events of type "discover" are collected together and are checked to see if $e_{hall}$ is found as the subject role value of any of them. If so, *True* is returned.

when did hall discover $\Rightarrow$ *1877*

The *year* property of the events returned by "hall discover" (treated as "hall discovered") are returned.

phobos was discovered $\Rightarrow$ *True*

All of the events of type "discover" are collected together and are checked to see if $e_{phobos}$ is found as the *object* role value of any of them. If so *True* is returned.

earth was discovered $\Rightarrow$ *False*

Earth was not discovered by anyone, according to our data.

did hall discover phobos $\Rightarrow$ *True*

All of the events of type "discover" are collected together and are checked to create a pair (*s*, *evs*) for each value of the *subject* property found in the set of events. *evs* is the set of events to which the *subject* property is related through a discovery event. Each pair is then examined to see if the function denoted by the object termphrase (in this case `phobos`) returns a non-empty set when applied to a set (called an *FDBR*, which is described in Sect. 6) generated from the set of *evs* in the pair, and if so the subject of the pair is added to the set which is returned as the denotation of the verbphrase part of the query. The denotation of the termphrase at the beginning of the query is then applied to the denotation of the verbphrase to obtain the answer to the query.

Owing to the fact that our semantics is compositional, the *subject* and *object* termphrases of the query above can be replaced by any termphrases, e.g.:

```
a person or a team discovered every moon that orbits mars
```
⇒ *True*
```
who discovered 2 moons that orbit mars ⇒ hall
```

"who", "what", "where", "when" and "how" can be used in place of the *subject* termphrase. Different role values are returned depending on which "*wh*"-word is used in the query:

```
where discovered by galileo ⇒ padua
when discovered by galileo ⇒ 1610
every telescope was used to discover a moon ⇒ True (w.r.t. our data)
a moon was discovered by every telescope ⇒ False
a telescope was used by hall to discover two moons ⇒ True
which moons were discovered with two telescopes
⇒ halimede laomedeia sao themisto
who discovered deimos with a telescope that was used   to
discover
every moon that orbits mars ⇒ hall
who discovered a moon with two telescopes
⇒ nicholson science_team_18 science_team_2
how was sao discovered ⇒ blanco_telescope canada-france-hawaii_telescope
how discovered in 1877 ⇒ refractor_telescope_1
how many telescopes were used to discover sao ⇒ 2
who discovered sao ⇒ science_team_18
how did science_team_18 discover sao
⇒ blanco_telescope canada-france-hawaii_telescope
which planet is orbited by every moon that was discov-
ered by two people ⇒ saturn; none (ambiguous because "by two people"
could apply to "discovered" or "orbited")
which person discovered a moon in 1877 with every tele-
scope that was used to discover phobos ⇒ hall; none (ambiguous because
"to discover phobos" could apply to "used" or "discovered")
who discovered in 1948 and 1949 with a telescope ⇒ kuiper
```

## 5.2  Queries with "Non-compositional" Structures

We agree that natural language has non-compositional features but believe that the non-compositionality is mostly problematic when the objective is to give a meaning to an arbitrary NL expression (i.e. an NL expression without a context). It is less problematic when answering NL queries. As illustrated below, the person posing the query, or the database or triplestore can provide contexts that help resolve much of the ambiguity resulting from non-compositional features. The advantages of a using a compositional semantics include:

1. The answer to a query is as correct as the data from which it is derived,
2. The meaning of sub phrases within a query can be discussed formally,
3. The query language can be extended such that all existing phrases maintain their original meanings,
4. The definition of syntax and semantics in the compositional semantics can be used as a blueprint for the implementation of the query processor.

Some researchers have provided examples of what they claim to be non-compositional structures in NL. For example, Hirst [16] gives the example of the verb "depart" which he states is not compositional because its meaning changes with the prepositional phrase(s) which follow it, and that the definition of compositionality needs to be modified to include the requirement that the function used to compose the meaning of parts must be systematic. We claim that our semantics for verbs is systematic as the denotations of subject and object termphrases, and the possibly empty list of prepositional phrases following the verb, are treated equally and are all used in the same way to filter the set of events of the type associated with the verb, before that set is returned as the denotation of the verb phrase. This is illustrated in the following queries:

who discovered ⇒ *bernard bond cassini cassini_imaging_science_team christy dollfus galileo etc ...*

No *subject, object* or prepositional phrase is given in the query, and so all events of type "discover" are returned by the verbphrase and the denotation of the word who picks out the *subjects* from those events.

where discovered io ⇒ *padua*

No *subject,* or prepositional phrase is given in the query, and so all events of type "discover" are considered and filtered by the denotation of the *object* termphrase io and then, those that pass the filter are returned by the verbphrase and the word where picks out the location from those events.

who discovered in 1610 ⇒ *galileo*

No *subject* or *object* is in the query so all events of type "discover" are considered and only those with the *year* property equal to 1610 pass the filter and then the denotation of the word who selects the subject which is returned.

who discovered every moon that orbits mars with one
telescope or a moon that orbits jupiter with a telescope ⇒ *one.* ;
*none.* ; *none.* ; *bernard galileo kowal melotte nicholson perrine science_team_-
1 science_team_2 ; hall ; hall ; none.*

As shown above, in our semantics, the *subject* and *object* termphrases are
treated as filters, as are all prepositional phrases. Note that several results are
returned here because the query is syntactically ambiguous. We discuss solutions
on how to best present the results of ambiguous queries to the user in Sect. 10.3.

where discovered in 1610 ⇒ *padua*
how discovered in padua ⇒ *galilean_telescope_1*

## 5.3    Extensions to the Semantics

Some phrases containing nested quantifiers are given by some researchers as
examples of non-compositionality. For example: "a US diplomat was sent to every
capital" is often read as having two meanings which can only be disambiguated
by additional knowledge. We argue that the person posing a query can express
the query unambiguously if they are familiar with quantifier scoping conventions
used by our processor, as illustrated in the following:

christy or science_team_19 or science_team_20 or science_team_21
discovered every moon that orbits pluto ⇒ *False*

In our semantics, quantifier scoping is always leftmost/outermost, and an unam-
biguous query can be formulated as follows:

every moon that orbits pluto was discovered by christy or
science_team_19 or science_team_20 or science_team_21 ⇒ *True*

Some examples of non-compositionality involve polysemantic superlative
words such as "most" in, for example:

*"Who discovered most moons that orbit P. Where P is a planet."*

If "most" is treated as "more than half" then:

who discovered most moons that orbit mars ⇒ *hall*

However, consider the answer to the alternate reading "who discovered the
most moons that orbit $P$" - i.e. more than anyone else who discovered a moon
that orbits $P$.:

what discovered the most moons that orbit jupiter
⇒ *science_team_4*

Here, the *subjects* of the "discover" events are sorted based on the cardinality of the number of things they discovered after filtering the events for
objects which are moons that orbit jupiter. Of the 50 moons that orbit jupiter,
science_team_4 discovered 12 of them.

`how was every moon that orbits saturn discovered` $\Rightarrow$ *cassini reflector_telescope_1 aerial_telescope_1 refractor_telescope_4 etc...*

It may be surprising that *cassini* is returned in the answer since it is not a `telescope`, but is instead a `spacecraft`. However, since it was used to discover at least one `moon` that orbits `saturn`, it is considered to have fulfilled the *implement* role and is encoded as such in the triplestore.

# 6 The FDBR: A Novel Data Structure for Natural Language Queries

## 6.1 Quantifiers and Events

In 2015, Champollion [5] stated that, at that time, it was generally thought by linguists that integration of Montagovian-style compositional semantics and Davidsonian–style event semantics [7,18] was problematic, particularly with respect to quantifiers. Champollion did not agree with that analysis and presented an integration which he called "quantificational event semantics" which he claimed solved the difficulties of integration by assuming that verbs and their projections denote existential quantifiers over events and that these quantifiers always take lowest possible scope.

In this paper, we borrow much from Montague Semantics (MS), Davidsonian Event Semantics, and Champollion's Quantificational Event Semantics. However, we provide definitions of our denotations in the notation of set theory, which improves computational efficiency and, we believe, simplifies understanding of our denotations. We also believe that our semantics is intuitive, systematic, and compositional.

## 6.2 Montague Semantics

All quantifiers, such as "a", "every" and "more than two" are treated in MS as functions which take two characteristic functions of sets as arguments and return a Boolean value as result. Our modifications to MS are to use sets of entities instead of predicates/characteristic functions of those sets, and to pair sets of events with each entity; the set of events paired with an entity justify the entity's inclusion in the denotation. For example:

$$\|propernoun\| = \lambda p.\{(e, evs) \mid (e, evs) \in p \ \& \ e = \text{the entity associated}$$
$$\text{with the proper noun}\}$$

$$\|spins\| = \{(e_{phobos}, \{ev_{1360}\}), (e_{deimos}, \{ev_{1332}\}), etc \ldots\}$$

Therefore,

$$\|phobos \ spins\|$$
$$\Longrightarrow \|phobos\| \ \|spins\|$$
$$\Longrightarrow \lambda s.\{(e, evs) \mid (e, evs) \in s \ \& \ e = e_{phobos}\} \ \|spins\|$$
$$\Longrightarrow \{(e, evs \mid (e, evs) \in \|spins\| \ \& \ e = e_{phobos}\}$$
$$\Longrightarrow \{(e_{phobos}, \{ev_{1360}\})\}$$

We call this set of pairs of entities and events an *FDBR*, and describe it in more detail in Sect. 6.3. In the following example, we show how the FDBR can be used to denote the quantifier **a**. The function *intersect* computes the intersection of two FDBRs based on their entities, keeping the events of the second FDBR and discarding those of the first in the result.

$$intersect = \lambda m \lambda s.\{(e_1, evs_2) \mid (e_1, evs_1) \in m \ \& \ (e_2, evs_2) \in s \ \& \ e_1 = e_2\}$$
$$\|a\| = intersect$$

Therefore,

$$\|a \ moon \ spins\|$$
$$\implies \|a\|\|moon\|\|spins\|$$
$$\implies \{(e_1, evs_2) \mid (e_1, evs_1) \in \|moon\| \ \& \ (e_2, evs_2) \in \|spins\| \ \& \ e_1 = e_2\}$$
$$\implies \{(e_{phobos}, \{ev_{1360}\}), (e_{deimos}, \{ev_{1332}\}), \ etc \ldots\}$$

We can define the denotations of other quantifiers in terms of *intersect* as well. For example, consider the denotation of **every**, where *ents m* denotes the set of entities that appear in the first column of the FDBR $m$:

$$ents = \lambda m.\{ent \mid (\exists evs) \ (ent, evs) \in m\}$$
$$\|every\| = \lambda m \lambda s. \begin{cases} intersect \ m \ s, & ents \ m \subseteq ents \ s \\ \emptyset, & otherwise \end{cases}$$

Therefore,

$$\|every \ moon \ spins\|$$
$$\implies \|every\|\|moon\|\|spins\|$$
$$\implies intersect \ m \ s, \quad since \ ents \ \|moon\| \subseteq ents \ \|spins\|$$
$$\implies \{(e_{phobos}, \{ev_{1360}\}), (e_{deimos}, \{ev_{1332}\}), \ etc \ldots\}$$

Note that the events *evs* paired with the entities returned in the denotation of "was every moon that orbits saturn discovered" are a subset of the events of type "discover" where the *object* property of those events are moons, since the result of *intersect_fdbr* takes the events of from its second argument. This enables additional data to be accessed from those events, as illustrated in the last example query in the previous section, where "how" retrieves the *implement* property from those events. This allows all "*wh*"-style questions to be handled compositionally, selecting the desired properties from the events as needed.

## 6.3   The FDBR

In order to generate the answer to "hall discovered every moon that orbits mars", $\|every\|$ is applied to $\|moon \ that \ orbits \ mars\|$ (i.e. the set of moons that orbit `mars`), as first argument, and the set of entities that were discovered by `hall`, as the second argument. Our semantics generates this set from the set of events of type "discover" whose the subject property is *"hall"*, as discussed below:

Every set of $n$-ary events (i.e. events with $n$ roles) of a given type, e.g. discovery, defines $n^2 - n$ binary relations. For example, for discovery events:

$$discover\_rel_{subject \rightarrow object} \; discover\_rel_{subject \rightarrow year} \; discover\_rel_{subject \rightarrow implement} \cdots$$

$$discover\_rel_{object \rightarrow subject} \; discover\_rel_{object \rightarrow year} \; discover\_rel_{object \rightarrow implement} \cdots$$

$$discover\_rel_{year \rightarrow subject} \; \; discover\_rel_{year \rightarrow object} \; \; discover\_rel_{year \rightarrow implement} \cdots$$

$etc \ldots$ to 20 binary relations for the set of discovery events or an 5-ary discovery relation. For example:

$$discover\_rel_{subject \rightarrow object} =$$
$$\{(ev_{1045}, e_{hall}, e_{phobos}), (ev_{1046}, e_{hall}, e_{deimos}), etc \ldots\}$$

If we collect all of the values from the range of a relation that are mapped to by each value $v$ from the domain (i.e. the image of $v$ under the relation $r$) and create the set of all pairs $(v, image\_of\_v)$, we obtain a *Function Defined by the Relation $r$*, i.e. the FDBR. For example:

$$\text{FDBR}(discover\_rel_{subject \rightarrow object})$$
$$= \Big\{(e_{hall}, \{(e_{phobos}, \{ev_{1045}\}), (e_{deimos}, \{ev_{1046}\})\}), etc \ldots \Big\}$$

It is these functions that are created, and used, by the denotation of the transitive verb associated with the type of the events. For example in calculating the value of $\|who\ discovered\ every\ moon\ that\ orbits\ mars\|$, $\|every\|$ is applied to the set of entities which is the denotation of "`moon that orbits mars`" (i.e $\{(e_{phobos}, \{ev_{1045}\})$ , $(e_{deimos}, \{ev_{1046}\})\}$ ) and all of the images that are in the second field of the pairs in FDBR($discover\_rel_{subject \rightarrow object}$). For the pair $(e_{hall}, \{(e_{phobos}, \{ev_{1045}\}), (e_{deimos}, \{ev_{1046}\})\})$, $\|every\|$ returns the nonempty set $\{(e_{phobos}, \{ev_{1045}\}), (e_{deimos}, \{ev_{1046}\} )\}$, and the value in the first field, i.e. $e_{hall}$, is subsequently returned with the answer to the query.

The various FDBRs are used to answer different types of queries. For example:

`who discovered phobos and deimos` $\Rightarrow$ *hall*
    uses FDBR($discover\_rel_{subject \rightarrow object}$)
`where discovered by galileo` $\Rightarrow$ *padua*
    uses FDBR($discover\_rel_{location \rightarrow subject}$)
`how discovered in 1610 or 1855` $\Rightarrow$ *galilean_telescope_1*
    uses FDBR($discover\_rel_{implement \rightarrow year}$)

## 7 Handling Prepositional Phrases

Prepositional phrases (PPs) such as "`with a telescope`" are treated similarly to the method above, except that the termphrase following the preposition is applied to the set of entities that are extracted from the set of events in the FDBR function, according to the role associated with the preposition. The result is a "filtered" FDBR which is further filtered by subsequent PPs.

## 8    Handling Superlative Phrases

A novel feature of our semantics is that we can directly accommodate superlative phrases such as "most" and "the most" inside chained prepositional phrases. Here, we take "most" to mean "more than half" and "the most" to mean "more than anything else". This makes it possible to answer queries such as "who discovered a moon using the most telescopes" and "most planets are orbited by a moon" with our NLQI.

Superlatives can be placed nearly anywhere a determiner can exist. This makes it possible to nest superlatives inside chained prepositional phrases, a property we believe to be novel in our semantics. For example, consider "what discovered at the most places using the most telescopes", where "the most" occurs inside both prepositional phrases "at the most places" and "using the most telescopes". The query is always evaluated in left-to-right order, and results are sorted by each superlative phrase in the order they appear. In this case, the results are first sorted by the number of places, followed by the number of telescopes, both in descending order. First, the denotation for "most" (as in "more than half") is defined as follows:

$$\|most\| = \lambda m \lambda s. \begin{cases} intersect\ m\ s, & |intersect\ m\ s| > |s|/2 \\ \emptyset, & \text{otherwise} \end{cases}$$

Providing a denotation for superlative phrases such as "the most" is more challenging. To achieve this and maintain compositionality, the superlatives are handled in the denotation for the transitive verbs. First, we introduce the denotation for "the most":

$$\|the\ most\| = \lambda m.(\text{GT}, intersect\ m)$$

"the most" takes a nounphrase as an argument and returns a pair consisting of the ordering $GT$ (i.e. "greater than"), and a termphrase created using partial application of the *intersect* function. This ordering describes how the results should be sorted – in this case, in descending order.

The denotation for prepositional phrases is modified to include an ordering as third parameter, which may take on the special value *None* if the prepositional phrase does not contain a superlative phrase within it. However, if it does contain a superlative phrase, the ordering of the prepositional phrase is set to the ordering specified in the denotation of the superlative phrase.

The denotation for transitive verbs is modified such that, at the end of the prepositional phrase evaluation performed previously, where the filtered FDBR is obtained (containing only *relevant* events [19]), the resulting FDBR is passed to a new function, filter_super, which handles superlative evaluation. The behavior of this function is as follows. First, if no superlatives are present (i.e. the ordering in the denotation of each prepositional phrase is *None*), nothing more is done, and the behavior of the new denotation is identical to the previous one.

If superlatives are present, however, they are evaluated in the order they appear. For each superlative phrase present in the chain of prepositional phrases, the FDBR is expanded to a new data structure called a *Generalized FDBR* (or *GFDBR*) which is similar to an FDBR, except that instead of having a set of events in its second column, it has an FDBR instead. The GFDBR is formed by taking the set of events in each row of the original FDBR, and expanding them into an FDBR using the role attached in the prepositional phrase. This is used to obtain the cardinality of the number of entities that the subject is related to in that role under the FDBR (called the *object cardinality*). Now, these object cardinalities are used to partition the GFDBR into a set of GFDBRs, where the set with the highest (or lowest) object cardinality is chosen to replace the original GFDBR, depending on the ordering in the denotation of the prepositional phrase (i.e. the ordering denoted by the superlative phrase). For "the most", it would be the set with the highest object cardinality (since the ordering is $GT$). In the future, for "the least", it would be the set with the lowest object cardinality. The GFDBR is then converted back into an FDBR by keeping only the events in each row, and the process repeats until no more superlative phrases are remaining. The final FDBR is returned as the result.

This allows superlative phrases to still be handled in left-to-right evaluation order, and it also allows results to be sorted by multiple columns. For example "who discovered the most moons in the most places" would first sort by "the most moons", and following that, would sort by "the most places". Currently, we are not able to accommodate "the least", as the semantics filters out rows with empty sets of events in FDBRs before superlatives work on them. For example, if a user were to ask "which planet has the least moons", the answer currently would be "earth", as it has only one moon, and our system filters out both "venus" and "mercury" (which have no moons) before they have a chance to affect the result. This seems to be related to our original Open World Assumption, where we only include results in the result set if there is at least one accompanying event in the FDBR to justify its inclusion. It is possible that if negation could be accommodated in the semantics, then "the least" could be handled as well, since they seem to be related problems.

## 9  Our Approach with Relational Databases

Our NLQI can be easily adapted for use with conventional relational databases. First, note that each event at minimum contains a role *ev_type* that identifies the type of event, and as noted in Sect. 4, there is a general expectation that events of the same type should contain similar roles. Second, note that the event identifier in each triple is a URI and is therefore unique by definition.

Assume the roles that events of a particular type $t$ are fixed, including optional roles. Let $N$ be the number of roles, including optional roles, that an event of type $t$ contains. Then an event of type $t$ can be described as a row in a relation with $N$ columns, each role occupying one column respectively, with optional roles taking on a special value NULL if they are not present in that particular event. Let this relation be called $ev\_type$.

Store this relation in a relational database as a table using the event identifier as the primary key. Now, only the triple retrieval functions in Sect. 10.2 need to be modified to use this database in place of a triplestore. This architecture allows the denotations to remain unchanged and yet still work with different types of databases. Note that triplestores do have an advantage in that they need not be rebuilt if a new role is added to the event. The decision to choose one approach over the other needs to be weighed based on application specific factors.

## 10    Implementation of Our NLQI

We built our query processor as an executable attribute grammar using the *X-SAIGA* Haskell parser-combinator library package [15]. The *collect* function which converts a binary relation to an FDBR is one of the most compute intensive parts of our implementation of the semantics. However, in Haskell, once a value is computed, it can be made available for future use. We have developed an algorithm to compute FDBR($rel$) in $O(n \lg n)$ time, where $n$ is the number of pairs in $rel$. Alternatively, the FDBR functions can be computed and stored in a cache when the NLQI is offline. Our implementation is amenable to running on low power devices, enabling it for use with the Internet of Things. A version of our query processor exists that can run on a common consumer network router as a proof of concept for this application. The use of Haskell for the implementation of our NLQI has many advantages, including:

1. Haskell's "lazy" evaluation strategy only computes values when they are required, enabling parser combinator libraries to be built that can handle highly ambiguous left-recursive grammars in polynomial time.
2. The higher-order functional capability of Haskell allows the direct definition of higher-order functions that are the denotations of some English words and phrases.
3. The ability to partially apply functions of $n$ arguments to 1 to $n$ arguments allows the definition and manipulation of denotation of phrases such as "every moon", and "discover phobos".
4. The availability of the *hsparql* [25] Haskell package enables a simple interface between our semantic processor and SPARQL endpoints to our triplestores.

## 10.1  System Architecture

A flowchart of our system architecture is presented in Fig. 1.

The query begins as a string of text as sent to the semantics, which is then sent directly to the parser, as described in Sect. 3.1. This produces two results:

(1) A function that, given a set of triples, will evaluate the query with respect to that set of triples and return the result
(2) A *"Memo Tree"* that roughly follows the syntax tree resulting from the parse of the input string. In addition to providing a unique name to each sub-expression of the parsed input, it is also used to determine which queries need to be evaluated against the remote triplestore.

The function produced in (1) requires a set of triples to produce a result. While it is possible, given sufficient time and resources, to directly retrieve all triples from the remote triplestore and pass them directly into this function to evaluate the input, in practice it is cost prohibitive to do so.

Instead, we retrieve only *relevant triples* [19] from the remote triplestore and we create a *reduced* triplestore from them which is then passed into (1).

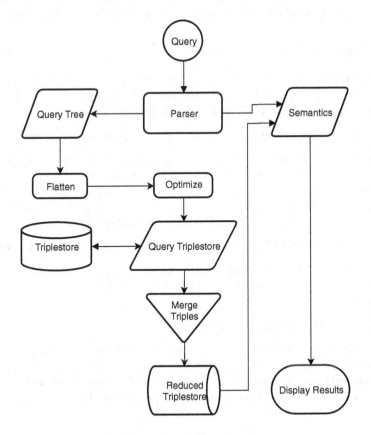

**Fig. 1.** Application architecture.

The Memo Tree obtained in (2) is traversed to obtain the set of all triplestore queries that are required to evaluate each sub-expression of the parsed input. These queries correspond to the `getts` family of functions described in Sect. 10.2. The results of these queries may *overlap*, i.e. share triples in common with those of other queries in the set. An optimization step is performed to eliminate these redundant queries. Domain specific knowledge could be used to improve this process where appropriate. Finally, these optimized queries are evaluated against the remote triplestore and the results are merged and stored locally in the reduced triplestore. These triples are then passed to the function produced in (1), yielding the final result. This is one area where our NLQI differs from other NLQIs to the Semantic Web – notice that nowhere do we attempt to directly translate the NL query into SPARQL or any other querying language. Instead, we rely on simple triple querying primitives which are embedded in the semantics to perform this task for us.

The architecture presented in this section lends itself to a very clean implementation in Haskell, where the semantics themselves can be written as pure functions, with the only impure parts of the NLQI being those that directly deal with querying the triplestore and with presenting these results to the user. We expand on the individual sub-components of the NLQI in the following sections.

## 10.2   Triple Retrieval

**Remote Triplestore.** Our semantics does not directly depend upon any particular query language. When querying remote triplestores, the NLQI requires only two conceptually simple functions. The first is:

```
getts_triples_entevprop_type ev_data prop_names ev_type
```

This function is used to retrieve triples belonging to the relation `ev_type`. `prop_names` is a list of columns of the relation to retrieve. Only the names of the columns of the relation that are actually required are listed here. Finally, `ev_data` is the URL used to access the remote triplestore or database. For example, in the query **what discovered**, it may be invoked as follows:

```
getts_triples_entevprop_type url ["subject"] "discover_ev"
```

This would retrieve the triples of all "discover" events that contain a *subject* property, including the triples describing the type of those events. The second function is:

```
getts_triples_members ev_data set
```

Here, `ev_data` performs the same function as it did previously, and "set" indicates the name of a set, for example the moons or the set of things that spin. This retrieves the triples of all "membership" events whose *object* property corresponds to that set, including the triples describing the type of those events.

Together, these two primitives can be used to retrieve triples from event-based triplestores, provided the names of the roles to be queried are known. This would typically be described in a schema, but in simple cases may be feasible to hard-code into a program. To see how these two primitives work in action, consider the following complex query, featuring chained prepositional phrases:

which person discovered a moon in 1877 with a telescope

This would invoke the following queries to the database:

```
getts_triples_entevprop_type url ["subject", "object",
"year", "implement"] "discover_ev"
  getts_triples_members url "moon"
  getts_triples_members url "telescope"
  getts_triples_members url "person"
```

These four queries to the remote triplestore, taken together, will retrieve enough information to answer the user's query. Transitive and intransitive verbs are implemented in terms of `getts_triples_entevprop_type`. Common nouns and adjectives are implemented in terms of `getts_triples_members`. These conceptually simple functions are easy to implement in SPARQL, SQL, and as Triple Pattern Fragments [23]. An example implementation is provided in our source code, available on Hackage [15] for both Triple Pattern Fragments and SPARQL.

After all "getts" queries are evaluated, their results are merged together into a local *reduced* triplestore. The idea behind this triplestore is that it contains enough triples to evaluate the correct result, but no more than that. In other words, the results from passing in the entire triplestore to the semantic function in (1) and the results from passing in the reduced triplestore should be equivalent.

**Reduced Triplestore.** Once the reduced triplestore is passed into the semantics, however, it still needs to be queried by the semantic functions in the denotations. This is where the boundary of the impure code of the NLQI meets the pure code of the semantics. At this higher level, there are three primitives that are used to query the reduced triplestore:

- `pure_getts_triples_entevprop_type ev_data prop_names ev_type`
- `pure_getts_triples_entevprop ev_data prop_names evs`
- `pure_getts_members ev_data set`

These are very similar functions to those described previously, however they are implemented as pure functions in Haskell. The actual implementation of the reduced triplestore is opaque to the semantics, which rely strictly on these three functions to retrieve triples from the reduced triplestore. Implementing these as pure functions allows them to be embedded in the semantics, which are implemented as pure functions themselves. This provides a number of benefits, including allowing the semantics and queries to be lazily evaluated.

pure_getts_triples_entevprop_type performs a similar role as it did previously. pure_getts_triples_entevprop is a new function that, instead of specifying an event type parameter, specifies a set of events instead. This is used to implement chained prepositional phrases, where sets of events are honed down in the order that the phrases occur in (from left to right). Finally, pure_getts_members performs a similar function as it did previously, except this time it directly returns an FDBR from the members of the set given to the events in which the set membership is recorded.

## 10.3   Handling Ambiguity in the Query Interface

**Syntactic Ambiguity.** As queries may be ambiguous, it's important that users see how their queries were parsed to understand the result given. Our system displays the parse tree along with the query result to assist with this. The parse tree is presented in a familiar Haskell syntax to indicate scoping. As an example, consider the scoping of the simple query "who discovered a moon that orbits mars":

```
who (discovered (a (moon `that` (orbits mars))))
```

Here, we see that scoping of denotations is shown with parentheses. Prepositional phrases are enclosed inside square brackets, with commas to delimit chained prepositional phrases:

who discovered a moon in 1877 with a telescope

$\Rightarrow$ who (discovered (a moon) [in 1877, with (a telescope)])

This mirrors the familiar list syntax that Haskell offers and suggests to the user that the prepositional phrases will be evaluated in the order presented (left to right), allowing users to understand exactly how their query is evaluated by the system. Now, consider the following ambiguous query:

who discovered a moon that orbits in 1877

There are two possible parses of this query, depending on which transitive verb the prepositional phrase "in 1877" is applied to:

who (discovered (a (moon `that` (orbits [in 1877]))))) $\Rightarrow$ *none*

who (discovered (a (moon `that` orbits)) [in 1877]) $\Rightarrow$ *hall*

In the first case, the prepositional phrase "in 1877" is treated as though it applies to "orbits". However, the result is "*none*" because orbit events do not have a concept of time in our database. If we were to add a *year* role to the "orbit" relation, then all planets and moons in the solar system would be returned. In the second case, "in 1877" applies to "discovered", a relation which has the concept of a time of discovery (the *year* role). As hall is the only person that discovered anything in 1877, only they are included in the result.

Our system permits highly ambiguous input, providing a result for each possible parse of that input. However, it may be the case that a user has a clear understanding of how they want their query to be parsed and would gain no benefit from seeing other possible parses of their query. Fortunately, this use case is easily accommodated with a simple extension to our NLQI: allowing the scoping syntax as presented above directly in the query interface itself. For example, a user could directly query "what (discovered (a (moon 'that' orbits)) [in 1877])", which would exclude the other parse as mentioned in the example above. In fact, the query need not even be fully explicitly scoped to benefit from this. A partial scoping such as "what discovered (a moon that orbits) in 1877" would be sufficient to exclude the other undesirable parses from the result. We intend to implement this functionality in our NLQI in the very near future.

It may also be worthwhile to implement a simple dialogue-based approach to disambiguation, where the system could simply provide the possible parses to the user and allow them to choose which one they intended. This approach may be beneficial when using speech to interact with the system, as providing scoping with the above method directly with speech would be very inconvenient. An example dialogue could be:

**User:**

what discovered a moon that orbits mars in 1877 with a telescope

**Interface:**

There are three possible ways I can interpret this query.

Which one do you mean?

1) what (discovered (a (moon 'that' (orbits mars [in 1877, with (a telescope)])))))

2) what (discovered (a (moon 'that' (orbits mars)))) [in 1877, with (a telescope)])

3) what (discovered (a (moon 'that' (orbits mars [in 1877])))) [with (a telescope)])

**User:**

2

**Interface:**

OK -- the result of the second interpretation is ''hall''

If the modality of the interface is by voice, reading the scoping directly as presented above may be inconvenient to users. Fortunately, it is possible to verbally state the scoping in an intuitive way:

**User:**

```
what discovered a moon that orbits mars in 1877 with a
telescope
```

**Interface:**

```
I can interpret this three different ways. In the first
interpretation, the prepositions ``in 1877'' and ``with a
telescope'' apply to the verb ``orbit''. Is that what you
meant?
```

**User:**

```
no
```

**Interface:**

```
In the second interpretation, the prepositions ``in
1877'' and ``with a telescope'' apply to the verb ``discov-
ered''. Is that what you meant?
```

**User:**

```
yes, that's what i meant
```

**Interface:**

```
OK -- the result of that interpretation is ``hall''
```

Given the different nature of the user's responses compared to the queries themselves, they may be subject to a different grammar or may be handled by a different system entirely that permits more free-form responses to be given. This could be a good opportunity to integrate Machine Learning-based NLP approaches in the NLQI in the future, as they are ideally suited to use cases involving loosely structured input.

**Semantic Ambiguity.** Semantic ambiguity may also be accommodated by permitting multiple definitions of the same terminal in the grammar, augmenting it with a human readable description of what the terminal means. Each definition would be evaluated as though it were a different parse of the query, although each parse would have the same syntax tree. To avoid confusion, the human readable definition of the word could be printed below the tree.

## 10.4   Semantic Implementation

The semantics themselves are completely unaware of the structure of the underlying triplestore or the methods and query languages used to retrieve triples from it. Recall from Sect. 10.1 that the result of a parse of user input produces two items: a pure function that, given a triplestore as input will produce the result of a query and a tree that represents the query itself, including the types of queries that are required from a remote triplestore.

**Applying Multiple Semantics in Parallel.** The Biapplicative Bifunctor in Haskell, which is inspired from its counterpart in category theory, can serve as a generalization of function application. One possible use for it is to apply pairs of values to pairs of functions. Briefly, given two arbitrary functions $f$ and $g$ and two values $a$ and $b$ we can use the biapplicative operator `<<*>>` to apply $a$ and $b$ both functions in parallel: $(f, g)$ `<<*>>` $(a, b) = (f\ a, g\ b)$. The functions themselves need not be related.

First, we introduce an operator, `>|<`, that allows us to bridge together two semantics such that they can be applied using `<<*>>`:

$$a >|< b = (a, b)$$

This allows these two independent functions to be applied in parallel while parsing the input string using the exact same grammar and no code duplication, provided the `<<*>>` is used in place of function application. For example, "a moon spins" is evaluated as though it were written as "a `<<*>>` moon `<<*>>` spins" under this approach. Our NLQI uses this to construct the Memo Tree in parallel while applying the denotations of the words in the query. Consider the following example, where GIntersect and GMembers are constructors of the Memo Tree:

```
a' = a >|< GIntersect
moon' = moon >|< GMembers "moon"
spins' = spins >|< GMembers "spins"
```

Therefore,

$$a' \lll* \ggg moon' \lll* \ggg spins'$$
$$\Rightarrow (\text{a moon spins, GIntersect (GMembers "moon") (GMembers "spin")})$$

However, this is somewhat inconvenient and unfamiliar syntax to work with. Fortunately, it is trivial to define a set of "wrapper" functions to restore the original function application syntax:

$$wrap_N\ (f, g)\ (a_1, b_1)\ (a_2, b_2)\ \ldots\ (a_N, b_N) = (f\ a_1\ a_2 \ldots a_N,\ g\ b_1\ b_2 \ldots b_N)$$

Here, the function $wrap_N$ takes a pair of functions $(f, g)$ with arity $N$ and then $N$ pairs of arguments to be applied in order to $f$ and $g$ respectively. This allows " $a'$`<<*>>` moon' `<<*>>` spins'" above to be written as "a' moon spins", where $a'' = wrap_2\ a'$. Therefore, we can retain the familiar function application syntax in the semantics while taking advantage of parallel function application. By itself, this is a convenience, but let us revisit the Memo Tree once more. It has two uses. The first is as stated previously, in determining which queries need to be performed against the remote triplestore. The second is that this allows us to assign a unique identifier to each sub-expression of the parsed input.

**Memoized Compositional Semantics.** Consider the query "what is orbited by a thing that was discovered by a person that discovered phobos", containing three nested transitive verbs. One possible parse of this query yields:

```
what (is orbited [by (a (thing 'that' (was discovered [by
    (a (person 'that' (discovered phobos)))])))])
```

A query's sub-expressions may be evaluated multiple times during the prepositional filtering of a transitive verb (i.e one evaluation for each row of the FDBR denoted in that transitive verb). This has a compounding effect when transitive verbs are nested as sub-expressions in prepositional phrases of other transitive verbs. In general, if there are $m$ nested transitive verbs in a query, each having an FDBR with $n$ rows. Then the complexity for evaluation is $O(n^m)$.

As it turns out, we can use the Memo Tree to memoize the results of the sub-expressions of a query, drastically reducing the number of re-evaluations performed. The memoization occurs in a more sophisticated version of the $wrap_N$ functions described previously, which use the unique identifier provided by the Memo Tree to memoize the results of the semantic functions as they are evaluated. This is completely transparent to the user, and the familiar function application syntax used in all previous examples still remains. This reduces the complexity to $O(mn)$, where $m$ is the number of nested transitive verbs, each having an FDBR with $n$ rows. All sub-expressions in the query are memoized, including the final result of the query expression itself.

The State monad in Haskell is used to thread the memoized state throughout the execution of the semantics. This mirrors the memoization technique used in the parser itself to provide efficient parsing using combinators [13]. We believe this two-pronged approach to triplestore retrieval and memoization is novel and has not been used in any other Compositional Semantics-based systems. We intend to expand more on our approach in a future publication, as we believe it to be useful for creating modular and efficient compositional NLQIs that can scale to the needs of the Semantic Web.

## 11   Related Work

Orakel [6] is a portable NLQI which uses a Montague-like grammar and a lambda calculus semantics. Our approach is similar in this respect. Queries are translated to an expression of first order logic enriched with predicates for query and numerical operators. These expressions are translated to SPARQL or F-Logic. Orakel supports negation, limited quantification, and simple prepositional phrases.

YAGO2 [17] is a semantic knowledge base containing reified triples extracted from Wikipedia, WordNet and GeoNames, representing nearly 0.5 billion facts. Reification is achieved by tagging each triple with an identifier. However, this is hidden from the user who views the knowledge base as a set of "SPOTL" quintuples, where T is for time and L for location. The SPOTLX query language is used to access YAGO2. SPOTLX can handle queries with prepositional aspects involving time and location. However, no mention is made of chained complex PPs.

Alexandria [24] is an event-based triplestore, with 160 million triples (representing 13 million n-ary relationships), derived from FreeBase. Alexandria uses a neo-Davidsonian [18] event-based semantics. In Alexandria, queries are parsed to a syntactic dependency graph, mapped to a semantic description, and translated to SPARQL queries containing named graphs. Queries with simple PPs are accommodated. However, no mention is made of negation, nested quantification, or chained complex PPs.

The systems referred to above have made substantial progress in handling ambiguity and matching NL query words to URIs. However, they appear to have hit a roadblock with respect to natural-language coverage. Most can handle simple PPs such as in "who was born in 1918" but none can handle chained complex PPs, containing quantifiers, such as "in us_naval_observatory in 1877 or 1860".

Blackburn and Bos [4] implemented lambda calculus with respect to natural language, in Prolog, and Van Eijck and Unger [22] have extensively and clearly discussed such implementation in Haskell. Implementation of the lambda calculus for open-domain question answering has been investigated by [1]. The SQUALL query language [10,11] is a controlled natural language (CNL) for querying and updating triplestores represented as RDF graphs. SQUALL can return answers directly from remote triplestores, as we do, using simple SPARQL-endpoint triple retrieval commands. It can also be translated to SPARQL queries which can be processed by SPARQL endpoints for faster computation of answers. SQUALL can handle quantification, aggregation, some forms of negation, and simple unchained prepositional phrases containing the word "at" and "in". It can also handle superlative phrases as long as they are not nested under a prepositional phrase. Notably, the scope of prepositional phrases in SQUALL are the entire sentence they reside in. It is also written in a functional language. However, some queries in SQUALL require the use of variables and low-level relational algebraic operators (see for example, the queries on page 118 of [11]).

## 12   Future Work

**Negation.** Our system currently relies on the Open World Assumption, where the absence of evidence cannot be treated as having evidence of absence. As a consequence of this, the system currently is unable to handle negation, and does not have a denotation for the words "no" and "not".

However, there is a clear need for handling negation in our semantics where the Closed World Assumption holds. For example, it should be possible to answer queries such as "who did not discover a moon "or" what discovered no moon". Work has been done on event-based semantics that can handle negation [5]. We believe it should be possible to accommodate negation in our semantics as well using a similar approach, and in turn provide a denotation for "the least" as well, as noted in Sect. 8.

**DBPedia.** With the addition of memoization in our semantics, we feel our approach is now scalable enough to work directly with DBPedia. We intend to expand on how our semantics can handle large triplestores such as DBPedia in a future publication. In particular, an interface to DBPedia will allow our approach to be directly evaluated with existing systems in use, such as YAGO [17].

**Hardware Acceleration.** Consider that the reduced triplestore described in Sect. 10.2 is stored locally in the query interface and is queried with the pure "getts" functions. These could make good candidates for offloading to FPGA fabric or a GPU for hardware acceleration. Work has been done in developing on FPGAs using Haskell [3]. This could allow for both low latency and low power consumption in embedded consumer devices, such as those that operate on the Internet of Things.

**Non-Event-Based Triplestores.** We also believe it should be possible to handle non-event based triplestores as well using our approach using a translation layer. It may be possible to use ontological information to provide an event-based view to many kinds of non-event based data. Machine Learning approaches could provide a way forward in the absence of or lacking sufficient ontological information about a triplestore.

## 13   Conclusions

This work comes at an appropriate time when massive triplestores, such as DBpedia [2] are being created containing billions of verified facts. We are currently looking at how such facts can be converted to event-based triples which can be queried by our interface. We are confident that, after we accommodate negation, our compositional semantics is appropriate for answering most queries that are likely to be asked of data stores containing everyday knowledge. We have shown how the FDBR data structure presented in this paper can be used to handle many kinds of complex language features, including chained prepositional phrases and superlatives. The way quantification is handled within the semantics is consistent with other work in this area, as discussed in Sect. 6.1. Our approach is extensible enough that it can accommodate queries to both relational and non-relational types of database, including Semantic Web triplestores. Our approach is also suitable for use on low power devices, which may be useful for applications on the Internet of Things (IoT).

We have shown how our system is tolerant of highly ambiguous user input and we discussed possible ways to present this in Sect. 10.3. In particular, we discussed how both semantic and syntactic ambiguity could be handled. We also presented a novel approach to memorizing compositional semantics using unique identifiers attached to sub-expressions in a query, substantially improving the time complexity of evaluation. We also showed how those unique identifiers are also useful to determine the set of queries that need to be made to the remote database.

Our next goal is to provide an NLQI to DBPedia using our approach with the techniques described here, and then evaluate the effectiveness of our system relative to other NLQIs using established benchmarks, such as QALD [21].

# References

1. Ahn, K., Bos, J., Kor, D., Nissim, M., Webber, B.L., Curran, J.R.: Question answering with QED at TREC 2005. In: TREC (2005)
2. Auer, S., Bizer, C., Kobilarov, G., Lehmann, J., Cyganiak, R., Ives, Z.: DBpedia: a nucleus for a web of open data. In: Aberer, K., et al. (eds.) ASWC/ISWC -2007. LNCS, vol. 4825, pp. 722–735. Springer, Heidelberg (2007). https://doi.org/10. 1007/978-3-540-76298-0_52
3. Baaij, C.: CΛash: from Haskell to hardware. Master's thesis, University of Twente (2009)
4. Blackburn, P., Bos, J.: Representation and Inference for Natural Language. A First Course in Computational Semantics, CSLI (2005)
5. Champollion, L.: The interaction of compositional semantics and event semantics. Linguist. Philos. **38**(1), 31–66 (2014). https://doi.org/10.1007/s10988-014-9162-8
6. Cimiano, P., Haase, P., Heizmann, J., Mantel, M.: ORAKEL: a portable natural language interface to knowledge bases. Technical report, Institute AIFB, University of Karlsruhe (2007)
7. Davidson, D.: The logical form of action sentences (1967)
8. Earley, J.: An efficient context-free parsing algorithm. Commun. ACM **13**(2), 94–102 (1970). https://doi.org/10.1145/362007.362035
9. Erling, O., Mikhailov, I.: Virtuoso: RDF support in a native RDBMS. In: de Virgilio, R., Giunchiglia, F., Tanca, L. (eds.) Semantic Web Information Management, pp. 501–519. Springer, Heidelberg (2010). https://doi.org/10.1007/978-3-642-04329-1_21
10. Ferré, S.: SQUALL: a controlled natural language for querying and updating RDF graphs. In: Kuhn, T., Fuchs, N.E. (eds.) CNL 2012. LNCS (LNAI), vol. 7427, pp. 11–25. Springer, Heidelberg (2012). https://doi.org/10.1007/978-3-642-32612-7_2
11. Ferré, S.: SQUALL: a controlled natural language as expressive as SPARQL 1.1. In: Métais, E., Meziane, F., Saraee, M., Sugumaran, V., Vadera, S. (eds.) NLDB 2013. LNCS, vol. 7934, pp. 114–125. Springer, Heidelberg (2013). https://doi.org/10.1007/978-3-642-38824-8_10
12. Frost, R., Launchbury, J.: Constructing natural language interpreters in a lazy functional language. Comput. J. **32**(2), 108–121 (1989)
13. Frost, R.A., Hafiz, R., Callaghan, P.: Parser combinators for ambiguous left-recursive grammars. In: Hudak, P., Warren, D.S. (eds.) PADL 2008. LNCS, vol. 4902, pp. 167–181. Springer, Heidelberg (2007). https://doi.org/10.1007/978-3-540-77442-6_12
14. Frost, R.A., Peelar, S.M.: A new data structure for processing natural language database queries. In: Proceedings of the 15th International Conference on Web Information Systems and Technologies, WEBIST 2019, Vienna, Austria, 18–20 September 2019, pp. 80–87 (2019). https://doi.org/10.5220/0008124300800087
15. Hafiz, R., Frost, R., Peelar, S., Callaghan, P., Matthews, E.: The XSaiga package (2018)
16. Hirst, G.: Semantic Interpretation and the Resolution Of Ambiguity. Cambridge University Press, Cambridge (1992)

17. Hoffart, J., Suchanek, F.M., Berberich, K., Weikum, G.: YAGO2: a spatially and temporally enhanced knowledge base from Wikipedia. Artif. Intell. **194**, 28–61 (2013)
18. Parsons, T.: Events in the Semantics of English, vol. 5. MIT Press, Cambridge (1990)
19. Peelar, S.: Accommodating prepositional phrases in a highly modular natural language query interface to semantic web triplestores using a novel event-based denotational semantics for English and a set of functional parser combinators. Master's thesis, University of Windsor, Canada (2016)
20. Tomita, M.: Efficient Parsing for Natural Language: A Fast Algorithm for Practical Systems. Kluwer Academic Publishers, Boston (1985)
21. Usbeck, R., Gusmita, R.H., Ngomo, A.C.N., Saleem, M.: 9th challenge on question answering over linked data (QALD-9). In: Semdeep/NLIWoD@ ISWC, pp. 58–64 (2018)
22. Van Eijck, J., Unger, C.: Computational Semantics with Functional Programming. Cambridge University Press, Cambridge (2010)
23. Verborgh, R., Vander Sande, M., Colpaert, P., Coppens, S., Mannens, E., Van de Walle, R.: Web-scale querying through linked data fragments. In: LDOW. Citeseer (2014)
24. Wendt, M., Gerlach, M., Düwiger, H.: Linguistic modeling of linked open data for question answering. In: Proceedings of Interacting with Linked Data (ILD 2012) [37], pp. 75–86 (2012)
25. Wheeler, J.: The hsparql package. In: The Haskell Hackage Repository (2009). http://hackage.haskell.org/package/hsparql-0.1.2

# Towards a Context-Sensitive User Interaction Framework for Information Systems

Stephan Kölker[1(✉)], Felix Schwinger[1,2(✉)], and Karl-Heinz Krempels[1,2(✉)]

[1] Information Systems, RWTH Aachen University, Aachen, Germany
`stephan.koelker@rwth-aachen.de`, {`schwinger,krempels`}`@dbis.rwth-aachen.de`
[2] Fraunhofer Institute for Applied Information Technology FIT, Aachen, Germany

**Abstract.** With the rise of mobile devices, users operate applications in a large variety of contexts. In each of these contexts, a user may have different requirements and preferences regarding an application's user interface. The context describes the current physical and social environment of the user, his activity and locomotion, as well as the current location and time. Hence, different user interfaces may be more suitable in specific contexts than others. At the moment, a user interface is an integral part of an application, consequently also limiting its usefulness in certain contexts as the information is not presented in the best possible way. Therefore, we propose a way to decouple the user interface from a specific form of representation. Through this decoupling, it is possible to dynamically adapt user interfaces to the user's specific needs in a context, to increase the value of the application for the user. In this paper, we introduce a general framework for the context-dependent adaptation of user interfaces and evaluate it in the specific context of travel information systems. Travel information systems are particularly suited to evaluate such a framework, as they are usually operated in many different contexts – before a trip, during a trip, and after a trip. The adaptation framework transforms between system-oriented messages and user-oriented messages. The user's context, the output device capabilities, and the user's preference, all influence the choice of the actual representation for user-oriented messages. We implemented a prototype of the proposed system and conducted an experimental evaluation focusing on scenarios from the domain of travel information systems.

**Keywords:** Context · Context-aware applications · User interface · Human-computer interaction · Adaptation

## 1 Motivation and Introduction

In the last two decades, smartphones have emerged and had since become widely adopted. A survey from 2019 by the Pew Research Center showed that 81% of U.S. adults own a smartphone[1]. With the rise of the adoption rate, the

---

[1] Pew Research Center, "Mobile Fact Sheet", https://www.pewresearch.org/internet/fact-sheet/mobile/, viewed January 15, 2020.

© Springer Nature Switzerland AG 2020
A. Bozzon et al. (Eds.): WEBIST 2019, LNBIP 399, pp. 195–217, 2020.
https://doi.org/10.1007/978-3-030-61750-9_9

importance of applications for smartphones also grows. People use these mobile devices mainly as a means for communication and entertainment – but also as mobile information systems. Owing to their high portability, users employ devices in diverse contexts and environments, such as at home, at work, or while traveling.

Users of mobile applications may have specific preferences and requirements in different contexts regarding the *user interface (UI)*. For example, the interaction with a *graphical user interface (GUI)* of a navigation system usually distracts the vision of the driver. The consequence is a highly increased crash potential [38]. Hence, to maximize the UI's utility and minimize the distraction level, the inclusion of the user's context is essential. In this paper, we define *context* as a set of information describing the environment, time and location and activity of an entity. It consists of information about the object itself, its physical and social environment, and all other entities that currently exert an influence on it. Such an entity may be a human, an inanimate object, or a place [11,40].

Manufacturers of mobile devices equip their devices with a wide variety of different sensors, including accelerometers, gyroscopes, magnetometers, GPS, thermometers, WiFi and Bluetooth, cameras, microphones, or light sensors. The data from those sensors allow mobile applications to sense parts of the current context of use [24]. Through sensor fusion, the data from the sensors is correlated and verified to increase the accuracy of the context detection. While the discovery of the current context is crucial for the framework, we do not further discuss the actual context detection and elicitation itself in this paper, but instead, require that such a context detection system exists.

In addition to the context derived from the environment through the sensors, users may also have a domain-specific context. In this paper, we primarily examined contexts of trips from one location to another location, as a traveler has a variety of different contexts during such a trip [22,46]. These contexts include, among others, the situations before a trip, during a trip, and after a trip. Each of these contexts require different kinds of UIs [26]. While, for example, a car navigation system is suited very well for the context of not distracting the driver, it is not well suited for other, more general purposes [36]. When regarding public transportation, there are a variety of contexts that favor certain representations of the information system to the users. For example, when walking with luggage in both hands, using a GUI-based information system on the mobile phone is cumbersome. In such a scenario, a voice- and audio-based information system is more suitable.

UIs of nearly all mobile applications, including most mobile information systems, are predesigned in the form of GUIs. With the appearance of smartphones, the input for those GUIs is mostly tactile, while the output is nearly always graphical [15]. However, as illustrated by the examples above, the hard-coding of UIs with tactile input and graphical output impacts the usability of the information system in certain contexts. In specific contexts, the usage of particular UIs may even be dangerous, e.g., interacting with a GUI while driving. Additionally, such an approach cannot be generalized to run the same program on, for example, a smart speaker.

Most mobile devices nowadays do not only contain a variety of sensors, but also different output modalities. These include, among others, the display, the speaker, and notification lights. Specific applications already support separate input and output modalities. Voice Assistants such as Apple Siri, Google Assistant, or Microsoft Cortana already support the microphone coupled with speech-detection as an input modality. Furthermore, the output modality depends on the answer of the system; the system sometimes answers using the speaker, while it displays others graphically on the device. Similarly, an application may choose the output modality based on the current context of the user.

To aid the development of such applications, we propose a framework to decouple an application from the way the application communicates with the user. Hence, our proposed framework can render messages between the user and the system in different modalities. The system chooses the currently best available modality for the current context as the output modality. Additionally, a user may also interact with the system using various input modalities. As a consequence, a method for finding the best available output modality, based on the user's context, their preferences, and device capabilities is required. Such an adaptation framework can increase the number of situations where users can effortlessly access information systems.

With our previous research, we sketched and described a framework for the adaptation of user interfaces to the current context of use, the capabilities of the available devices and the user's preferences [25]. Hereby, we extend this work by introducing the framework itself in more detail and by presenting a first evaluation of the proposed methods.

The remainder of the paper is structured as follows: Sect. 2 introduces the current State-of-the-Art regarding multimodal UIs and adaptation systems. In Sect. 3, we present our approach to the problem, whereas Sect. 4 evaluates this approach. Finally, Sect. 5 concludes the paper with a summary and highlights future work.

## 2   State of the Art

Currently, most developers use a predesigned UI for travel information systems that are optimized for specific contexts. Applications, such as a car navigation system or Google Maps, are optimized for a specific context of use. For smartphones, GUIs are the predominant form of presenting information to the user, whereas the user commonly interacts with the system using tactile feedback [15]. Car navigation systems, optimized for a single use case, also make use of bidirectional speech-based interaction between system and user as not to distract the driver from the road [36]. While we focus on a framework for the automatic adaptation of user interfaces, it is still essential to look at the wider literature of context-aware computing. As context-aware computing, in general, is already well-studied, we refer the reader to recent surveys in the area for a broader overview of the subject: [5,14,21,23]. The following excerpt of related work either focuses on context-aware travel information systems or the automatic adaptation of user interfaces. This section is also largely adapted from our previous work [25].

Mitrevska et al. developed a context-aware in-car information system [29]. Users can interact with particular entities in the environment of the car, e.g., a restaurant. They can either retrieve additional information about these entities or access associated services for this entity, e.g., reserving a table in a specific restaurant. Users can interact with the system via speech, gesture, and displays. However, the UI is not dynamically adapted to the context of use and focuses on being used while driving a car.

Vanderdonckt et al. introduced a language for describing multimodal UIs on different levels of abstraction [42]. The XML-based language allows supporting a device- and modality-independent development of UIs. Furthermore, it can transform a UI from one representation to another one. Lemmelä et al. proposed a manual iterative process for designing multimodal mobile information systems [28]. During the design process, UI developers create multiple UIs, where each of these UIs are manually adapted to different contexts of use. The automated synthesis or transformation of UIs for the different contexts is, however, not examined.

Falb et al. proposed a system to automatically synthesize UIs using a discourse model [17]. This discourse model is a meta-model for the description of interactions. It allows representing human-computer interaction with communicative acts. The system can automatically generate UIs for various devices based on the interaction description. However, it does not take the usage context into account.

Currently, researchers are experimenting with novel device classes for travel information systems. One of these device classes are, for example, *smartwatches* [32, 35, 45]. Smartwatches have a reasonably small display but are more easily accessible compared to a smartphone. Additionally, Pielot et al. examined the suitability of *vibration* for communicating the next navigational instructions to travelers [31]. The main advantage here is that the traveler is not distracted by this communication form. Eis et al. introduce a travel navigation system with *smart glasses* [16]. Smart glasses have the advantage that information can be overlayed onto a view of the real-world and thus creating an augmented reality view. Finally, Rehman et al. compare navigation on hand-held devices with navigation on smart glasses [33].

Moreover, there is also literature on the dynamic adaptation of UIs to some external circumstances. Baus et al. presented a pedestrian navigation system in 2002 [3]. Their system automatically provided the user with context-depending information, while also adapting the presentation form to the capabilities of the employed hardware and the current information needs of the user.

Christoph et al., in turn, described a process for the dynamic adaptation of UIs to hardware capabilities and user preferences [6,7]. They represent UIs as a sequence of so-called elementary interaction objects *(eIOs)*. A system based on XSLT rules dynamically adapts these XML-based eIOs. Lastly, Criado et al. discussed a model-driven approach for the dynamic adaptation of GUIs [8]. They present a meta-model for the description of GUIs. This meta-model allows the incremental adjustment of GUIs while they are running.

# 3   Approach

In this section, we present our previous work, the automated *user interface* (UI) adaptation system from Kölker et al. [25], in more detail. This system is responsible for suitably giving the message content from an information system to the user, and for providing an information system with, optionally inferred, user input. Since generalizability is one of the leading design goals of the system, we designed it as an independent service that interacts with various client systems and other system components through specified interfaces.

Figure 1 shows an outline of the adaptation system and its interfaces. In order to present information to the user, a client information system sends its information as a message to the UI adaptation service. The multimodal fission component of the UI adaptation service is then responsible for the transformation of this message into a context-dependent and user-friendly representation. To this end, the multimodal fission component utilizes conversation information from the dialogue manager and information about the context of use from the context manager. The dialogue manager keeps track of the state of all ongoing and past conversations between the client application and the user and thus, is capable of providing information about the conversational context. The context manager interacts with an external context detection service to retrieve information about the current context of use, including user and device profiles and characteristics

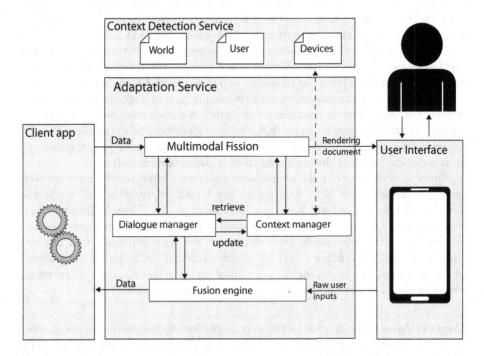

**Fig. 1.** Overview over the components of the UI adaptation service, from [25].

of the physical and social environment of the user. An external rendering engine then renders the output of the multimodal fission component according to the previously determined appropriate representation to present the information to the user.

The UI adaptation service always listens for user inputs. When user input is registered, the UI adaptation service extracts the information from the user input and provides the targeted information service with that information. The fusion engine component of the UI adaptation service is responsible for integrating the information from multiple sources, such as the user input and conversational information, to interpret the information.

## 3.1   Service Interfaces

The UI adaptation service acts as a broker between the client information system and the user while utilizing an external renderer to render the user interface. Besides the client information system and the renderer, it interfaces with a context detection service. The context detection service provides context information to the UI adaptation service. This context information is the basis for the UI adaptation.

**The Information Service Interface.** The interface to the information service treats messages as communicative acts. Communicative acts are messages between intelligent agents. They were formalized in the *Agent Communication Language* (ACL) by the *Foundation for Intelligent Agents* (FIPA) [18].

By performing a communicative act, an agent can execute a specific action (performative). These actions may include informing the recipient about a fact, querying information from the recipient, or requesting the recipient to perform a particular action. Communicative acts are usually part of a conversation between agents. Conversations are sequences of communicative acts between a set of agents. In the framework of the ACL, unique identifiers in messages allow the mapping of communicative acts to conversations. Conversations can adhere to an interaction protocol that imposes rules on this communication.

Ontologies ensure that the recipient can correctly interpret the message content of communicative acts. Ontologies are formal representations of specific domains and define concepts and their interrelations [19]. They facilitate knowledge exchange and reuse due to their formality [40,43]. Consequently, the content of communicative acts should be a document that can be parsed and inferred with a pre-defined ontology that all communication participants have access to. Widely used languages for defining ontologies are the *Resource Description Framework* (RDF) [9] and the *Web Ontology Language* (OWL) [37].

**Context Interface.** A vital factor to consider for the adaptation is the current context in which a user operates an application. This context consists of not only the device-internal context information, such as active applications, available resources, and user profiles but also the broader environmental context of use, such as the current weather, traffic information, the currently used means of transport, the social environment and the constitution of the user itself. Within the UI adaptation service, information on the context of use is retrieved and maintained by a context manager in the form of context models. An external context detection service provides this information.

At the context detection interface, ontologies are used to represent the context of use. Several works have shown that ontologies are especially useful for describing contexts due to their formality and knowledge exchange capabilities [40, 43]. The formality also allows the automated deduction of implicit knowledge from explicitly provided knowledge by inference rules. Commonly used ontology languages already contain a specific set of built-in inference rules [20]. However, in the case that more expressivity is needed, logical rules can be used to infer implicit knowledge based on ontologies because ontologies are a specialization of logic programs [2, 43].

**The Renderer Interface.** The UI adaptation service uses an abstract representation of UIs during the adaptation process. The framework translates the abstract UI representation into a language that can be rendered by an external rendering engine. This process allows the utilization of standard renderers to present the information to users. This language is usually highly platform-specific.

### 3.2 Transformation of Information into a User-Friendly Representation

The transformation of information into a user-friendly representation is a function $\text{trans}_{out}$ that maps a tuple of documents in the language of *communicative acts* ($\mathcal{D}_{\mathcal{L}CA}$), the *context detection service* ($\mathcal{D}_{\mathcal{L}CDS}$), *user preferences* ($\mathcal{D}_{\mathcal{L}UP}$), and *device profiles* ($\mathcal{D}_{\mathcal{L}DP}$) into documents in a language that the *renderer* can render ($\mathcal{D}_{\mathcal{L}out}$) [6, 25]:

$$\text{trans}_{out} : \mathcal{D}_{\mathcal{L}CA} \times \mathcal{D}_{\mathcal{L}CDS} \times \mathcal{D}_{\mathcal{L}UP} \times \mathcal{D}_{\mathcal{L}DP} \rightarrow \mathcal{D}_{\mathcal{L}out},$$

This transformation process consists of several distinct steps. Hence, $\text{trans}_{out}$ can be implemented as a composition of the following functions:

- $\text{trans\_pui} : \mathcal{D}_{\mathcal{L}CA} \rightarrow \mathcal{D}_{\mathcal{L}PUI}$: transforms communicative acts to *prototypical UIs* (PUI),
- $\text{adapt} : \mathcal{D}_{\mathcal{L}PUI} \times \mathcal{D}_{\mathcal{L}CDS} \times \mathcal{D}_{\mathcal{L}UP} \times \mathcal{D}_{\mathcal{L}DP} \rightarrow \mathcal{D}_{\mathcal{L}PUI}$: adapts the prototypical UI according to the context, the device profile and the user profile
- $\text{inst\_ui} : \mathcal{D}_{\mathcal{L}PUI} \rightarrow \mathcal{D}_{\mathcal{L}out}$: instantiates the output document

Instead of directly representing the UI in a platform-specific UI language, an abstract platform-independent language is chosen for this task. Here, this language is referred to as *"prototypical UI"* and is further explicated in the next subsection. Figure 2 gives a visual summary of the implementation of the function $\text{trans}_{out}$.

**Representation of Prototypical User Interfaces.** Christoph et al. describe user interfaces in terms of *elementary interaction objects* (eIOs) [6]. We define elementary interaction objects as "non-decomposable objects that enable a user to interact with a system" with the following properties [25]:

- *Type* of the eIO, one of the following:
  - *Single select*: selection of one single element from a given list
  - *Multiple select*: selection of multiple elements from a given list
  - *Input*: input of information into the system
  - *Inform*: output of information to the user
  - *Action*: initiate an action in the system
- Optionally, a *description* of the interaction object
- Optionally, a *content* of the object
- A *content representation*, consisting of
  - *Output device*: on which device the eIO is presented to the user,
  - *Presentation medium*: which medium is used to present the eIO to the user, e.g., display or speaker,
  - *Modality*: the way the information is represented [4], e.g., text, image, or speech, and
  - *Modality properties*: specific modality-dependent representation parameters, e.g., font color, size, or voice
- *Natural language* of the content, e.g., English (en), German (de), Chinese (zh), ...
- *Unique identifier* of the element for reference

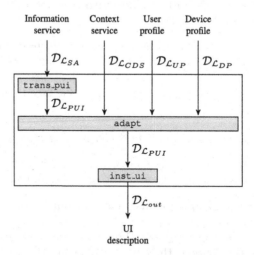

**Fig. 2.** Implementational view on **trans**$_{out}$ as a composition of partial transformations. This visualization is from our previous work [25].

For the task of adaptation, the eIO type and content representation are of particular interest. Therefore, the focus of the following descriptions lies on these two properties.

**Transformation of Communicative Acts into Prototypical User Interfaces.** Communicative acts from the client have to be transformed into prototypical user interfaces to generate an adaptable user interface. The transformation depends on the performative, the direction of the communication, and the corresponding interaction protocol. For this transformation, only two different classes of performatives need to be considered: *informative* and *requesting* performatives. The former class of performatives consists of all performatives that are used to inform other agents about a given subject without requesting any specific action. Conversely, all performatives that are used to request an action from other agents are assigned to the latter class.

Depending on the direction of the communicative act, a different set of eIOs is available for the transformation. If the recipient of the communicative act is the user, the communicative act is transformed into an *inform* eIO because the other eIO types are for inputting information into the system. Hence, a communicative act from the user to the system can be either translated into a *select, input,* or *action* eIO. The system translates communicative acts with an informative performative into either select or input eIOs depending on the message content. In contrast, communicative acts with a requesting performative are translated into action eIOs. The mapping of communicative acts to eIOs is visualized in Table 1.

Besides generating eIOs for presenting the message content to the user, possible further eIOs are includable to provide the user with means to respond, such as input or action eIOs. The inclusion of these eIOs depends on whether feedback from the user is expected. This inclusion can be checked based on the interaction protocol, the conversation history, and the current communicative act.

**Table 1.** Characterization of eIOs by the direction of the communication and the interaction type [25].

|  |  | Direction | |
|---|---|---|---|
|  |  | System → User | User → System |
| Performative class | Inform | Inform | Input, selection |
|  | Request (without feedback) | Inform | Action |
|  | Request (with feedback) | Inform with inputs and selections | Action |

**Adaptation of Prototypical User Interfaces.** After the translation of communicative acts into eIOs, a suitable user interface representation is to be determined. To this end, the framework adapts the content representation of every eIO to the context of use, device, and user profile.

The implications to the user interface from each of those documents are assigned an importance value to avoid ambiguous or contradictory information.

If information from one document is conflicting with information from another, the information from the more important document is considered relevant. The implications from the device profile are the most important because the device profile defines the technically possible means of communication. The second most important information comes from the user profile. The user profile contains information about how the user can and wants to communicate. The context of use has the least significant impact on the user interface.

On a high level, the UI adaptation procedure works as follows:

1. Calculate the *adjusted user profile* by removing all preferences from the original user profile that are conflicting with the device profile,
2. Determine the set of all admissible content representations $R_{admissible}$ from the set of all theoretically possible content representations based on the device profile(s), the user profile, and the message content,
3. Determine the most suitable content representation(s) $r_{best}$ from $R_{admissible}$ for the current context of use $C$ according to an evaluation function `eval`:

$$r_{best} = \underset{r \in R_{admissible}}{argmax} \ \texttt{eval}(C, r)$$

4. Adapt the properties of all eIOs according to $r_{best}$, the device profile and the adjusted user profile

The set of admissible content representations is determined based on the available output devices, their interaction capabilities, the abilities of the user, and the message content. The latter restricts the possible modalities. For example, vibration is usually unsuitable to represent textual information.

If multiple different content representations have an equally optimal rating, the message is represented in all optimal content representations concurrently. Thus, one copy of the respective eIOs for each optimal content representation is created.

*Representation of Contexts.* In this work, we represent context as a consistent knowledge-base with context information. Then, a logical expression $\alpha$ defines a context class consisting of all contexts that entail $\alpha$. We refer to such logical expressions $\alpha$ as *partial context descriptions* because they are used to define context classes by describing parts of a context [25]. For example, the logical expression $\alpha = weather(rainy) \land environment(crowded)$ defines the class of all contexts with rainy weather and a crowded environment. The advantage of this approach over the manual classification of distinct context classes is its flexibility and the possibility to define very fine-grained context classes. These properties are required in this use case due to the complex relationship between contexts of use and user interfaces.

*Evaluation Function.* Let $C$ denote the set of all possible contexts, $R$ the set of all content representations and $E \subseteq \mathbb{R}$ the set of all ratings ranging from "unsuitable" to "suitable". Then, the following function assigns a rating to each admissible combination of context and content representation:

$$\texttt{eval} : C \times R \to E \subseteq \mathbb{R},$$

To combine different ratings into a single one, we define a combination function. Ideally, this combination function $\oplus$ is chosen such that the result of combining different ratings is consistent with the definition and semantics of ratings.

**Instantiation of the User Interface.** Since the UI description languages differ among different mobile device platforms [10,41], the translation of the prototypical UI into a final UI is highly platform-specific. As an alternative to the native UI description languages of widely used mobile device platforms, developers can also write applications in HTML, CSS, and JavaScript by using techniques like Progressive Web Apps [1] or specific frameworks [44]. Besides, renderers and interpreters for HTML, CSS, and JavaScript are available on all major mobile platforms because they are one of the core components of Web browsers. Therefore, the translation of the prototypical UI into a UI described by HTML, CSS, and JavaScript reduces implementation effort because a broad range of platforms is supported by default. HTML and CSS mainly describe the visual appearance of a UI, while JavaScript code snippets can achieve auditive and tactile outputs. Therefore, a mapping from a prototypical UI in terms of eIOs to a collection of HTML, CSS, and JavaScript documents can be defined.

### 3.3   Transformation of Information from the User

Assuming that the user will, by default, choose the most suitable communication channel to communicate with an information system, the communication channel for user input does have to be selected by the UI adaptation service. Instead, the UI adaptation service needs to be able to receive input from all possible inbound communication channels simultaneously. Specifically, this means that input, selection, and action eIOs will always be rendered on all possible incoming communication channels concurrently and that only the modality and modality properties need to be selected for them.

From the perspective of the user, one can distinguish between *proactive* and *reactive* communication. Proactive communication is initiated by the user, while the user only responds to messages from the system in a reactive communication. Both communication modes have to be handled differently by the adaptation service. The adaptation service has to provide the user with access to the currently available functions of the client information system to allow the user to initiate a communication. The inclusion of additional interaction objects enables reactive communication that give the user the possibility of reacting to a message from the client information system. The necessity of including these other interaction objects depends on the communicative act, the conversation history, and the interaction protocol of the respective conversation.

**Processing User Input.** Generally, inputs from the user are received either as GUI interaction or raw data. The user generates GUI events during the interaction with a GUI. Recording the real world directly produces raw data, e.g., by recording audio or video data. The system forwards the data that is input at the UI to the UI adaptation service for further processing. This additional processing depends on whether the data type of the input data matches the expected data type in the interaction protocol of the associated conversation. In case of a match, the data can be directly sent to the client information service. Otherwise, the data has to be interpreted by the UI adaptation service. For example, if the user inputs spoken words, although textual data is required according to the interaction protocol, the adaptation service needs to transcribe the words and send the transcription to the client. Similarly, GUI events, such as touches or clicks, can be mapped to intents. The interpretation procedures are designed as pre-defined building blocks by the developer of the adaptation service with a specific input and output data type. Then, a suitable interpretation pipeline can be generated automatically by assembling several of such building blocks to a pipeline.

According to Dumas et al., the coordination of multiple incoming data streams is the task of a fusion engine [14]. For the proposed adaptation service [25] such coordination is not necessary because it only supports concurrent multimodality [30]. Therefore, the only task of the fusion engine [25] is to link the incoming messages from the user to conversations by storing the corresponding conversation ID in every interaction object.

After the incoming data has been processed successfully, the adaptation service generates a communicative act containing the processed data and sends it to the client information service.

### 3.4 Dialogue Manager

As stated by Dumas et al., the task of a dialogue manager is to provide and manage information about conversations [14]. Specifically, the dialogue manager maintains the communication history, keeps track of the states of all conversations, and provides information about the associated interaction protocols. Additionally, based on the interaction protocol, the dialogue manager can also check the validity of communicative acts in a conversation. It can also provide the expected data type of the content of the next communicative act in a conversation.

### 3.5 Implementation

For the evaluation of the proposed UI adaptation system, we implemented a prototype for the adaptation procedure. This prototype transforms messages from client information systems into descriptions of the output representation together with a suitability rating using the previously described function $\text{trans}_{out}$. Device profiles, user profiles, and descriptions of the context of use influence the adaptation process. In the following, some implementational details are presented.

**Evaluation Function.** In the prototype, we represent a rating as a real value in $[0, 1]$ [25]. A rating of $\texttt{eval}(C, r) = 1$ means that the representation $r$ is suitable in context $C$, whereas $\texttt{eval}(C, r) = 0$ means that it is unsuitable. For the selected range of ratings, the multiplication function is a reasonable choice for the combination function [25].

**Evaluation of User Interfaces in Contexts.** The evaluation function, as listed before, assigns a rating to a tuple of context and content representation. However, since the number of possible contexts is generally infinite and the number of content representations high, such an assignment is impossible to define manually. As a simplification, only a rating for the combination of a specific context class and a component of a content representation is set, while all other combinations are rated as "suitable" ($r = 1$) by default. Therefore, the evaluation function is decomposable as follows:

$$\texttt{eval}(C, r) = \bigoplus_{\gamma: C \models \gamma} \bigoplus_{cm \in r} \texttt{eval}'(\gamma, cm).$$

Here, $\texttt{eval}'(\gamma, cm)$ is the evaluation of a single communication mean $cm$ in a context class defined by $\gamma$. In our prototype, this evaluation is defined by lookup tables.

In the prototype, three different tables are used: a table for evaluating devices, communication channels, and modalities, respectively. The evaluation of modality properties is omitted here due to a large number of possible modality properties. Table 2, Table 3, and Table 4 show the lookup tables. The values in the lookup tables are based on common knowledge and thought experiments.

According to the communication infrastructure, a presentation medium addresses a specific communication channel. Since presentation media with the same addressed communication channel share essential properties concerning their suitability during a journey, presentation media are evaluated according to the channel that they address.

In the experimental evaluation, we consider five major classes of mobile devices: tablets, smartphones, smart watches and smart glasses. The evaluation of devices in Table 2 is mainly based on their accessibility in the given contexts. For example, when transporting luggage, hand-held devices are far less accessible than wearables and, thus, are assigned a considerably worse rating. Furthermore, the general accessibility determines the ranks of the devices in all contexts.

Table 3 introduces the evaluation of communication channels. We chose the visual, auditive and the tactile communication channel because they are the main communication channels in contemporary information systems [13]. Various environmental factors have a considerable impact on the human-device communication. Consequently, their existence results in a reduction of the rating. For example, a noisy environment halves the rating of all content representations using the auditive channel. Thus, it becomes unlikely for the system to choose such a content representation in that situation.

**Table 2.** Evaluation of information devices.

| Context | Tablet | Smart-phone | Smart watch | Smart glasses | Board computer |
|---|---|---|---|---|---|
| All contexts | 0.96 | 0.97 | 0.98 | 1.0 | 0.99 |
| One-handed luggage transport | 0.1 | 0.25 | 1.0 | 1.0 | 1.0 |
| Two-handed luggage transport | 0.1 | 0.1 | 0.5 | 1.0 | 1.0 |
| Standing inside a moving vehicle | 0.1 | 0.25 | 1.0 | 1.0 | 1.0 |
| Standing inside a moving vehicle ∧ one-handed luggage transport | 0.1 | 0.1 | 0.5 | 1.0 | 1.0 |
| Active movement ∧ smartphone not in visual field | 0.0 | 0.0 | 0.75 | 1.0 | 1.0 |
| Active movement ∧ smartphone in visual field | 0.0 | 1.0 | 0.75 | 1.0 | 1.0 |

**Table 3.** Evaluation of communication channels.

| Context | Visual | Auditive | Tactile |
|---|---|---|---|
| All contexts | 1.0 | 1.0 | 1.0 |
| High ambient light level | 0.5 | 1.0 | 1.0 |
| No sight contact | 0.0 | 1.0 | 1.0 |
| Vibrating environment | 0.75 | 1.0 | 0.75 |
| No body contact | 1.0 | 1.0 | 0.0 |
| Noisy environment | 1.0 | 0.5 | 1.0 |
| "Do not disturb" | 1.0 | 0.0 | 0.5 |
| Active movement ∧ device not in visual field | 0.9 | 1.0 | 1.0 |

Table 4 presents the evaluation of modalities. We distinguish between nine major classes of modalities: texts, structured texts, diagrams, pictograms, images, lamps, speech, sounds, and vibration. Texts are sequences of symbols and words that express information in a natural language. Structured texts consist of short portions of text that are structured in a two-dimensional space (e.g., tables). Diagrams are arrangements of various geometric shapes, pictographs and short portions of text to communicate messages or thoughts or to illustrate information (e.g., a map). Pictograms are simplified, symbolic graphical representations of objects and concepts (e.g., application icons). Images are naturalistic graphical representations of objects and scenes in the real world and lamps are simple binary or multi-valued light emitters. Speech is the audible representation of human language and all non-speech auditive signals are referred to as "sounds".

The ratings for those modalities were determined based on multiple aspects: the accessibility of a modality in a given context, the acceptance of them by the social environment, and the compatibility of the modality with the current activity of the user. For example, when the user is watching a movie, the information representation should preferably be short, concise, and silent. Otherwise, the information might harm the activity of the users by interfering with the visual or auditive channel of the movie Consequently, the modalities (structured) text and vibration are assigned to a high rating in this context.

**Table 4.** Evaluation of modalities.

| Context | Text | Structured text | Diagram | Pictogram | |
|---------|------|-----------------|---------|-----------|---|
| All contexts | 0.98 | 0.99 | 1.0 | 0.0 | |
| Active movement | 0.0 | 0.25 | 1.0 | 1.0 | |
| Visual entertainment | 0.99 | 1.0 | 0.5 | 0.5 | |

| Context | Image | Lamp | Speech | Sound | Vibration |
|---------|-------|------|--------|-------|-----------|
| All contexts | 0.75 | 1.0 | 1.0 | 0.99 | 0.99 |
| Active movement | 0.5 | 1.0 | 1.0 | 1.0 | 1.0 |
| Auditive entertainment | 1.0 | 1.0 | 0.98 | 0.99 | 1.0 |
| Visual entertainment | 0.5 | 1.0 | 1.0 | 1.0 | 1.0 |
| Noisy environment | 1.0 | 1.0 | 0.25 | 0.75 | 1.0 |
| Hearing impaired | 1.0 | 1.0 | 0.1 | 0.8 | 1.0 |
| No headphones in the public | 1.0 | 1.0 | 0.5 | 1.0 | 1.0 |
| Display on | 1.0 | 0.0 | 1.0 | 1.0 | 1.0 |

**Implementation of the Content Representation Search.** We implemented the search for suitable content representations as a uniform-cost search [34] on a graph representation of the space of all admissible content representations [25]. In this graph, each node represents a component of a content representation, such as an output device, a presentation medium, a modality, or a modality property. The algorithm assigns a suitability rating $eval(C, b)$ for the current context $C$ to each edge $(a, b)$. The graph structure follows the *RDF schema* depicted in Fig. 3.

The RDF schema for the communication structure has a class for each component of a content representation. Naturally, a device can have one or multiple presentation media. A presentation medium can output information in one or various modalities, and a modality can have one or multiple properties. Specializations of the `hasComponent` relationship in the schema represent these relationships. Additionally, a presentation medium can address various communication channels, and a modality can use a specific communication channel to represent information.

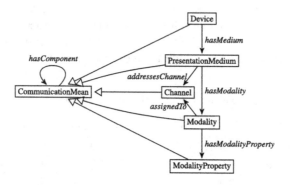

**Fig. 3.** Visual depiction of an RDF schema for content representations [25].

For simplicity, we introduce a virtual root node that is connected to each instance of `Device` via `hasComponent` relations. The uniform-cost search can then start on this root node. For the search, only on the edges referring to `hasComponent` relations or its specializations are considered. During the search, all best-rated paths from this root node to a leaf node are determined.

The representation of the search space as a graph enables the application of this search method to different device configurations [25]. Therefore, this algorithm is applicable to use cases with automated device recognition and customized user preferences.

## 4   Evaluation

In this section, we present the conducted experiments and results in detail.

### 4.1   Evaluation Setup

For the evaluation, the prototype described in Sect. 3.5 was used. To obtain sensible contexts and profiles, we extract them from typical use cases of a travel navigation system. After this, we compare the result of the adaptation to a manually determined optimal user interface.

We derived the following use cases for travel information systems from a study by the Association of German Transport Companies (Verband Deutscher Verkehrsunternehmen e.V., VDV) [39]:

- Navigation for public transport
- Navigation for individual transport
- Navigation for shared vehicles

Furthermore, the VDV defined persona in [39]. We then identified four relevant groups of users among those personas:

- Unimpaired public transport users
- Mobility-impaired public transport users
- Perception-impaired public transport users
- Individual transport users

We selected these user groups because they have different communication needs in several contexts during a journey. They are the basis for the user profiles in the experiments.

## 4.2   Evaluation Results

This section shows the results of the evaluation grouped by use case. First, the situation of each use case is described in general. More specific situations serve as the basis of the evaluation. For each situation, we list the result of the UI adaptation. Here, the best-rated modalities are shown for each device class to provide an overall result. Hence, no assumption about the availability of specific devices is necessary. Finally, we evaluate the result by comparing it with a manually determined optimal user interface for that situation.

**Navigation for Public Transport.** The main task of a travel navigation system in public transport is to notify the user about arriving vehicles of interest, the next station, and when to alight from the vehicle. Optionally, it provides the user with the possibility of checking in manually or for signaling the driver to stop at the next station.

When using means of public transport, the user is located either at a public transport station or inside a public service vehicle [22]. The environment in public transport stations and public service vehicles is often noisy due to traffic and other passengers. Inside a public service vehicle, passengers have to either stand or sit. Standing passengers usually need to hold somewhere to avoid falling.

Consider the following situation: an unimpaired public transport user waits at a noisy bus station for the next bus. In this situation, the travel information system's task is to notify the user about the next vehicle of interest. Based on the context information (noisy environment, public service station, unimpaired user), the UI adaptation service selects the following representations for each device class:

- Smartwatch, vibration (rating: 0.9702)
- Smartphone, vibration (rating: 0.96029)
- Tablet, vibration (rating: 0.95039)
- Smart glasses, sound (rating: 0.73507)

To summarize, the system chooses tactile communication means on each of the given devices that support tactile information output. If no tactile information output is available, an auditive signal notifies the user. The noisy environment severely impacts the auditive communication channel between the user and the device. Therefore, the user might not register an auditive notification. Consequently, this situation favors the usage of the tactile communication channel. Furthermore, the visual channel is unsuitable in a situation in which the user does not pay attention to the device. Consequently, the result of the adaptation system is optimal in this situation.

After the vehicle arrived, the user enters the vehicle, but no free seats are available. Therefore, the user is standing inside the vehicle and holds the handrail. The information system's next task is to notify the user about the station where alighting a vehicle is necessary. The UI adaptation service selects the following representations for each device class:

- Smart glasses, sound (rating: 0.9801)
- Smartwatch, vibration (rating: 0.9702)
- Smartphone, sound and vibration (rating: 0.24)
- Tablet, sound and vibration (rating: 0.0950)

In short, easily accessible devices, such as smart glasses and smartwatches, are preferred in this situation, and the system avoids the visual communication channel. This behavior is suitable in the given situation because the user is not already watching the device and has to hold the handrail with one hand. This selection ensures that the user will receive the notification.

**Navigation for Individual Transport.** In individual transport, the primary use case for travel information systems is navigational instructions. Usually, navigational instructions consist of a notification and further information on the action to be performed by the user. The modalities speech, diagram, or text represent navigational instructions well and provide the user with additional information.

The act of active movement mainly characterizes contexts of individual transport by the user. Consequently, the user has to spend a considerable amount of mental resources on the task of controlling the movement. This limitation holds true especially for the vision of the driver [27]. Apart from that, those contexts can be very diverse. For example, while the car protects the driver from many environmental influences, such as noise and rain, a cyclist usually exposed to those influences.

The context under consideration in this use case is the following: the user is driving the car (active movement). In this context, the UI adaptation service will select the following representations for a navigational instruction:

- Board computer, speech and diagram (rating: 1.0)
- Smart glasses, speech and diagram (rating: 0.99)
- Smartwatch, diagram (rating: 0.882)

- Smartphone, speech and diagram (rating: 0.485)
- Tablet, speech and diagram (rating: 0.24)

The proposed UI adaptation system yields a configuration that is mostly employed in state-of-the-art navigation systems: speech commands with visualization in the form of a diagram (e.g., a map view with short amounts of text in the form of annotations). Again, easily accessible devices are preferred, such as a board computer or smart glasses that enable the user to retrieve information without the need for using a hand-held device. It is important not to distract the driver in this context because the driver has to focus on controlling the movement of the car. However, reading text demands the visual resources of a reader for a considerable amount of time, and consequently, text is generally unsuitable during acts of active movement. While speech commands are a generally acceptable representation of a navigational instruction, it might be easier for a user to map them to the real world when accompanied by a visual representation. Furthermore, map-based navigation systems have been proven to be suitable for this type of context [12]. Consequently, the modality selection of the adaptation system is reasonable in this context.

**Navigation for Shared Vehicles.** In the next use case [39], the tasks of the travel information system are:

- to announce the vehicle position, properties and access code,
- to provide the user with the possibility to read and agree to the terms and conditions of the data transfer from a mobile device to the board computer, and
- to offer alternatives in case of deviations from the schedule.

Similar to the use case "individual transport", the user is notified about an event and provided with further information. Furthermore, the set of possible contexts in this use case can be very diverse and could be possibly intersecting with the earlier mentioned use cases (e.g., a user receives a notification about the position of an ordered shared vehicle while sitting on the bus).

Consider the following situation: a user just ordered a shared vehicle and is now standing near the vehicle. The travel information system needs to announce the vehicle position and properties to the user. According to the UI adaptation system, the following representations for each device class are optimal:

- Smart glasses, speech and diagram (rating: 0.99)
- Smartwatch, diagram (rating: 0.98)
- Smartphone, speech and diagram (rating: 0.97)
- Tablet, speech and diagram (rating: 0.96)

Here, the UI adaptation system selects the modalities "speech" and "diagram" for the representation of the information. This selection is generally useful in the given context because the information to be communicated to the user is complex and cannot be represented by modalities with a low information capacity, such as vibration. Besides, the environment is not restricting the communication, and therefore, the system can choose the best matching modalities.

**Conclusion.** As shown in the examples above, the proposed UI adaptation system can flexibly provide reasonable user interfaces for a diverse set of contexts based on the given evaluation rules. However, this pen-and-paper evaluation of the adaptation service should be complemented by a user study in the future to cover more aspects of real-life contexts and to be able to adapt the evaluation function to the diverse contexts in the real world.

## 5    Conclusion and Future Work

In this work, we extended our previous work of a context-dependent UI adaptation system [25]. It is helpful for the UI to regard the current context of the user, the available device capabilities, and the user's personal preferences to increase the usefulness of applications in various situations. We sketc.hed a service that transforms messages between a system- and a user-oriented representation and adapts them according to the factors mentioned earlier.

We modeled the messages between the application and the sketc.hed adaptation service as communicative acts. These messages can then be translated into a prototypical UI. An ontology models context of use, whereas elementary interaction objects (eIOs) describe prototypical UIs. A uniform-cost search on the communication infrastructure graph adapts the content representation of the eIOs to the current context of use with the help of evaluation functions. Lastly, the targeted rendering engine renders the document that the system generated from the prototypical UI. As the framework is also applicable to bidirectional communication, it also needs to consider the messages from the user to the system. The adaptation service receives these messages and processes them according to the current state of the associated conversation and forwards them to the client application as communicative acts. This work additionally shows a first evaluation of the adaptation system that indicates that a dynamic adaptation of UIs is feasible. Future work should define suitable evaluation functions for the adaptation system. Test cases with real-life environments and potential users must be described. The user groups consist of application developers on the one hand, and end-users of the UI, on the other hand. After obtaining the first evaluation results, the evaluation function can be refined based on the user's feedback.

Currently, the adaption rate of smart speakers and smartwatches is rising. Potentially, also smart glasses will become more widespread. In such a scenario, it is most likely that users will regularly interact with multiple devices. Here, it is not sensible to have a distinct information state on each device but to regard the interaction as communicative acts that are shared between all devices. Such a seamless interaction between multiple devices of the user is particular important for travel information systems, as the user may use hand-held devices or maybe in-vehicle devices. The proposed system provides a framework for seamless interaction across different devices.

# References

1. Ater, T.: Building Progressive Web Apps: Bringing the Power of Native to the Browser. O'Reilly Media, Sebastopol (2017)
2. Baader, F.: The Description Logic Handbook. Cambridge University Press, Cambridge (2010)
3. Baus, J., Krüger, A., Wahlster, W.: A resource-adaptive mobile navigation system. In: Proceedings of the 7th International Conference on Intelligent User Interfaces, IUI 2002, pp. 15–22. ACM, New York (2002). https://doi.org/10.1145/502716. 502723
4. Bernsen, N.O.: A reference model for output information in intelligent multimedia presentation systems. In: Proceedings of the ECAI 1996 Workshop on: Towards a Standard Reference Model for Intelligent Multimedia Presentation Systems (1996)
5. Chen, G., Kotz, D.: A survey of context-aware mobile computing research. Technical report, Department of Computer Science, Dartmouth College, Hanover, NH, USA (2000)
6. Christoph, U., Krempels, K.H.: Automatisierte Integration von Informationsdiensten. PIK - Praxis der Informationsverarbeitung und Kommunikation **30**(2), 112–120 (2007). https://doi.org/10.1515/piko.2007.112
7. Christoph, U., Krempels, K.H., von Stulpnagel, J., Terwelp, C.: Automatic context detection of a mobile user. In: Proceedings of the International Conference on Wireless Information Networks and Systems (WINSYS), 2010, pp. 1–6 (2010)
8. Criado, J., Vicente Chicote, C., Iribarne, L., Padilla, N.: A model-driven approach to graphical user interface runtime adaptation. In: CEUR Workshop Proceedings, vol. 641 (2010)
9. Cyganiak, R., Wood, D., Lanthaler, M.: Rdf 1.1 concepts and abstract syntax. Technical report, World Wide Web Consortium (W3C) (2014). http://www.w3. org/TR/2014/REC-rdf11-concepts-20140225/. Accessed 3 Jan 2019
10. D'areglia, Y.: Learning iOS UI Development. Packt Publishing, Birmingham (2018)
11. Dey, A.K.: Understanding and using context. Pers. Ubiquit. Comput. **5**(1), 4–7 (2001). https://doi.org/10.1007/s007790170019
12. Dingus, T.A., Hulse, M.C., Antin, J.F., Wierwille, W.W.: Attentional demand requirements of an automobile moving-map navigation system. Transp. Res. Part A General **23**(4), 301–315 (1989). https://doi.org/10.1016/0191-2607(89)90013-7
13. Varela, E., Gabriel, I., Quiroz, A., Báez, L.A., Salazar, H., Villaseñor, L.: Artificial neural networks for the study of cosmic rays. In: Ruiz, P.H., Agredo-Delgado, V. (eds.) HCI-COLLAB 2019. CCIS, vol. 1114, pp. 113–123. Springer, Cham (2019). https://doi.org/10.1007/978-3-030-37386-3_9
14. Dumas, B., Lalanne, D., Oviatt, S.: Multimodal interfaces: a survey of principles, models and frameworks. In: Lalanne, D., Kohlas, J. (eds.) Human Machine Interaction. LNCS, vol. 5440, pp. 3–26. Springer, Heidelberg (2009). https://doi.org/ 10.1007/978-3-642-00437-7_1
15. Edwards, W.K., Mynatt, E.D.: An architecture for transforming graphical interfaces. In: Proceedings of the 7th Annual ACM Symposium on User Interface Software and Technology - UIST 1994. ACM Press (1994). https://doi.org/10.1145/ 192426.192443
16. Eis, A., Klose, E.M., Hegenberg, J., Schmidt, L.: Szenariobasierter Prototyp für ein Reiseassistenzsystem mit Datenbrillen. In: Burghardt, M., Wimmer, R., Wolff, C., Womser-Hacker, C. (eds.) Mensch und Computer 2017 - Tagungsband, vol. 17, pp. 203–214. Gesellschaft für Informatik e.V., Gesellschaft für Informatik e.V., Regensburg, Germany (2017). https://doi.org/10.18420/muc2017-mci-0164

17. Falb, J., Rock, T., Arnautovic, E.: Using communicative acts in interaction design specifications for automated synthesis of user interfaces. In: 21st IEEE/ACM International Conference on Automated Software Engineering (ASE 2006), IEEE (2006). https://doi.org/10.1109/ase.2006.71
18. FIPA: FIPA ACL message structure specification. Technical report SC00061G, Foundation for Intelligent Physical Agents (FIPA), Geneva, Switzerland (2002)
19. Gruber, T.R.: A translation approach to portable ontology specifications. Knowl. Acquis. **5**(2), 199–220 (1993). https://doi.org/10.1006/knac.1993.1008
20. Hitzler, P., Krotzsch, M., Rudolph, S.: Foundations of Semantic Web Technologies. Taylor & Francis Ltd. (2009)
21. Hong, J., Suh, E., Kim, S.: Context-aware systems: a literature review and classification. Expert Syst. Appl. **36**(4), 8509–8522 (2009). https://doi.org/10.1016/j.eswa.2008.10.071
22. Hörold, S., Mayas, C., Krömker, H.: Analyzing varying environmental contexts in public transport. In: Kurosu, M. (ed.) HCI 2013. LNCS, vol. 8004, pp. 85–94. Springer, Heidelberg (2013). https://doi.org/10.1007/978-3-642-39232-0_10
23. Jaimes, A., Sebe, N.: Multimodal human–computer interaction: a survey. Comput. Vis. Image Underst. **108**(1–2), 116–134 (2007). https://doi.org/10.1016/j.cviu.2006.10.019
24. Johnson, D.A., Trivedi, M.M.: Driving style recognition using a smartphone as a sensor platform. In: 2011 14th International IEEE Conference on Intelligent Transportation Systems (ITSC), pp. 1609–1615 (2011). https://doi.org/10.1109/ITSC.2011.6083078
25. Kölker, S., Schwinger, F., Krempels, K.H.: A framework for context-dependent user interface adaptation. In: Proceedings of the 15th International Conference on Web Information Systems and Technologies. SCITEPRESS - Science and Technology Publications (2019). https://doi.org/10.5220/0008487204180425
26. Kolski, C., Uster, G., Robert, J.-M., Oliveira, K., David, B.: Interaction in mobility: the evaluation of interactive systems used by travellers in transportation contexts. In: Jacko, J.A. (ed.) HCI 2011. LNCS, vol. 6763, pp. 301–310. Springer, Heidelberg (2011). https://doi.org/10.1007/978-3-642-21616-9_34
27. Lansdown, T.C., Brook-Carter, N., Kersloot, T.: Distraction from multiple in-vehicle secondary tasks: vehicle performance and mental workload implications. Ergonomics **47**(1), 91–104 (2004). https://doi.org/10.1080/00140130310001629775
28. Lemmelä, S., Vetek, A., Mäkelä, K., Trendafilov, D.: Designing and evaluating multimodal interaction for mobile contexts. In: Proceedings of the 10th international conference on Multimodal interfaces - IMCI 2008. ACM Press (2008). https://doi.org/10.1145/1452392.1452447
29. Mitrevska, M., et al.: SiAM - situation-adaptive multimodal interaction for innovative mobility concepts of the future. In: 2015 International Conference on Intelligent Environments. IEEE (2015). https://doi.org/10.1109/ie.2015.39
30. Nigay, L., Coutaz, J.: A design space for multimodal systems. In: Proceedings of the SIGCHI Conference on Human Factors in Computing Systems - CHI 1993, Amsterdam, The Netherlands, pp. 172–178. ACM Press (1993). https://doi.org/10.1145/169059.169143
31. Pielot, M., Poppinga, B., Heuten, W., Boll, S.: PocketNavigator: studying tactile navigation systems in-situ. In: Proceedings of the SIGCHI Conference on Human Factors in Computing Systems, CHI 2012, pp. 3131–3140. ACM, New York (2012). https://doi.org/10.1145/2207676.2208728

32. Pielot, M., Poppinga, B., Vester, B., Kazakova, A., Brammer, L., Boll, S.: Natch: a watch-like display for less distracting pedestrian navigation. In: Ziegler, J., Schmidt, A. (eds.) Mensch & Computer 2010: Interaktive Kulturen, pp. 291–300. Oldenbourg Verlag, München (2010)

33. Rehman, U., Cao, S.: Augmented-reality-based indoor navigation: a comparative analysis of handheld devices versus google glass. IEEE Trans. Hum.-Mach. Syst. **47**, 1–12 (2016). https://doi.org/10.1109/thms.2016.2620106

34. Russell, S., Norvig, P.: Artificial Intelligence: A Modern Approach, Global Edition. Addison Wesley, Boston (2018)

35. Samsel, C., Dudschenko, I., Kluth, W., Krempels, K.H.: Using wearables for travel assistance. In: Proceedings of the 11th International Conference on Web Information Systems and Technologies (2015). https://doi.org/10.5220/0005481306350641

36. Samsel, C., Thulke, D., Beutel, M.C., Kuck, D., Krempels, K.H.: In-car intermodal travel assistance using mobility service platforms. In: 2018 21st International Conference on Intelligent Transportation Systems (ITSC), pp. 800–805. IEEE (2018)

37. Schreiber, G., Dean, M.: OWL web ontology language reference (2004). https://www.w3.org/TR/owl-ref/. Accessed 6 Nov 2018

38. Smith, A.: More than half of cell owners affected by 'distracted walking' (2014). http://www.pewresearch.org/fact-tank/2014/01/02/more-than-half-of-cell-owners-affected-by-distracted-walking/. Accessed 15 Sept 2018

39. Steinert, T., et al.: VDV-Mitteilung 7046: Definition und Dokumentation der Nutzeranforderungen an eine offene Mobilitätsplattform. Technical report, Verband Deutscher Verkehrsunternehmen (VDV) e. V., Köln, Germany (2018)

40. Strang, T., Linnhoff-Popien, C.: Service interoperability on context level in ubiquitous computing environments. In: International Conference on Advances in Infrastructure for Electronic Business, Education, Science, Medicine, and Mobile Technologies on the Internet (2003)

41. Thornsby, J.: Android UI Design. O'Reilly Media, Sebastopol (2016)

42. Vanderdonckt, J., Limbourg, Q., Michotte, B., Bouillon, L., Trevisan, D.Q., Florins, M.: USIXML: a user interface description language for specifying multimodal user interfaces. In: Proceedings of W3C Workshop on Multimodal Interaction WMI (2004)

43. Wang, X.H., Zhang, D.Q., Gu, T., Pung, H.K.: Ontology based context modeling and reasoning using OWL. In: Proceedings of the Second IEEE Annual Conference on Pervasive Computing and Communications Workshop. IEEE (2004). https://doi.org/10.1109/percomw.2004.1276898

44. Wargo, J.M.: PhoneGap Essentials: Building Cross-platform Mobile Apps. Addison-Wesley Professional, Boston (2012)

45. Zargamy, A., Sakai, H., Ganhör, R., Oberwandling, G.: Fußgängernavigation im urbanen Raum - Designvorschlag. In: Boll, S., Maaß, S., Malaka, R. (eds.) Mensch & Computer 2013: Interaktive Vielfalt, pp. 365–368. Oldenbourg Verlag, Munich (2013)

46. Zauner, F.J., Radermacher, B.: VDV-Mitteilung 7047: itcs-Nutzungsfälle/Betriebsfälle in der praktischen Anwendung - Methodik und Praxisbeispiele. Technical report, Verband Deutscher Verkehrsunternehmen (VDV) e. V., Köln, Germany (2019)

# Paid Advertising on Social Media: Antecedents and Impacts of General and Specific Attitudes

Maria Madlberger[1]([✉]) [iD] and Lisa Kraemmer[2]

[1] Webster Vienna Private University, Praterstr. 23, 1020 Vienna, Austria
maria.madlberger@webster.ac.at
[2] Mediaplus Digital, Mediaplus Gruppe, Brienner Str. 45 a-d, 80333 Munich, Germany
lisa.kraemmer@gmail.com

**Abstract.** Social media platforms have become important channels of promotional communication from marketers to users with the goal of enhancing purchase intention. One important element of the communication mix is paid advertising on social media. In this context, the interplay between general attitude towards advertising on social media and specific attitude towards an individual advertisement as drivers of purchase intention has not yet been addressed in extant social media research. This study investigates this issue by distinguishing between these two levels of attitude and examining their antecedents as well as their impacts on purchase intention. The empirical test of the nomological network with survey data shows that platform enjoyment is an antecedent of general attitude towards social media advertising whereas perceived meaningfulness and brand awareness drive specific attitude towards the individual advertisement. Perceived intrusiveness has no impact in a social media setting. Specific attitude shows a stronger impact on purchase intention than general attitude although both are significant. The findings point at the need for a clear conceptual differentiation between both levels of attitudes and the role of their antecedents for an appropriate design of paid social media advertisements.

**Keywords:** Social media advertising · General attitude towards advertising · Specific attitude towards advertisements · Purchase intention · Social media platforms

## 1 Introduction

Social media have become a significant part of the everyday life worldwide. The number of users of social media platforms has sharply increased since the early 2000s, hence nowadays billions of Internet users have signed up for one or more social media platforms. Facebook alone has counted more than 2.2 billion users as of 2018; in the same year, around 1.9 billion individuals have used YouTube and one billion used Instagram. Besides the large, globally used social media platforms, also smaller or regional platforms enjoy large and increasing user numbers, such as WeChat with one billion, Tumblr with 624 million, Reddit with 355 million, or Twitter with 330 million users in 2018 [1]. Since their emergence, social media have evolved from their initial idea

© Springer Nature Switzerland AG 2020
A. Bozzon et al. (Eds.): WEBIST 2019, LNBIP 399, pp. 218–237, 2020.
https://doi.org/10.1007/978-3-030-61750-9_10

of enabling socializing and sharing content with others to serving as communication channels for the dissemination of promotional and commercial contents. Hence, the different social media platforms such as Facebook, YouTube, Instagram, or Twitter have not only transformed the way Internet users are communicating amongst each other but also how advertising messages can be spread among relevant target groups. Social media largely influence consumer behavior in many respects, from empowering consumers by serving as a channel for word-of mouth via allowing for personalized messages to the strengthening of business-to-consumer relationships. The importance of social media for promotional communication is showcased by the increasing financial volume of social media advertising. In 2019, the expenditures for advertising on social media platforms has surpassed the expenditures for print advertising. They have grown to 13% of all advertising expenditures to an overall amount of 84 billion US$ worldwide, turning social media advertising into the third-largest advertising channel behind television and paid search [2].

Against this background, a comprehensive understanding of drivers of the effectiveness of social media advertising becomes a crucial insight. However, despite an active research agenda within this domain, there are still several indications of relevant conceptualizations of key variables that received little attention in research so far. In particular, there is evidence from related domains in three issues [3–5]: First, there is an interplay between social media platforms as the advertising medium and the advertised product or brand. Second, consumers' simultaneous perception of the advertising medium and individual advertisements suggests the existence of consumer attitude on different levels, especially on the level of general attitude towards advertising in the respective medium and specific attitude towards an individual advertisement on this medium [6]. Third, perceptions related to the advertisement itself are drivers of attitudes towards the advertisement and finally the resulting purchase intention. All three issues have not been exhaustively investigated within the context of social media advertising. The resulting research gap in this relevant area of application forms the motivation to pursue the following research goals.

The first goal is gaining an understanding of consumers' attitude towards advertising on social media on two different levels, i.e., the level of the social media platform and the level of the individual advertisement. This goal draws on extant research that has addressed consumer attitudes on different levels by distinguishing between more general media-specific attitudes and individual brand-specific attitudes. Second, the study aims at investigating how different antecedents that are related (1) to the social media platform, (2) the advertisement, and (3) both impact attitude on both levels. Third, the study intends to reveal whether and to what extent attitudes on both levels impact a key dependent variable in consumer behavior research, i.e., purchase intention. The resulting research questions of this study are the following:

1. How do platform-specific influencing factors impact consumers' attitude within the context of social media advertising on different levels?
2. How do advertisement-specific influencing factors impact consumers' attitude within the context of social media advertising on different levels?
3. How do consumer attitudes on both levels within the context of social media impact purchase intention?

To answer these research questions, the study at hand develops and empirically tests a research framework that is formulated as a nomological network. To empirically test this model, survey data has been collected from social media users located in Austria. The study seeks to contribute to a better understanding of the drivers of effectiveness of social media advertising by identifying and evaluating the impact of platform and advertisement-specific antecedents as well as the in-depth examination of consumer attitudes on different levels. In doing so, it investigates the conceptual differences between these two levels of attitude as well as draws conclusions on particular interactions on social media platforms that influence the formation of attitudes. The findings allow to derive relevant theoretical and managerial implications for social media advertising.

This chapter is an extension of the work provided by [6] that further extends the notion of the distinction between attitude in the context of social media advertising on two levels, i.e., general attitudes towards advertising on social media and specific attitudes towards an individual advertisement. It further deepens the investigation of antecedents of the specific attitude towards an individual advertisement by elaborating a more comprehensive conceptual framework on its drivers so that novel conclusions are drawn from the results. The chapter is organized as follows: The following section provides a literature review on social media advertising and the formation of consumer attitudes. On this basis, the conceptual framework of general versus specific attitudes and their antecedents is developed. Section three elaborates the research model and formulates the hypotheses that propose drivers of attitudes on both levels as well as their impact on purchase intention. Section four reports on the research methodology, followed by the presentation of the analysis results obtained by PLS data analysis in section five. Section six discusses research and managerial implications of the study.

## 2 Conceptual Background

### 2.1 Social Media Advertising

Social media have become established Internet-based networks that allow users to communicate with a large variety of different actors simultaneously. This has largely altered the way individuals are interacting with friends, but also different types of organizations. As a result, social media have become a communication channel that allows individuals, organizations, and public bodies to communicate on personal, social, political, but also commercial issues [7, 8]. This way, social media establish a new hybrid element in the promotion mix [9]. There is a multitude of different ways social media can be used for promotional purposes, such as customer relationship management, advertising, electronic word of mouth, or branding [10]. In contrast to classical mass media communication, advertisers can establish an interactive and more personalized communication with their audiences [9]. A particular attribute of social media communication is the increase of reach of larger groups of audiences, but at the same time a decrease in control over the content and timing of disseminated messages. Hence, shaping consumer impressions on social media platforms needs to be coordinated with a companies' overall mission, message strategy, and performance goals, resulting in the need for an integrated marketing communications approach [11]. More specifically, it is important to integrate social media into companies' promotional marketing mix by applying networking platforms, blogs, or social media tools in order to engage customers with the companies' advertisements, products, and services [9].

There are three ways social media marketing can be used within the online marketing context: owned media, paid media, and earned media [12]. Owned media are characterized by a corporate presence in the form of a company's website or an own page on a social media platform. Examples are a corporate Facebook page or an Instagram business account. Paid media are an analogy to traditional mass media advertising where the marketer pays other companies, i.e., the media owners, to provide a space to disseminate promotional content for reaching their audience [11, 12]. Examples of online paid media are display advertisements that appear on webpages, paid search entries on search engines, or paid advertisements and sponsored posts in social media. The last category is earned media where promotional or brand-related contents are disseminated by Internet users themselves without a compensation. Earned media include word of mouth, comments and shares, ratings, and generally any content generated by people online, to mention a few [11]. Since users determine the content of these messages themselves, the marketer's control over these messages is very limited. Earned media can also lead to the dissemination of content that is negative to the marketer. In this context, research revealed the existence of a trust hierarchy. Recommendations from real-life friends enjoy the highest degree of trust, followed by recommendations from users who are only known from the Internet, but not in person. The lowest level of trust is attributed to recommendations on the brand's website generated by individuals who are unknown to the users [13]. Due to their credibility, earned media are an especially powerful communication tool but also one that requires a high degree of incentives and positive relationship with the users to trigger the dissemination of positive content [11].

## 2.2 Two Levels of Attitude Towards Advertising on Social Media

The effectiveness of advertising is strongly associated with consumer attitudes. Since advertisements are always bound to the media they appear in, consumer attitudes towards the medium influence attitudes towards individual advertisements on this medium [6]. Research has made a conceptual distinction between consumer evaluations of advertising in general and individual advertisements in the context of advertising value and attitude towards advertising [14, 15]. Hence, attitudes towards advertising in general impact attitudes towards individual advertisements [16].

In a most general level, attitude towards social media is largely related to users' perception of the social media platform itself whereby individual platforms (such as Facebook, Instagram, YouTube) show substantial individual differences [17]. Key factors that influence users' attitudes towards social media platforms are perceived ease of platform use, usefulness, enjoyment, social influence, and drama [18]. The first three stem from the Technology Acceptance Model that consistently turned out to explain acceptance of information systems in many domains [19]. Ease of use denotes the extent to which a user perceives the social media platform to be free from effort when using it. Usefulness is the degree to which the social media platform is perceived to be appropriate to improve the user's intended tasks. Platform enjoyment refers to the emotional component of social media usage and denotes the affective expression of joy and entertainment on social media. The social influence describes a user's perception of engagement with others on the social media platform. Lastly, drama summarizes users' evaluation of social media postings to be spectacular and hence refers to their ability to gain attraction. Compared to other information system types, perceived enjoyment has turned out to show the largest impact on attitude towards the social media platform [18]. Users can make large differences between individual social media platforms so that attitudes towards social media need to be related to the individual social media platforms [17].

Within the specific context of advertising, a distinction between consumer attitudes towards advertising on the medium in general as well as attitude towards individual advertisements can be made [5]. These two levels of attitude have been shown within the context of offline print media. Survey participants who were exposed to magazine advertisements content expressed positive (e.g., feeling of being kept up-to-date by ads) and negative (e.g., mistrust about truthfulness of claims made in ads, annoyance) attitudes towards advertising on the medium in question. Individual effectiveness measures on advertisements, such as intrusiveness, recall, or persuasion, turned out to be related to these attitudes [5]. These effects could also be shown in research on online advertising. Contrasting attitude towards advertising on the Internet with attitude towards advertising on a specific social media platform reveals that both are connected and can provide users with a sense of belonging and an interpersonal utility, turning users' perception of advertisements on the social media platform more positive [3].

On the even more specific level of advertising on social media, research has shown that users' general engagement with a social media platform impacts their engagement with advertising on this platform. These carryover effects can be explained by the context theory which posits the existence of three main theoretical explanations for the importance of context, i.e., the attitude towards a social media platform [17]. These three factors are priming, mood, and congruity. Priming leads to an interpretation of a specific content (e.g., an advertisement) in a way that is consistent with the interpretation of contents within the context (the social media platform). In the context of mood, a social media platform makes certain moods (e.g., relaxation) more accessible to users and if a specific content such as an advertisement also evokes the same mood, the effectiveness is increased. Finally congruity denotes that the social media platform and the provided advertisements appear consistent to users as the advertisement is perceived as a part of the overall social media platform content [20, 21]. As a result, users perceive a certain kind of "fit" between a social media platform and advertisements on this platform.

Within the context of attitudes towards advertising on social media platforms, users can be largely divided into three groups: individuals who are clearly negative about social media advertising, individuals who are neutral, and individuals who show positive attitudes towards social media advertisements and their likelihood to engage with them [4]. Concluding from context theory, we posit that these general attitudes towards advertising on the social media platform will influence the specific attitude towards individual advertisements that are posted on the social media platform.

## 2.3   General Attitude Towards Advertising on a Social Media Platform

A large number of activities that take place on social media show relations to commercial and promotional contexts which establishes a connection and a blurred line between personal communication and the exchange of promotional content. A study on 15 specific activities on social media shows that all kinds of social media activities, i.e., information processing, entertainment activities, and social connection, can be related to consumers' perception of products. Examples are retrieval of product information or sharing product information and experiences as information processing activities, self-expression or managing one's self-image activities as entertainment activities, and sharing of content with others or feelings of belonging and bonding with brands as social connection activities. All of these activities are often revolving around the ideas of consumption and consumer input so that companies need to design and adapt their social media marketing strategies accordingly [22].

Attitude towards the social media platform is an important antecedent of purchasing behavior. Users' attitude towards using a social media platform as a tool to make purchases is driven by several factors. This includes usefulness perception of recommendations and suggestions, users' perception of platform enjoyment when searching for information on products and brands, and users' perceived ease of use of the platform. Perceived platform enjoyment has turned out to show a direct impact on purchase intention as the only factor. Hence, the social media platform can motivate users to obtain product information, but also make purchases. The more users like advertisements on the social media platform in general, the more they are likely to purchase advertised products [23].

A major impacting factor of purchasing behavior related to social media is advertising value [24]. The value of advertising is contingent upon its perceived interactivity, relevance, hedonic motivation, performance expectancy, and informativeness, which are this way driving purchase intention based on social media advertising [7]. Also social media previews of products and a social media platform's ability to support purchase processes quickly can stimulate actual online purchases [25]. A survey-based study in the context of Facebook shows that advertising has a positive attitudinal influence on purchase intention and actual purchases amongst Millennials. Within this context, advertising on Facebook shows the largest impact on users' purchase intention if users spend two or more hours at a time on the platform. The larger exposure gives the users more time to interact with advertisements on the platform, hence there are more opportunities to form positive attitudes towards the advertisements and ultimately increase willingness to purchase the advertised products or services [26].

## 2.4   Specific Attitude Towards Individual Advertisements on Social Media

Attitudes towards individual advertisements are driven by cognitive as well as affective factors and include informativeness, irritation, and entertainment [14]. In an online and particularly social media setting, entertainment has turned out to significantly gain in importance compared to other drivers of attitude [27]. Further, purchase intention is impacted by advertising informativeness and credibility [28]. In contrast to the positive impact of entertaining and informativeness, a negative driver of advertising effectiveness is irritation [29].

An advertisement's perception of informativeness is dependent on whether an advertisement is considered meaningful and reasonable. As advertisements on social media are usually intended to be short and entertaining, the amount of information that can be transferred is limited and hence meaningfulness is particularly important in this setting. Perceived meaningfulness of an advertisement refers to how an ad is understood by users. This variable generally influences individuals' evaluation of advertisements [30]. Humans remember words or sentences that are meaningful to a larger extent than in case of meaningless content [31]. Meaningfulness can be derived from a dictionary meaning, i.e., whether the wording relates to generally known terms or a business meaning that is based on the knowledge of established companies or brands [32]. Hence, meaningfulness has turned out to be a relevant attribute of messages and contents in many contexts, including websites [32, 33]. In the advertising context, meaningfulness denotes the extent to which an advertisement contains elements that are relevant to the message that is conveyed as well as the intention of the advertisement. Hence, it reflects how effectively an advertisement supports the goal of the respective brand [34, 35]. Consumers perceive meaningful advertisements as appropriate, useful, or in some way valuable [36] so that it establishes a connectedness between the advertiser and the consumer [34]. Several researchers identify a relationship between an advertisement's meaningfulness and its creativity in a way that the latter is contingent upon the existence of the former [37]. Meaningfulness is also highly associated with the perceived authenticity of an advertisement which is another key driver of attitude towards advertisements [38].

Irritation is related to the perceived intrusiveness of an advertisement and denotes the degree to which an ad is seen as distracting from the intended usage of the platform. Irritation has turned out to have little impact on the overall attitude towards social media ads [4], however, several studies show that a related construct, intrusiveness, does negatively impact attitude towards the respective individual advertisement [5, 30, 39]. With a growing amount of advertising clutter, consumers are getting increasingly involved in the experience of advertising intrusiveness. This results in a negative reaction as consumers perceive advertisements as a forced message that interrupts or distracts them from their actual media usage goal and can cause annoyance. This can further result in an advertisement avoidance behavior [39]. Intrusiveness is a driver of negative reactions associated with an advertisement, but not the experience of any negative feelings themselves [40]. It is rather the perception that the intended cognitive process (e.g., reading a message) is interrupted. Hence, intrusiveness is defined as an interruption of the perception of editorial content by advertisements [41]. The existence of perceptions of advertisement intrusiveness has been investigated in various offline and online contexts whereby intrusiveness turned out to be higher online as many online interactions are associated with a flow whose interruption leads to a stronger perception of intrusiveness [42]. Despite the negative nature of advertisement intrusiveness, advertised brands are still preferred over brands that are not advertised [43].

Lastly, also the advertised brand plays a role for the formation of attitude towards an advertisement on social media. The more users are engaged with a marketer's brand, the more likely they are to make repeat purchases from that brand and communicate their brand awareness with others. In contrast, dissatisfaction or annoyance with a brand negatively impacts purchase intention on social media platforms [22]. In this context, the familiarity with the respective marketing companies or brands has turned out to be a relevant antecedent of attitude towards advertisements on social media platforms [4]. The latter finding is consistent with insights into the role of brand awareness for the formation of attitudes towards online advertisements [44].

## 3   Research Model and Hypotheses Development

The proposed research model is a nomological network that investigates antecedents of purchase intention triggered by advertising on a social media platform. It specifically considers general attitudes towards social media advertising and specific attitudes towards an individual advertisement. Figure 1 graphically shows the research model and the hypotheses.

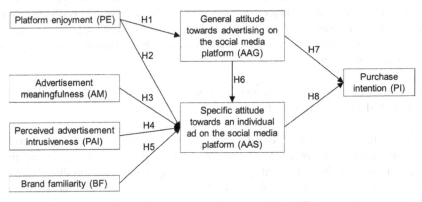

**Fig. 1.** Research model (extended from [6]).

The conceptualization of the general and specific attitudes is derived from the notions of [3, 4, 26] and distinguishes between attitude towards advertisements on the social media platform in general (AAG) and specific attitude towards an individual advertisement on the social media platform (AAS). Overall attitude towards advertising is understood as a "learned predisposition to respond in the consistently favorable or unfavorable manner to advertising in general" [15]. Attitude towards the specific advertisement is defined as the users' predisposition towards one individual advertisement that is displayed on the particular social media platform.

Based on evidence on the predominant role of entertainment in social media, we consider perceived platform enjoyment a relevant antecedent of attitudes in respect of advertising [18, 23]. Users' experience of enjoyment on social media platforms turned out to show a significant impact on attitude towards stimuli shown on the platform [18]. If a social media platform is seen as enjoyable to the users, they are more likely to positively perceive advertising on the platform [23]. Hence, we conclude that platform enjoyment has a positive influence on both forms of attitude relating to social media advertising, i.e., the general attitude towards advertising on the platform and the specific attitude towards an individual advertisement. Therefore, we propose the following hypotheses:

H1: Perceived platform enjoyment positively impacts general attitude towards advertising on the social media platform.

H2: Perceived platform enjoyment positively impacts specific attitude towards an individual advertisement on the social media platform.

Besides entertainment, informativeness is a key antecedent of attitude towards an advertisement. However, within the context of social media, advertising messages are usually designed in a way that their messages are entertaining and at the same time can quickly be understood. Hence it is of major importance that users understand an advertisement's intention despite entertainment and simplification elements that may distract from the actual meaning of the message. Therefore, we consider meaningfulness of an advertisement a key factor that serves as an appropriate proxy of informativeness and entertainment of an advertisement. Perceived meaningfulness has been identified as a relevant mediator between objective features of an advertisement and attitude towards it. It shows a direct impact on attitude towards an advertisement [38]. Since perceived meaningfulness is inherent to an individual advertisement, we hypothesize an impact on the specific attitude only:

H3: Perceived advertisement meaningfulness positively impacts specific attitude towards the individual advertisement on the social media platform.

One of the most relevant negative drivers of attitude in the context of advertising on social media is perceived intrusiveness [45]. Although not a negative feeling itself, perceived intrusiveness is associated with negative experiences such as distracting, disturbing, forced, interfering, intrusive, and obtrusive [40]. As research has shown, perceived intrusiveness is driven by perceptions about individual advertisements such as the obvious use of personal information, the fit of the advertised offer, or financial incentives [46]. Therefore, we propose that perceived intrusiveness only affects the specific attitude towards the individual advertisement:

H4: Perceived advertisement intrusiveness negatively impacts specific attitude towards the individual advertisement on the social media platform.

As research on advertising, including social media advertising, has shown, users' relation with the advertised brand plays a key role in attitude formation [4]. High brand familiarity can increase the positive experience with the brand and also trust in it [44], ultimately positively affecting attitude. Since brand familiarity is specifically addressing the advertised brand, we hypothesize a positive impact of this factor on the specific attitude towards the individual advertisement, but not on general attitude towards advertising on the social media platform.

H5: Brand familiarity positively impacts specific attitude towards the individual advertisement on the social media platform.

Finally, we are drawing on research that makes the distinction between general attitude towards advertising on a medium and specific attitude towards an individual advertisement [3–6, 14, 47]. In line with this research and concluding from the temporal sequence of impacts we propose that this relationship comes in a form that the more general construct, general attitude towards advertising on the medium, impacts the specific attitude towards the individual advertisement. Within a social media context, it has been demonstrated that general attitudes towards advertising on social media, i.e., whether users generally like or dislike social media advertising, are transferred to specific advertisement types, such as display ads [27, 48] which supports this notion. Hence, we hypothesize:

H6: General attitude towards advertising on the social media platform positively impacts specific attitude towards the individual advertisement on the social media platform.

The entire premise of the marketing mix, including the element of social media marketing [9] is aiming at ultimately influencing consumer behavior in a way that the advertised product is purchased. We are drawing on the seminal theory of planned behavior [49, 50] by proposing that purchase intention is a strong antecedent and therefore an appropriate proxy for actual purchasing behavior and that both forms of attitude impact purchase intention. This relationship has also been demonstrated by previous research in the context of social media [26, 51]. Hence, we propose the following two hypotheses:

H7: General attitude towards advertising on the social media platform positively impacts purchase intention.
H8: Specific attitude towards the individual advertisement on the social media platform positively impacts purchase intention.

## 4   Research Methodology

### 4.1   Instrument Development

The constructs that have been applied in the study were all adapted from existing multi-item scales published in the literature (see Table 2 below). All items have been measured on a five-point Likert scale where 1 represents "Strongly Disagree" and 5 represents "Strongly Agree". To establish a clear context with a concrete scenario and address the differentiated view users have on individual social media platforms [17], respondents were requested to consider Facebook as the relevant social media platform. In addition, participants were shown a screenshot of a real paid Facebook advertisement that was posted by a well-known consumer goods brand [6].

Perceived platform enjoyment (PE) was measured using three items adapted from [18]. Advertisement meaningfulness (AM) has been based on the scale developed by [30]. Perceived advertisement intrusiveness (PAI) was measured by adapting the scale developed by [39]. Brand familiarity (BF) was captured using three items adapted from

[44]. General attitude towards advertisements on the social media platform (AAG) was measured with two items from [5]. Specific attitude towards the individual advertisement on the social media platform (AAS) was measured using two items adapted from [3]. Finally, purchase intention (PI) was measured with three items adapted from [26].

## 4.2 Data Collection and Sample Description

The research model has been tested on data that has been collected through an online, self-administered, anonymous questionnaire implemented with the online survey tool Qualtrics. The geographic focus of the study is Austria. Filter questions ensured that respondents were using Facebook as a social media platform as well as able to recognize the advertised brand used in the survey.

In total, 211 questionnaires were completed. After 26 questionnaires have been removed due to incomplete answers, a sample size of 185 questionnaires has been used for further analysis. Table 1 shows the sample description.

**Table 1.** Sample description.

| Category | Values | Relative frequency |
|---|---|---|
| Gender | Male | 46.7% |
| | Female | 53.3% |
| Age | Less than 25 years | 70.7% |
| | 25 to 25 years | 9.4% |
| | 36 to 42 years | 5.5% |
| | 43 or more years | 14.4% |
| Highest completed level of education | High school | 55.2% |
| | Bachelor's degree | 26.5% |
| | Master's degree | 11.1% |
| | PhD | 3.3% |
| | Others | 3.9% |
| Experience with Facebook usage | Less than 3 years | 4.4% |
| | 3 to 6 years | 19.9% |
| | 6 to 9 years | 60.2% |
| | More than 9 years | 15.5% |

# 5 Results

## 5.1 Measurement Model

The research model has been tested by means of a Partial Least Squares (PLS) analysis with the analysis software tool SmartPLS [52]. The test of the measurement model consists of analyzing the consistency (Cronbach's Alpha), the convergent validity, and the discriminant validity. Table 2 shows the Cronbach's Alpha and AVE values of the variables.

**Table 2.** Reliability measures of variables.

| Variable | Number of items | Cronbach's Alpha | AVE |
|---|---|---|---|
| Platform enjoyment (PE) | 3 | .896 | .826 |
| Advertisement meaningfulness (AM) | 3 | .734 | .651 |
| Perceived ad intrusiveness (PAI) | 2 | .844 | .731 |
| Brand familiarity (BF) | 3 | .764 | .678 |
| General attitude towards advertising on the social media platform (AAG) | 2 | .823 | .850 |
| Specific attitude towards the individual ad on the social media platform (AAS) | 2 | .758 | .805 |
| Purchase intention (PI) | 2 | .875 | .889 |

The Cronbach's Alpha values all exceed the recommended value of 0.7 [53]. Convergent validity is satisfactory if the average variance extracted (AVE) is higher than 0.5 [54]. Also, this condition is met for all variables. Table 3 displays the numbers concerning discriminant validity.

**Table 3.** Correlation matrix.

|  | PE | AM | PAI | BF | AAG | AAS | PI |
|---|---|---|---|---|---|---|---|
| PE | *.909* | | | | | | |
| AM | .086 | *.807* | | | | | |
| PAI | .090 | −.053 | *.855* | | | | |
| BF | .147 | .498 | .048 | *.823* | | | |
| AAG | .503 | .110 | .045 | .143 | *.922* | | |
| AAS | .191 | .558 | .098 | .552 | .291 | *.897* | |
| PI | .057 | .406 | .131 | .457 | .446 | .653 | *.942* |

In Table 3, the correlations of the variables are shown. The numbers on the diagonal in italics are the square roots of the AVE. For adequate discriminant validity, these values should exceed the interconstruct correlations. This condition is met for all constructs. Further, the loadings of the individual items on the corresponding variables are well above the recommended value of 0.5 for appropriate discriminant validity. They range between .790 and .949. Thus, the measurement model is highly satisfactory.

## 5.2 Hypotheses Tests

The PLS analysis comprises the computation of the path coefficients, their p-values, and the R-square values of the dependent variables. The p-values have been computed by bootstrapping with 100 cases and 1,000 samples. The R-square values are the following: .253 for AAG, .460 for AAS, and .498 for PI. Figure 2 shows the results of the PLS analysis along with the p-values of the path coefficients.

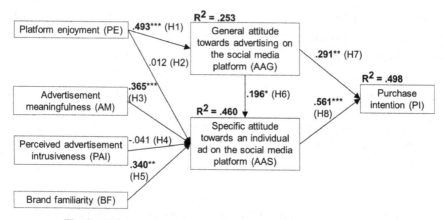

**Fig. 2.** PLS analysis results. p-values: *** < .001, ** < .01, * < .05

As the analysis results show, six out of eight hypotheses are supported by data and significant on a 5% p-level or lower. Platform enjoyment significantly impacts general attitude towards advertising on the social media platform, supporting H1. However, it does not significantly impact specific attitude towards the individual advertisement, so that H2 is rejected. Advertisement meaningfulness shows a significant positive impact on the specific attitude towards the advertisement which leads to the support of H3. Conversely, the data does not support the existence of an impact of perceived advertisement intrusiveness on the specific attitude towards the advertisement, hence H4 is rejected. The final independent variable, brand familiarity, again shows a significant and positive impact on specific attitude towards the advertisement which supports H5. The remaining three hypotheses are supported as the respective path coefficients are all significant at least on the 5% level. Since all impacts are positive, H6, H7, and H8 are supported.

The analysis has been complemented by several control variables. We controlled for the socio-demographic variables gender, age, and education as well as Facebook experience. This analysis did not show any significant impact of these variables on the outcome of the hypothesis tests.

## 6 Discussion

### 6.1 Discussion of Findings

The empirical test of the research model shows that the majority of the hypotheses is supported by data. The predominant role of perceived enjoyment of the social media platform and its impact on general attitudes towards advertising on the social media platform could be confirmed. With a path coefficient of .493, this impact is the second strongest throughout the research model and the data shows that more than 25% of the variance in general attitude towards advertising on the social media platform can be explained by this factor. This finding is consistent with previous research that has shown that the more enjoyable a platform is to the users the more likely the users are to appreciate the platforms' advertising [23]. On the other hand, the hypothesized impact of platform enjoyment on the specific attitude towards the individual advertisement could not be found in the data. Although this outcome counters the initially proposed assumption, this finding renders a noteworthy insight as it points at the conceptual difference between general and specific attitudes. The fact that platform enjoyment shows different degrees of influence on attitude in both respects strengthens the notion that users differentiate between advertising in general and specific advertisements. This confirms previous research in other domains [14, 15] and supports the transfer of these insights into the social media context. Furthermore, platform enjoyment and specific attitude are related to two different sources from the user's perspective, namely the social media platform and the advertisement. The findings suggest that users evaluate both independently from each other. Additionally, although a direct impact of platform enjoyment on attitude towards the individual advertisement does not exist, there is a mediated impact via general attitude towards advertising on the social media platform. Hence, users' formation of attitudes follows a kind of sequence from more platform-related issues to more advertisement-related ones.

Among the other antecedents that are related to attributes of the individual advertisement the majority show a significant impact on attitude towards the advertisement. Advertisement meaningfulness and brand familiarity both show a significant positive impact and are of a similar strength. This finding is consistent with related work within the context of online advertising [32, 33, 41] and points in case of advertisement meaningfulness at the importance of a careful design of social media advertising content. The significant impact of brand familiarity is an important implication as is clearly shows that social media advertising is more effective for established brands or brands which show a strong relationship with its customer target groups. The proposed negative impact of perceived intrusiveness of the advertisement on attitude could not be supported by the data. This result differs from related findings in online advertising contexts [5, 39, 40]. Although contradicting the original assumption on this impact, this result allows drawing a conclusion concerning the specifics of advertising on social media [11]. A possible explanation lies in the specific type of interaction on social media platforms. Whereas many interactions on the Internet are mainly pull-oriented, i.e., carried out to pursue a certain goal and retrieve a certain informational or entertaining content, social media platforms are usually used for push-oriented purposes. This means that in case of information push, users are open to the delivery of various contents without actively searching for them [55]. In such a context, users may be more open to unexpected and surprising content, but may also not feel interrupted by advertising messages since they are not involved in completing a task. Unlike in other entertainment settings, e.g., watching TV, advertisements on social media platforms are not providing a forced exposure to such a large extent, so that users seem to experience an interruption to a lesser extent.

## 6.2   Research Implications

The study at hand provides several implications that contribute to a better theoretical understanding of consumer behavior in social media advertising. First, the notion of attitude towards advertising on two different levels within the context of social media could clearly be demonstrated. This is not only evident by the different impact strengths of platform enjoyment, but also the significant impact of general attitude on specific attitude towards the individual advertisement. This impact is the weakest throughout the model, yet still significant. As proposed in previous research in related online advertising contexts, a more distinct conceptualization of attitudes is necessary for a complete understanding of consumer behavior in social media advertising. Attitude towards advertising on social media platforms can affect user behavior in various ways, as research on engagement has shown [17]. Hence, the transfer of general attitude on specific attitude towards an individual advertisement exists in social media and hence should be considered a key factor in research on social media advertising.

Second, the overall explanatory power of the nomological network, as demonstrated by the R square values, stresses the relevance for social media advertising. Together with advertisement meaningfulness and brand familiarity, general attitude towards advertising on social media explain 46% of the variance of attitude towards the individual advertisement. The different strengths of impact show that marketers have a larger control over attitude towards the advertisement than the social media platform. The model also shows that attitude towards the individual advertisement shows a substantially larger impact on purchase intention than general attitude towards social media advertising. This outcome is consistent with the findings obtained by [26] and [51]. Both factors together explain almost 50% of the variance in purchase intention. The identification of these impacts is consistent with prior research within and outside the social media context [3–5] and calls for a distinction between these two types of attitude in future research. It stresses the importance of perceptions on individual advertisements rather than attitude towards advertising on a certain medium in general.

Third, we could identify three relevant antecedents of attitude on both levels, i.e., platform enjoyment, advertisement meaningfulness, and brand familiarity. These factors stress the importance of attributes that are related to the individual advertisement rather than advertising on the respective medium in general. This aspect is further strengthened by the strong impact of specific attitude towards an individual advertisement on purchase intention. Like the two levels of attitude, the antecedents highlight the relevance of users' perception of the social media platform itself (platform enjoyment), but even more the relevance of the advertisement attributes (perceived meaningfulness and brand familiarity). Especially perceived meaningfulness has so far received little attention in advertising and social media advertising research and should be investigated to a larger degree.

Finally, the study also shows that social media establish a context that differs from other media by showing that the otherwise significant impact of perceived intrusiveness does not hold in the study's social media context. This finding suggests that more knowledge is needed on users' perception of interruption and perceptions that are felt in a negative way. In this context, also the very nature of different social media platforms [17] should be considered, as they may be key drivers of users' perceptions of interactions and the resulting perception of an interruptive nature of advertisements. To summarize, the study at hand supports the notion of users' attitude towards advertising on different levels as well as the specific context of social media advertising.

## 6.3 Managerial Implications

There are several managerial implications this study can offer. They are especially related to the usage of social media advertising as a powerful tool to communicate with users. First, within the current debate about the key role of earned media communication, especially in social media, paid advertising still has its important place in the promotional mix. In contrast, the findings support the notion that owned, paid, and earned media in social media marketing [11] complement each other. Marketers should not underestimate the role of paid advertising and should pursue a careful design of advertising messages. This does not only refer to a clear adaptation to the specifics of the different social media platforms [17], but, as in the case of Facebook, also an advertisement design that enables users to quickly understand an advertisement's main message while at the same time being entertaining and not information-overloaded. Hence, the generally entertaining character of many social media platforms requires marketers to design their advertisements in a way that they are more entertaining than in other channels. At the same time, their main message needs to be grasped quickly, which poses a potential challenge to the meaningfulness of the advertisement.

Second, from a brand management perspective, the findings show that a high brand familiarity can positively influence the overall likelihood of purchase intention due to advertising. As a result, stronger brands will most likely be at an advantage compared to less popular brands. Hence, especially companies whose brands are well-known and established are recommended to make use of social media advertising to reach social media-affine target groups effectively.

Third, platform enjoyment is an important antecedent which has an indirect impact on attitude towards an individual advertisement. The study provides an implication for the choice of social media platforms. Marketers of less-known brands can increase awareness by exploiting the entertainment potential of social media.

Finally, users' preferences and attitudes towards social media platforms are subject to changes. For example, the increasing popularity of Instagram goes hand in hand with a decrease of Facebook especially among Millennials and younger generations. Therefore, marketers are recommended to constantly monitor their target groups' activities on different social media in order to regularly choose those platforms that allow for the highest possible effectiveness of their advertising campaigns.

# 7   Conclusion

This research has addressed the role of users' attitude in the context of social media advertising on two levels and it examined its antecedents as well as its impact on purchase intention. The study shows that it is crucial for a comprehensive understanding of consumer behavior related to social media advertising to apply the distinction of attitude towards advertising on the medium in general and towards individual advertisements that has been identified in research from related areas [3, 5, 14]. The study also high-lights the predominance of factors that are associated with the individual advertisement compared to those factors that relate to the social media platform. Further, the study stresses the existence of specific interactions of users on social media platforms that obviously differ from other advertising channels. The concluding takeaways from this study from a practitioners' view are the importance of paid media and the need for a careful design of advertisements that are posted on social media platforms to maximally influence purchase intention.

Like any research, this study has limitations that need to be considered when interpreting the findings. First, with 185 completed questionnaires, the sample size is relatively small. While it is sufficiently large to test the nomological network by conducting the PLS analysis, it offers only a limited degree of generalizability of results. Hence the conclusions drawn from the findings are mainly preliminary and need support on the basis of a larger sample. Second, the structure of the sample is not representative of social media users. It over represents younger social media users and under represents mid-aged and older ones. This issue may diminish with an increased number of digital natives over time, but it does not appropriately reflect the behavior of customer groups that are still very influential. Further, the respondents' genders are not fully balanced in the collected data. Like in many online surveys, the data may be affected by a self-selection bias due to the online survey design. Another limitation of the study is the focus on one specific social media platform, Facebook, as well as one specific brand used as a stimulus. Whereas Facebook is still by far the most widely-used social media platform, it does not necessarily allow to draw conclusions for other social media platforms, especially since individual social media platforms do have their unique characteristics.

The study allows for various directions in future research that should consider an extended set of variables stemming from different established theoretical bases, such as the stimulus-organism-response (S-O-R) theory or models that consider different stages in the purchase decision process. Further, possible impacts of involved product categories as well as users' personality traits should be considered for further inclusion in a research model. The study at hand provides initial insights into the specific role of attitude on different levels in social media advertising as well as their different impact paths from antecedents to purchase intention so that we hope to stimulate the academic debate on driving factors in paid advertising on social media platforms.

## References

1. Our World in Data, The rise of social media. https://ourworldindata.org/rise-of-social-media. Accessed 17 Jan 2020
2. Zenith Media, Social media overtakes print to become the third-largest advertising channel. https://www.zenithmedia.com/social-media-overtakes-print-to-become-the-third-largest-advertising-channel/. Accessed 17 Jan 2020
3. Celebi, S.I.: How do motives affect attitudes and behaviors toward internet advertising and Facebook advertising? Comput. Hum. Behav. 51(1), 312–324 (2015)
4. Lukka, V., James, P.T.J.: Attitudes toward Facebook advertising. J. Manage. Market. Res. 14(1–26), 1 (2014)
5. Mehta, A.: Advertising attitudes and advertising effectiveness. J. Advert. Res. 40(3), 37–72 (2000)

6. Madlberger, M., Kraemmer, L.: Social media advertising: the role of the social media platform and the advertised brand in attitude formation and purchase intention. In: Bozzon, A., Domínguez Mayo, F., Filipe, J. (eds.) 15th International Conference on Web Information Systems and Technologies (WEBIST), pp. 100–109. Scitepress (2019)

7. Alalwan, A.A.: Investigating the impact of social media advertising features on customer purchase intention. Int. J. Inf. Manage. 42(10), 65–77 (2018)

8. Hawkins, K., Vel, P.: Attitudinal loyalty, behavioural loyalty and social media: an introspection. Market. Rev. 13(2), 125–141 (2013)

9. Mangold, W.G., Faulds, D.J.: Social media: the new hybrid element of the promotion mix. Bus. Horiz. 52(4), 357–365 (2009)

10. Alalwan, A.A., Rana, N.P., Dwivedi, Y.K., Algharabat, R.: Social media in marketing: a review and analysis of the existing literature. Telematics Inform. 34(7), 1177–1190 (2017)

11. Strauss, J., Frost, R.: E – Marketing. Routledge, New York (2016)

12. Burcher, N.: Paid, Owned, Earned: Maximizing Marketing Returns in a Socially Connected World. Kogan Page, London (2012)

13. Harris, L., Dennis, C.: Engaging customers on Facebook: challenges for e-retailers. J. Consum. Behav. 10(6), 338–346 (2011)

14. Ducoffe, R.H.: Advertising value and advertising the web. J. Advert. Res. 36(5), 21–35 (1996)

15. Lutz, R.J.: Affective and cognitive antecedents of attitude toward the ad: a conceptual framework. In: Alwitt, L.F., Mitchell, A.A. (eds.) Psychological Processes and Advertising Effects. Theory, Research and Application, pp. 45–63. Lawrence Erlbaum, Hillsdale (1985)

16. Tan, W.J., Kwek, C.L., Li, Z.: The antecedents of effectiveness interactive advertising in the social media. Int. Bus. Res. 6(3), 88–99 (2013)

17. Voorveld, H.A.M., van Noort, G., Muntinga, D.G., Bronner, F.: Engagement with social media and social media advertising: the differentiating role of platform type. J. Advert. 47(1), 38–54 (2018)

18. Curran, J.M., Lennon, R.: Participating in the conversation: exploring usage of social media networking sites. Acad. Market. Stud. J. 15(S1), 21–38 (2011)

19. Davis, F.D.: Perceived usefulness, perceived ease of use, and user acceptance of information technology. MIS Q. 13(3), 319–340 (1989)

20. Dahlen, M.: The medium as a contextual cue. J. Advert. 34(3), 89–98 (2005)

21. Malthouse, E.C., Calder, B.J., Tamhane, A.: The effects of media context experiences on advertising effectiveness. J. Advert. 36(3), 7–18 (2007)

22. Heinonen, K.: Consumer activity in social media: managerial approaches to consumers social media behavior. J. Consum. Behav. 10(6), 356–364 (2011)

23. Pietro, L.D., Pantano, E.: An empirical investigation of social network influence on consumer purchasing decision: the case of Facebook. J. Direct Data Digit. Market. Pract. 14(1), 18–29 (2012). https://doi.org/10.1057/dddmp.2012.10

24. Hamouda, M.: Understanding social media advertising effect on consumers' responses. J. Enterp. Inf. Manage. 31(3), 426–445 (2018)

25. Forbes, L.P., Vespoli, E.M.: Does social media influence consumer buying behavior? An investigation of recommendations and purchases. J. Bus. Econ. Res. 11(2), 107–112 (2013)

26. Duffett, R.G.: Facebook advertising's influence on intention-to-purchase and purchase amongst millennials. Internet Res. 25(4), 498–526 (2015)

27. Taylor, D., Lewin, J., Strutton, D.: Friends, fans, and followers: do ads work on social networks? How gender and age shape receptivity. J. Advert. Res. 51(1), 258–275 (2011)

28. Dao, W.V.T., Le, A.N.H., Cheng, J.M.S., Chen, D.C.: Social media advertising value. The case of transitional economies in Southeast Asia. Int. J. Advert. 33(2), 271–294 (2014)

29. Saxena, A., Khanna, U.: Advertising on social network sites: a structural equation modelling approach. Vis. J. Bus. Perspect. 17(1), 17–25 (2013)

30. Haberland, G.S., Dacin, P.A.: The development of a measure to assess viewers' judgments of the creativity of an advertisement: a preliminary study. Adv. Consum. Res. **19**(1), 817–825 (1992)

31. Shepard, R.N.: Recognition memory for words, sentences and pictures. J. Verbal Learn. Verbal Behav. **6**(1), 156–163 (1967)

32. Mu, E., Galletta, D.F.: The effects of the meaningfulness of salient brand and product-related text and graphics on web site recognition. J. Electron. Commer. Res. **8**(2), 115–127 (2007)

33. Katerattanakul, P., Siau, K.: Measuring information quality of web sites: development of an instrument. In: Proceedings of the 20th International Conference on Information Systems, pp. 279–285. Association for Information Systems, Atlanta (1999)

34. Ang, S.H., Low, S.Y.M.: Exploring the dimensions of ad creativity. Psychol. Market. **17**(10), 835–854 (2000)

35. Lehnert, K., Till, B.D., Ospina, J.M.: Advertising creativity: the role of divergence versus meaningfulness. J. Advert. **43**(3), 274–285 (2014)

36. Smith, R.E., MacKenzie, S.B., Yang, X., Buchholz, L.M., Darley, W.K.: Modeling the determinants and effects of creativity in advertising. Market. Sci. **26**(6), 819–833 (2007)

37. Ang, S.H., Leong, S.M., Lee, Y.H., Lou, S.L.: Necessary but not sufficient: Beyond novelty in advertising creativity. J. Market. Commun. **20**(3), 214–230 (2014)

38. Cornelis, E., Peter, P.C.: The real campaign: the role of authenticity in the effectiveness of advertising disclaimers in digitally enhanced images. J. Bus. Res. **77**(8), 102–112 (2017)

39. Li, H., Edwards, S.M., Lee, J.-H.: Measuring the intrusiveness of advertisements: scale development and validation. J. Advert. **31**(2), 37–47 (2002)

40. Edwards, S.M., Li, H., Lee, J.-H.: Forced exposure and psychological reactance: Antecedents and consequences of the perceived intrusiveness of pop-up ads. J. Advert. **31**(3), 83–95 (2002)

41. Ha, L.: Advertising clutter in consumer magazines: dimensions and effects. J. Advert. Res. **36**(7), 76–83 (1996)

42. Goodrich, K., Schiller, S.Z., Galletta, D.F.: Consumer reactions to intrusiveness of online-video advertisements. J. Advert. Res. **55**(1), 37–50 (2015)

43. Bell, R., Buchner, A.: Positive effects of disruptive advertising on consumer preferences. J. Interact. Market. **41**(2), 1–13 (2018)

44. Ha, H., Perks, H.: Effects of consumer perceptions of brand experience on the web: brand familiarity, satisfaction and brand trust. J. Consum. Behav. **4**(6), 438–452 (2005)

45. McCoy, S., Everard, A., Polak, P., Galletta, D.F.: An experimental study of antecedents and consequences of online ad intrusiveness. Int. J. Hum. Comput. Interact. **24**(7), 672–699 (2008)

46. van Doorn, J., Hoekstra, J.C.: Customization of online advertising: The role of intrusiveness. Market. Lett. **24**(4), 339–351 (2012). https://doi.org/10.1007/s11002-012-9222-1

47. Lancelot Miltgen, C., Cases, A.-S., Russell, C.A.: Consumers' responses to Facebook advertising across PCs and mobile phones: a model for assessing the drivers of approach and avoidance of Facebook ads. J. Advert. Res. **59**(4), 414–432 (2019)

48. Zhang, J., Mao, E.: From online motivations to ad clicks and to behavioral intentions: an empirical study of consumer response to social media advertising. Psychol. Market. **33**(3), 155–164 (2016)

49. Ajzen, I.: From intentions to actions: a theory of planned behavior. In: Kuhl, J., Beckmann, J. (eds.) Action Control. SSSSP, pp. 11–39. Springer, Heidelberg (1985). https://doi.org/10.1007/978-3-642-69746-3_2

50. Ajzen, I.: Attitude structure and behavior. In: Pratkanis, A.R., Breckler, S.J., Greenwald, A.G. (eds.) Attitude Structure and Function, pp. 241–274. Lawrence Erlbaum, Hillsdale, NJ (1989)

51. Yang, T.: The decision behavior of Facebook users. J. Comput. Inf. Syst. **52**(3), 50–59 (2012)

52. Ringle, C.M., Wende, S., Will, A.: SmartPLS. www.smartpls.de. Accessed 25 Sept 2019

53. Nunnally, J.C.: Psychometric Theory. McGraw-Hill, New York (1978)

54. Fornell, C., Larcker, D.F.: Evaluating structural equation models with unobservable variables and measurement error. J. Mark. Res. **18**(1), 39–50 (1981)
55. Cybenko, G., Brewington, B.: The foundations of information push and pull. In: Cybenko, G., O'Leary, D.P., Rissanen, J. (eds.) The Mathematics of Information Coding, Extraction and Distribution. The IMA Volumes in Mathematics and its Applications, vol. 107, pp. 9–30. Springer, New York (1999). https://doi.org/10.1007/978-1-4612-1524-0_2

# Correction to: Web Information Systems and Technologies

Alessandro Bozzon, Francisco José Domínguez Mayo
and Joaquim Filipe

Correction to:
**A. Bozzon et al. (Eds.):** *Web Information Systems and Technologies*, **LNBIP 399,**
**https://doi.org/10.1007/978-3-030-61750-9**

In the originally published version of the book there was an error in the first name of the second volume editor: "José Francisco Domínguez Mayo" should have been "Francisco José Domínguez Mayo". This has now been corrected.

---

The updated version of the book can be found at
https://doi.org/10.1007/978-3-030-61750-9

# Author Index

Printed in the United States
By Bookmasters